NEW REALISM

Traditions in World Cinema

General Editors
Linda Badley (Middle Tennessee State University)
R. Barton Palmer (Clemson University)

Founding Editor
Steven Jay Schneider (New York University)

Titles in the series include:

edinburghuniversitypress.com/series/tiwc

NEW REALISM
Contemporary British Cinema

David Forrest

EDINBURGH
University Press

We publish academic books and journals in our selected subject areas across the humanities and social sciences, combining cutting-edge scholarship with high editorial and production values to produce academic works of lasting importance. For more information visit our website: edinburghuniversitypress.com

© David Forrest, 2020, 2022

Edinburgh University Press Ltd
The Tun – Holyrood Road
12 (2f) Jackson's Entry
Edinburgh EH8 8PJ

First published in hardback by Edinburgh University Press 2020

Typeset in 10/12.5 pt Sabon by
Servis Filmsetting Ltd, Stockport, Cheshire
and printed and bound by CPI Group (UK) Ltd,
Croydon, CR0 4YY

A CIP record for this book is available from the British Library

ISBN 978 1 4744 1303 9 (hardback)
ISBN 978 1 4744 9469 4 (paperback)
ISBN 978 1 4744 1304 6 (webready PDF)
ISBN 978 1 4744 1305 3 (epub)

The right of David Forrest to be identified as author of this work has been asserted in accordance with the Copyright, Designs and Patents Act 1988 and the Copyright and Related Rights Regulations 2003 (SI No. 2498)

.

CONTENTS

FIGURES

ACKNOWLEDGEMENTS

I would like to thank the following, who have contributed to and supported this project in a variety of ways: my colleagues and friends at the University of Sheffield, in particular Jonathan Rayner, Julia Dobson, Jo Gavins, Brendan Stone, Adam Piette, Joe Bray, Richard Steadman-Jones, Susan Fitzmaurice and, for all her continued support, advice and friendship, Sue Vice; the Beyond the Multiplex team, Peter Merrington, Matthew Hanchard, Helen Rana, Simeon Yates, Andrew Higson, Mike Pidd, and Bridgette Wessels, and all our wonderful focus group participants who taught me so much about the meaning of realism(s) and unexpectedly influenced the direction of this book; my students at Sheffield, particularly those who have taken modules on British cinema, for all their thoughtful challenges, critiques and validations; Jack Cortvriend, whose work made me re-assess my assumptions about realist cinema; David Tucker, who was there at the start of this project and did so much to get it off the ground; Clive Nwonka, whose thoughtful scrutiny, good humour and friendship are all that is good about academia; Beth Johnson, an inspirational colleague and a great friend, my family: Gemma, Mike, Emma, Teresa, Robert, Wendy, Christine, Martin, Chris, Becky, Sophie and Erin; and my extended family of friends, you know who you are.

TRADITIONS IN WORLD CINEMA

General editors: **Linda Badley and R. Barton Palmer**
Founding editor: **Steven Jay Schneider**

Traditions in World Cinema is a series of textbooks and monographs devoted to the analysis of currently popular and previously underexamined or under-valued film movements from around the globe. Also intended for general interest readers, the textbooks in this series offer undergraduate- and graduate-level film students accessible and comprehensive introductions to diverse traditions in world cinema. The monographs open up for advanced academic study more specialised groups of films, including those that require theoretically-oriented approaches. Both textbooks and monographs provide thorough examinations of the industrial, cultural, and socio-historical conditions of production and reception.

The flagship textbook for the series includes chapters by noted scholars on traditions of acknowledged importance (the French New Wave, German Expressionism), recent and emergent traditions (New Iranian, post-Cinema Novo), and those whose rightful claim to recognition has yet to be established (the Israeli persecution film, global found footage cinema). Other volumes concentrate on individual national, regional or global cinema traditions. As the introductory chapter to each volume makes clear, the films under discussion form a coherent group on the basis of substantive and relatively transparent, if not always obvious, commonalities. These commonalities may be formal, stylistic or thematic, and the groupings may, although they need not, be popularly identified as genres, cycles or movements (Japanese horror, Chinese martial arts cinema, Italian Neorealism). Indeed, in cases in which a group of films is not already commonly identified as a tradition, one purpose of the volume is to establish its claim to importance and make it visible (East Central European Magical Realist cinema, Palestinian cinema).

Textbooks and monographs include:

- An introduction that clarifies the rationale for the grouping of films under examination
- A concise history of the regional, national, or transnational cinema in question
- A summary of previous published work on the tradition
- Contextual analysis of industrial, cultural and socio-historical conditions of production and reception
- Textual analysis of specific and notable films, with clear and judicious application of relevant film theoretical approaches
- Bibliograph(ies)/filmograph(ies)

Monographs may additionally include:

- Discussion of the dynamics of cross-cultural exchange in light of current research and thinking about cultural imperialism and globalisation, as well as issues of regional/national cinema or political/aesthetic movements (such as new waves, postmodernism, or identity politics)
- Interview(s) with key filmmakers working within the tradition.

INTRODUCTION

In this book I identify a recurring set of emphases and features within a range of films produced in Britain over the first two decades of the twenty-first century that considered together form a new tradition of realist cinema. While not a concerted or self-defined cycle of films, viewed collectively they can be seen to have re-imagined, re-cast and re-enlivened realism, a mode that, while fundamental to the discourses of British cinema, is conceptually mutable, contested and ill-defined. This book aims to re-visit and re-ignite debates about the British realist screen text, and in the process to anatomise what I am here terming new British realism (new realism hereafter). The use of 'new' as an adjective is of course always already redundant, yet it is necessary to indicate the sense in which over the last twenty years something quite fundamental has altered in realist practice.

Here I examine the works of five film-makers: Duane Hopkins, Joanna Hogg, Andrea Arnold, Shane Meadows and Clio Barnard. This is not an exhaustive new realist cast list, and by no means do I attempt to cover every element of their oeuvres, but I draw out what is consistent across their work: a commitment to rendering depictions of the familiar and the tangible in ways that are best described as realistic, or, indeed, realist. While their methodologies vary and the nature of their reality effects are divergent – ranging from the intimate and participatory, to the painterly and observational, from the perceptually textured and phenomenological, to the stylised and referential – the films are united by broad but clearly recurrent characteristics, which will be identified and investigated here.

The book traces common areas and elements of form, style and method, and the thematic emphases that underpin the contemporary tradition of realist cinema in Britain. The films under consideration all undertake a concerted examination of the relationship between environment and identity – evolving beyond merely a deterministic account of social, economic and cultural forces – giving shape to the trajectories of the films' protagonists so that this dynamic is also *felt* at the experiential level, where multiple visual and aural registers of place, space and landscape are accented to invite spectatorial contemplation and empathetic participation. They are bound too by a meticulous, rhythmic poeticism, inculcated through recurring motifs of quotidian sound and imagery, constructing a mode of realism which we might understand as both image-led and attendant to the aural and to other forms of sensory engagement. These elements are combined to foster a mode of everyday poetics that are frequently enabled by and navigated through young protagonists, or at the very least individuals who are aimless, uncertain or half formed, and in turn these character portraits are repeatedly generated alongside refreshingly multi-dimensional portrayals of the non-human. A rich and multivalent authenticity is also foregrounded at the level of experience, with the directors frequently drawing on their personal biographies as stimuli, or at the very least, connecting the films' concerted emphases on place to their own personal geographies; this extends to the realm of performance, with the regular deployment of non-professional actors, individuals who are invited to bring their own narratives into dialogue with those that they are enacting on screen. Taken together, these features unite a range of seemingly divergent films and film-makers and point to a redefinition of this most contested and foundational tendency in British film culture.

IN, THROUGH AND BEYOND THE NATIONAL

The re-examination of realism that has occurred in British cinema in the twenty-first century presents broader questions for the ways in which national cinema is conceptualised and felt at the textual and institutional levels. While the films examined in this book can be seen to respond to cinemas and cultural traditions beyond Britain, managing, as Ezra and Rowden put it, to 'transcend [. . .] the national as autonomous cultural particularity while respecting it as a powerful symbolic force' (Ezra and Rowden 2006: 2), they are, because of their concerted emphasis on landscape, like many global 'new realisms', imbued with a referential specificity of nationhood. In this sense they can be aligned with and understood within those other emerging contemporary realist traditions that Tiago de Luca has called 'realist programmes in overt dialogue with their local realities' (de Luca 2014: 27). While it is productive to think of British cinema in global terms, not least to resist the 'homogenising and enclosing tendency' (Higson 2006: 22) of an essentialised conception of the national that Andrew Higson argues against, this book will seek to situate the films as projects which, while fuelled by global cinematic traditions, respond to and artistically interrogate a distinctly domestic set of iconographies. These films' very poetic stimuli are what Higson terms the 'familiar images, images of the mundane, the quotidian, the unremarkable [. . .] which are at the same time steeped in the habitual customs and cultural fabric of a particular nation' (Higson 2011: 1).

Realism is, then, by definition a cultural phenomenon that is intensely localised and one that asserts the familiar even in a globalised world. As Hallam and Marshment put it, 'all definitions of realism are locally (regionally, nationally) specific' (Hallam and Marshment 2000: x), and this is especially true of a realist tradition such as the one examined in this book which derives so much of its affective energies from lyrical encounters with distinctly national and often regional topographies. To return to Higson, I wish to make clear, however, that national cinema and national cinema traditions are in this book not 'used prescriptively rather than descriptively, citing what *ought* to be the national cinema, rather than describing the actual cinematic experience of popular audiences' (Higson 1989: 37). Instead, we need to conceptualise the national as fundamental to the aesthetic and more often than not political preoccupations of the contemporary realist text, rather than as a homogenising framework for idealising a fixed notion of 'British culture'.

The realist films examined here circulate against the backdrop of an uncertain and increasingly divisive political landscape that has nationhood at its very heart, and yet we must guard against an uncritical understanding of their status as statements on or reflections of national life. Indeed, the result of the 2016 referendum on Britain's membership of the European Union was nothing if not a reassertion of the national; a reminder that the local remains the primary means of experiencing and actualising one's identity, and yet, with a few exceptions (*Fish Tank* (Andrea Arnold, 2009), *This Is England* (Shane Meadows, 2006)), the films surveyed in this book have struggled to find a popular, national audience – in short, while these realist texts might speak of the nation, they do not speak to it.

Realism's status as an iteration of national cinema is thus complex – its intrinsic commitment to location defines its geographical and more broadly spatial parameters as necessarily narrow, limits that are felt, too, in terms of audience. As mentioned earlier, realism's relationship to the transnational is similarly complex and ambivalent. Many of the features of contemporary realist practice are echoed across the global media landscape, yet they are necessarily interwoven with and examined through the lens of localised locations and thematic contexts. The question of audience is again relevant here. As this book shows, the new realist tradition in Britain is formed from directors often working on superficially divergent subject matter but with common aesthetic strategies and/or artistic sensibilities. This textual unity however does not, as I have already suggested, result in anything like a consistent audience base in the UK, and, beyond, in Europe. Although *Fish Tank* (shown in Austria, Belgium, the Czech Republic, Germany, Denmark, Estonia, Spain, France [41% of admissions, 243023], UK [18%, 1110168], Greece, Hungary, Italy, Lithuania, Luxembourg, the Netherlands, Poland, Portugal, Sweden, Slovenia) and *This Is England* (Belgium, Denmark, Spain, France [21.967%], UK [40.972%] Greece, Italy, the Netherlands, Portugal, Romania, Sweden [15.143%], Slovenia), the two domestic successes that I mentioned earlier, can be viewed as transnational at both the industrial and the textual levels, many of the other films that I examine in this book have simply not travelled.[1] Indeed, the works of Joanna Hogg, arguably the director whose films most clearly speak to a particular tradition of European cinema, have received almost no circulation beyond Britain. Thus, while I seek to connect, cohere and conceive of a British tradition of new realism across these pages, I do so with an awareness that the boundaries of the national, with its essentialising and homogenising mythologies, should be approached with concerted critical scrutiny. The Britain of which new realism speaks is of course always partial; despite the progressive tendencies of these films, the nation is imagined as overwhelmingly white, and almost always English.

Mapping a Tradition

If new realism's status as and of national cinema is necessarily slippery, the very definition of what constitutes realist practice is equally and, I hope, productively, complex. My 'new' realist prefix adds to a long list of descriptive orderings of realism from the ubiquitous social and poetic, the moral, the emotional and so forth, each carrying their own definitions. As David Tucker argues:

> [p]art of the problem for realism, as for social realism, is one of definition. But whereas a lack of clear boundaries for social realism presents opportunities at the same time as it poses difficulties, the issue for realism is often one of too-simple definitions. (Tucker 2011: 11)

This simplicity manifests itself in multiple, reductive ways. As I will explore throughout this book, more often than not realism is evoked pejoratively as a generic framework against which a film-maker or cycle of films is contrasted

---

[1] Figures taken from Lumiere Database on admissions of films released in Europe: http://lumiere.obs.coe.int/web/search/

and marked as distinctive. In this way, British realism is constructed discursively as a homogeneous, aesthetically fixed paradigm. In contrast, this book argues that what is consistent about British realism is the maintenance of traditions of narrative film-making in Britain which are grounded in representations of common experience and everyday life, but which evolve dynamically, and are historically and culturally contingent. Realist traditions and cycles are thus always in processes and form porously against one another, reframing themselves against and within the shifting national and global contexts in which they operate. Realism, imagined as a static entity embodying fixed and specific conventions, simply does not and cannot exist.

As the recognition of a new and emerging realist impulse presented itself towards the end of the first decade of the twenty-first century, Nick Roddick, writing in *Sight and Sound*, inadvertently slipped into this critical blind alley:

> With film, realism is a necessary corollary of the photographic image. If we leave aside animation, narrative cinema – in Britain as much as anywhere else – is 'reality plus', with our spectre of that 'plus' running all the way from Grierson to Gilliam. (Roddick 2009: 20)

Roddick rightly suggests that film is always constructing rather than replicating reality and that there exists a broad British tradition of elevating the everyday for narrative ends. His argument about contemporary British films is that they are in fact 'anything but realistic' (2009: 19), before listing a range of films (including *Fish Tank*) that 'all have an almost adversarial relationship with the real, determined to see what lies beyond' (Ibid.: 19). What, however, is this 'realistic' cinema that Roddick describes? What are those films that do not 'go beyond the real'? Indeed, Roddick even cites Ken Loach – a film-maker who, as we will see, is profoundly connected to social realism – as part of this contemporary cycle of anti-realism. This apparently direct realist tradition, I argue, does not exist. In its place lies a persistent impulse in British cinema to conceive, interpret and confront 'the real' in multiple ways depending on a range of factors – thus, while we see shared points of emphasis in the film-makers covered in this book, there is, of course, no aesthetic consensus on what constitutes 'the real'. John Hill's argument that '[r]ealism, no less than any other type of art, depends on conventions, conventions which, in this case, have successfully achieved the status of being accepted as "realistic"' (Hill 1986: 57) is useful in that underlines realism as a constructed, considered practice rather than an unmediated representation of 'things as they really are', yet we can counter the pejorative implication of Hill's statement to suggest that these 'conventions' are enabling rather than obstructive. Contemporary realist film-makers are not illusionists who work to naturalise and flatten the dynamics of everyday experience to close off ambiguity and critical engagement.

Instead, they operate consciously and openly within such 'conventions' to ground their films through realism(s) and to represent differing levels of and perspectives on the familiar and the common; the very fabric of everyday life. The films explored in this book make no attempt to offer authoritative depictions of 'real life', they instead consciously admit and revel in the partialness of the 'realities' they depict, heightening and making emphatic selected elements of lived experience for their particular poetic and political ends. For example, while some of the films foreground intimate, subjectively tethered representations of their subjects, emphasising sensory encounters with their environment, others take that very environment as their centre point, enabling conspicuously observational and more distanced perspectives – both of these approaches demand an active participatory mode of spectatorship, predicated on what I have termed a sense of 'being with' and 'being there' respectively. Thus, our view of the characters and their locations is necessarily and wilfully restricted, depending on the particular 'conventions' of realism the film-makers choose to deploy.

The dynamics of realist texts are therefore dependent on the encounters they enable with the viewer – between the lived experience and the depiction of lived experience. This again runs counter to an understanding of realism as rigidly conceived and fixed to particular generic conventions and ideological effects. As Hallam and Marshment put it, '[p]re-knowledges and existing schemata are of particular importance in ascribing degrees of "realisticness" to film texts and assessing their "truth" to experience' (Hallam and Marshment 2000: 127), thus realist films in particular, with their focus on common, lived 'experience', appeal to spectatorial subjectivities, inviting the viewer to bring their narrative to the texts as interpretative resources and frameworks in order to situate the feeling of authenticity within the film. These encounters are of course also dependent on time, and the historical context that the film both depicts and is circulated within. As mentioned earlier, the contemporaneity of realism is always already fragmented – and realism, perhaps more than any other mode of filmic representation is historically contingent, as Paul Marris argues:

> [. . .] classically, 'realisms' are perceived as 'realistic' at the moment of their introduction. That is to say, in contrast to previously established artistic conventions, they are received as giving a more convincing and contemporarily relevant account of the social, offering new insights that speak to their times. Realism should not be taken as a fixed formal recipe. If so, it atrophies; over time, the formerly perceptive becomes routine and conventionalized and is no longer adequate to the changing situation. (Marris 2001: 250)

Multiple traditions of realism exist because they form around and as a response to the aesthetic trends of their period, themselves products of a range of environmental factors. What appears realistic in the contemporary moment, an age of the global and of the digital in which the very parameters of what is meant and felt by the real have been stretched and disrupted, would differ vastly from the conventions of, for example, 1960s realism, and of the fundamental experiences of reality in that period. That said, perhaps more than any other realist tradition, the films that are examined in this book foreground the physical nature of being in the world through highly textured emphases on space, place and the very experience of the landscape, and the haptic and sensory realm to emphasise the feeling of everyday life in ways which are not necessarily dependent for their meaning on a fixed sense of broader, contextual verisimilitude. Thus, many of the defining characteristics of the realism of the last twenty years can be seen to mitigate to an extent the trappings of temporal and historical specificity in their evolution of a more universal and fundamental emphasis on lived experience.

New realism should however not be seen as a consolidating or cumulative moment in the development of British realist traditions, but rather another iteration of a dynamically evolving impulse in British (and global) film culture. It is to acknowledge the dynamism and porosity of the realist mode that I offer no descriptive prefix beyond the assertion of these films' contemporaneity and to mark their difference to what has come before. This is an attempt to move away from the aforementioned monolithic understandings of, for example, 'social' realism, which, as I have argued here, have all too often come to function as a proxy mechanism to define rigidly an apparently fixed and conservative national cinema.

Although social realism is useful in so far as it does help us to understand and identify a particular iteration of and point of emphasis within the broad traditions of realism in Britain and beyond, it should not be seen as its defining framework. Hallam and Marshment's definition of the social realist mode usefully identifies a range of key features and thematic concerns:

> Social realism is a discursive term used by film critics and reviewers to describe films that aim to show the effects of environmental factors on the development of character through depictions that emphasise the relationship between location and identity. Traditionally associated in Britain with a reformist or occasionally revolutionary politics that deemed adverse social circumstances could be changed by the introduction of more enlightened social policies or structural change in society, social realism tends to be associated with an observational style of camerawork that emphasises situations and events and an episodic narrative structure, creating 'kitchen sink' dramas and 'gritty' character studies of the underbelly of urban life. (Hallam and Marshment 2000: 184)

For Hallam and Marshment, the social realist tradition is defined by its overt examination of the determining relationship between social (and economic and political) forces and the resultant circumstances and experiences of the film's protagonists and locations, aligning this logically with a distinctive and clearly articulated political project. Moreover, they identify particular aesthetic and formal elements that enable and authenticate social realism's 'reformist' project. Many of the new realist films that I discuss in this book can be understood within this definition. For example, the relationship between environment (at least in some form) and identity is, I argue, central both to the formal and thematic qualities of the films, and some of the films might, as I have already suggested, be seen to foreground a sense of the viewer as observer within the diegetic space. Yet, they are also films that invoke more subjectively orientated modes of address as routes into more empathic, sensory experiences and representations of reality. These films often seek to elevate through a range of means particular visual and or aural elements of their locations to invite broad interpretations and meaning making, and it is therefore often difficult to ascertain clear and specific socio-political prescriptions from their varying aesthetic strategies.

In this sense, then, new realism might be seen to evolve from and develop out of the social realist mode rather than operating as a continuation of it. While social realism is indeed used as a 'catch all' for the kinds of pejorative statements about realism that I have already described, Hallam and Marshment's definition is also useful because it clearly specifies conventions that this particular tradition can be identified by, and films that it can be identified with.

The centrality of the kind of social realism defined here within British culture is, I would argue, indelibly connected to the consistency and prominence of Ken Loach. While a rich tradition of television drama in Britain can also be seen to work within the particular conventions anatomised by Hallam and Marshment, in terms of film, Loach is the defining representative of the social realist tradition in Britain. As such, while they might not realise it, when critics speak of social realism in Britain they speak of Ken Loach. Although his collaborations with a diverse range of writers have placed multiple accents upon his oeuvre, his thematic preoccupations and his working methods are remarkably consistent. In line with Hallam and Marshment's definition, Loach's films are often driven by a didactic treatise on the relationship between economic forces and socially marginalised protagonists, with realist tools working to make authentic and to humanise a politically explicit analysis. Characters are necessarily representative figures, and narrative situations, while specific, can be extrapolated to unlock wider socio-economic issues in the national and geopolitical realms. This suggests a dynamic in which the effects of realism are directed towards the articulation of the films' primary political projects, and this is certainly true of Loach's work since the 1990s. Thus, the indeterminate qualities of the new realist film, their focus on physical and sensory experience, their lyrical and often opaque treatment of location, for example, are out of place in a social realist mould which depends on clarity rather than ambiguity for its meaning making. As Deborah Knight argues, Loach's films pursue very particular rhetorical strategies: 'discussions, meetings among co-workers, speeches, interviews, recollections, confrontations', and frequently see their protagonists 'asking questions of another character' (Knight 1997: 66). While delivered within the quotidian frame, these devices are designed clearly to generate a dialectic framework that locks in and makes visible the nature of the protagonists' struggle against the forces of capitalism, and it is this unambiguously and unapologetically didactic approach that defines his particular realist method.

Loachian social realism therefore exists as *a* and not *the* tradition of British realism, and it can and should be distinguished from the trends and characteristics traced across this book. This relationship of contrasting realisms is taken on by Stella Hockenhull in the context of her study of contemporary British women film-makers. Hockenhull notes the shared features of films by directors such as Lynne Ramsay, Andrea Arnold, Samantha Morton and Clio Barnard, and suggests that in contrast, Loach's films are defined by 'straightforward narratives in order to identify societal problems within a credible environment, and usually dialogue is the key vehicle for facilitating the narrative' (Hockenhull 2017: 20). The 'female film directors', Hockenhull argues, are progressing the Loachian realist tradition by 'making films not only with a bias towards societal concerns, but also through a poetic optic' (Ibid.: 20). It is this identification of the 'poetic' that is most frequently used as a mechanism for framing the films of new realism. Indeed, I use it throughout this book, and so it is necessary here to spend some time identifying what this pivotal adjective might constitute in practice, and how it has been deployed historically to examine and contextualise multiple realist traditions.

Hockenhull, for example, usefully substantiates the 'poetic optic' of the realist films examined in her book through textual analysis. Hockenhull's discussion of Morton's *The Unloved* (2009), a film about a child's experience of the care system and inspired by Morton's own childhood, analyses the 'lyrical' and 'poetic' framing of the protagonist Lucy's (Molly Windsor) solitary walks through the city of Nottingham (Ibid.: 133). Hockenhull notes the similarities between Morton's and Arnold's approach to location (in *Fish Tank*), describing how 'the backdrop of high-rise accommodation appears majestic and lyrical' and 'how the visual splendour is used to counteract Lucy's miserable existence' (Ibid.: 133). Hockenhull also notes Morton's use of sound to 'mobilise Lucy's feelings of alienation' (Ibid.: 133), and, as the analysis develops, registers the emphasis Morton places 'on the minutiae of Lucy's life via aspects of the *mise en scène*' (Ibid.: 134). This 'great attention' to quotidian detail is seen as the platform for a subjective examination of Lucy's memories, which in turn are presented in a sensually heightened manner through one particularly sensorially rich scene where Morton 'retains focus on the autumn leaves which swirl in the wind' as Lucy 'wanders around a churchyard with a deer grazing nearby', while 'Morton manipulates sound to interject the film with an atmospheric effect' (Ibid.: 134). Hockenhull sees this sensory, subjective impulse as central to the film's poetic examination of its subject matter. Crucially, Hockenhull cites Morton's own repudiation of the didactic model in favour of the lyrical approach: 'If I'd wanted to do that, I would have made a documentary. I didn't go for the jugular. I hope I've made a poetic statement if anything' (Ibid.: 134). Morton's own contrasting of the poetic against a more explicit and direct 'documentary' method, is another discursive framing of the qualities of the poetic (ambiguity, the invitation of contemplation, subjectivity, non-linearity) against the didactic or social (clarity, forcefulness, direction, coherence). More specifically, Hockenhull identifies a range of vehicles for and enablers of these poetic qualities: the child protagonist, the subtle transformation of the mundane location, the manipulation of sound design, the accented presence of the animal, the meticulous emphasis on the fragments and details of a character's existence. What emerges here, then, is a set of characteristics that help to substantiate the 'poetic' in realism, characteristics that are crucial in helping us to identify what is distinctive about the tradition of new realism in Britain.

Poetic realism is of course not exclusive to Britain, nor to the contemporary period. Indeed, it is perhaps best known as a descriptive label for French films of the 1930s and, while superficially these films are markedly different from those examined here, the fundamental connotations of the adjective are strikingly similar. Dudley Andrew's definitive study of French poetic realism, *Mists of Regret*, identifies in the genre 'a combined attention to the everyday and a heightened concern for subjective mood' (Andrew 1995: 14); a desire to 'deliver not a message about frustrated desire or expression or battered hopes or helplessness but the very experience of those feelings' (Ibid.: 20); and a concerted attempt to 'sublimate the everyday' (Ibid.: 336). These features clearly offer parallels to a contemporary British approach to the poetic which, as Hockenhull implies, is similarly defined by its roots in and subtle transformation of everyday processes and imagery; its atmospheric foregrounding of the experience of reality; and its elevation through formal means of quotidian details that would otherwise be overlooked or directed towards more prescriptive meaning. What emerges here then is a consensus of a particular set of aesthetic and philosophical practices that begin to define characteristics of the poetic and are subsequently visible across multiple realist traditions and modes of practices.

As mentioned, Lynne Ramsay is one of Hockenhull's key subjects, specifically Ramsay's film *Ratcatcher* (1999). This film, I want to argue, is a formative text in the tradition of new realism, not only as a direct influence on the likes of Arnold, Hopkins, and Barnard, but as a film which in broader terms opened up the possibilities of realist practice in Britain and unmoored the mode from its hitherto indelible association with the social realism of Loach. The film, a highly lyrical account of twelve-year-old protagonist James's (William Eadie) journey through grief and guilt against the backdrop of the Glasgow bin-men strike of 1975, condenses many of the features of new realism that will be examined and expanded upon as this book unfolds. Moreover, scholarly readings of *Ratcatcher* initiate a critical vocabulary that enables a renewed consideration of the features and formal elements of poetic realist practice. For example, Tina Kendall has described how the film 'registers a myopic attention to physical reality in all of its tactile detail', to invite the 'spectator into a sensory realm that is located below the threshold of ordinary aesthetic experience' (Kendall 2010: 180); how its 'lushly composed images with their emphasis on the static arrangement of people and things within the frame, offer evidence of the film's grounding in either a photographic or a painterly aesthetic' (Ibid.: 190), later arguing that conspicuous editing styles and lengthy shot duration encourage contemplative dialogues with the images on multiple levels. Again, then, these analyses open up the possibility of a realist practice which is at once rooted in a concrete evocation of physical *and* emotional experiences and which enables interpretative relationships with meticulously composed and yet everyday imagery. Annette Kuhn describes this in her book on *Ratcatcher* as cinema's ability to 'conjure a world that resembles the one we normally inhabit, and yet is at the same time self-evidently virtual' (Kuhn 2008: 11). Thus there is at once an engagement with the quotidian and the immediate and, through stylistic means, 'the exploration of a detail or a moment, that distinguishes poetry' (Ibid.: 12), since for Kuhn 'film can accommodate a meditative attitude that is akin to reverie' (Ibid.: 17), and it is the capacity for meditation on that which is familiar and authentic that defines poetic realism in contemporary cinema. Kuhn goes on to further anatomise what she terms 'film poetry and the poetic in film': 'lingering, thoughtfully composed, motionless or near-motionless images; slow, silent explorations of spaces; intense, searching close-ups; visual rhyme; recurrent visual and auditory motifs' (Ibid.: 12).

As we will see, these characteristics, here connected to *Ratcatcher*, are also fundamental features of the new realist tradition in British cinema. Indeed, Kuhn anticipates and contests the possible categorisation of *Ratcatcher* within the 'tradition of social realism', arguing instead that the film 'does set up and weave together several levels of "reality" (including a social realist one)' and that 'one of the film's unique qualities is the way its various levels of reality imbue each setting in overlapping, and sometimes changing ways' (Ibid.: 17). I would argue, however, that what was perhaps unique to *Ratcatcher* in 1999 is now one of the defining features of the tradition of new realism: that is, the evocation of multiple levels of and experiences of reality, which in turn invites active and engaged spectatorship. Just as Arnold, Meadows, Hopkins, Hogg and Barnard do, Ramsay's film evokes:

> realities – documentary, drama of working-class life, social history, referencing as they do an outer, social world – dominate the film, either separately or collectively. Rather, they are set against, and qualified by, 'realities' that are best described as inner, imaginal, even fantastic. (2008: 17)

To return to the historical traditions of poetic realism, this fragmentation of realism and multiplication of realisms is formed around and through lyrical encounters with 'the everyday' to 'explore the relationships and rifts between outer and inner worlds, worlds of external reality and worlds of imagination and fantasy' (Ibid.: 18). Realism is thus defined by its porousness and the non-hierarchical relationship between its many possible facets. As Ramsay herself describes it, this constitutes the movement from 'the mesmeric to hard reality; from internal reality to outside world, from internal [or] brutal to observational' (Ibid.: 85). Cinema, for Ramsay, is uniquely placed to enable this rendering of and dialogue with multiple realities:

> God is in the details. There is a lot of tenderness in the least obvious acts. A miniscule detail like [James pulling his mother's laddered tights over her toes] can say a lot about a relationship. I'm constantly trying to think cinematically. What can be shown instead of said. (Ibid.: 85)

Again, then, we are understanding the poetic through its emphasis on the indeterminate potentials of the image over the more prescriptive model of dialogue-driven realism:

> I love to see great dialogue in the cinema but I hate to see 'Film TV'. When I go to the cinema, I want to have a cinematic experience. Some people ignore the sound and you end up seeing something you might see on television and it doesn't explore the form. (Andrew 2002)

This again centres the poetic around an invitation for the spectator to interpret multiple meanings but to root these contemplations in the familiar and in the realm of common experience. Ramsay goes on: 'I try for sensuousness and, though it's difficult to express it, to reach for the sublime in the everyday. I believe you can approach a character's psychology through a detail or an action better than through a succession of sequences' (Kuhn 2008: 85). Here

Ramsay makes tangible a realist practice which operates vividly at the surface level – an affect-centred approach to the everyday and to direct experience – which, through its emphatic attention to detail, in turn unlocks that which lies beneath, in this case the internal realm.

THEORISING REALISM, RECOVERING REALISM

If Ramsay's film works as a manifesto for new realism, Andrea Arnold's *Fish Tank* (2009) and Clio Barnard's *The Selfish Giant* (2013) put its edicts into practice. Both films concern youthful protagonists struggling against harsh domestic situations, making sensorial and richly tactile encounters with their landscapes; both present their environments in heightened, accented ways, drawing the spectator into contemplative, non-prescriptive relationships with space, place and landscape; and both foreground material worlds which are multi-layered and which feel very tangible and authentic while also being able to accommodate subjective modes of narration, communicating powerful representations of their characters' inner worlds. I will go on to explore these films in more detail, but I mention them here because they illustrate in practical terms the poetic legacies of Ramsay and *Ratcatcher* and, owing to their relative prominence, they exist as totemic examples of the new realist tradition more broadly.

It is for this second reason, I think, that Clive Nwonka calls upon these films to structure his thoughtful critique of new realism, or as Nwonka calls it 'New British Social Realism' (Nwonka 2014: 2010). His own neologism is revealing in that it re-asserts the hierarchical presence of the 'social' in realism, rather than embracing the plurality of realisms that we have identified in *Ratcatcher* and that define the films that followed it. Indeed, tellingly, Nwonka's criticisms of the films emerge again from valorisation of Loach's particular and, as we have seen, apparently definitive brand of realism:

> The distinction between this period and contemporary accounts of realism is that, while Ken Loach's characters have always charted the erosion of the working class, his characters' decisions are not simply just a matter of personal morality but forced upon them by the socio-economic situation. (Ibid.: 207)

For Nwonka, then, the contemporary films are 'politically neutral', complicit in a 'decontextualisation of poverty' which reduces 'the filmic narrative of inequality to a behavioural rather than a socio-political consequence' (Ibid.: 206). The films represent and are instruments of 'Third Way ideology', with Nwonka connecting their apparent effacement of politics to the New Labour governments of 1997 to 2010. He sees the films as both illustrating and apparently complicit in an 'erosion of social collectivity' replaced by 'individualism, personal agency and the supposed disintegration of class identities' (Ibid.: 209).

Nwonka's analysis, while compelling, is dependent on a clear idea of what realism should be rather than what it is, one which is in turn reliant on the discursive contrast between on one hand a worthy social realist model typified by the films of Loach, which situate 'social realism within didactic contexts', meaning that 'socio-political epistemologies can emerge to counter hegemonic narratives held within the national sphere' (Ibid.: 207), and on the other, 'an anti-dialogical, static realism which produces a new modality of social realism where effects without cause become an important component of the New British Social Realism repertoire' (Ibid.: 210). Of course, *Fish Tank* and *The Selfish Giant* do not ignore the causal factors and contexts of their protagonist's situations, but perhaps what Nwonka is getting at is that this is not their dominant characteristic, rather, this examination of the socio-economic context unfolds alongside multiple other 'realities', in line with the characteristics of the 'poetic' that we have already begun to sketch out, denying the linear subordination of form to a prescriptive and specific end. It is this wilful plurality of realist accents that fully underlines the extent to which new realism is not 'static'. As I have already noted, and as we will see as this book develops, the films are defined by their deployment of multiple aesthetic registers that sees them resist staticity and the notion of an authoritative account or vision of reality. Nwonka's uncritical account of Loachian realism is reliant on a necessarily conclusive dismissal of Arnold's and Barnard's films and vice versa, and this means that we lose the possibility to disrupt the homogenising and monolithic understanding of a 'realism' in British film culture. For example, Nwonka argues that '*Fish Tank* and *The Selfish Giant* are comfortable in the mode of representation for the working class through sentimentality', and that while 'these sympathetic approaches have a clear narrative value in developing audience empathy, the very concept of the working class is reliant on there being a class-structured society' (Ibid.: 219). Nwonka conflates his critique of 'sentimentality' and 'empathy' inducing strategies with the often-repeated criticism of realism as a mode that naturalises rather than provokes critical dialogues with class structures. However, given the reliance of Nwonka's argument upon Loach as an exponent of the apparently necessary and ideal form of politically committed realism, this assumes that Loach's films eschew such emotive strategies.

Yet sentiment and empathy are fundamental components of Loach's method, as Deborah Knight argues:

> we observe and possibly also feel the frustrations such characters suffer, the aggravations they must tolerate, and the humiliations to which they

are subjected. We watch while things go wrong, despite the best efforts of characters to try to make things go right. (Knight 1997: 76)

Loach's characters do come up against the clearly defined and explicated structures of capitalism as they are found in every element of everyday life, but it is our emotional investment in their struggles that provokes both our realisation of these conditions and our outrage at them. This conjoined emotional and political currency is evident in a film like *I, Daniel Blake* (2016), where Loach clearly and pointedly invites our sentiment at the eponymous hero's death, the tragic culmination of the film's dialectic between his uncomplicated, virtuous nature and the labyrinthine and robotically unforgiving benefits system. We are able to feel both sadness and anger, just as we are able to feel with Mia, the young protagonist of *Fish Tank*, as she encounters her everyday life, to ponder the ambiguity of her fate as the film ends, and to understand the socio-economic determinants of her reality. The difference between these approaches to realism is one of emphasis, rather than the dichotomous relationship that Nwonka proposes.

However, Nwonka's argument builds on an important tradition in screen studies in terms of the historical development and theoretical interrogation of realist practice. Indeed, Nwonka re-ignites the binary between an aspirational, politically legitimate and vital encounter with the real and an existing realist film culture that is perceived to be innately conservative and reductive. It is one that catalysed Colin MacCabe's 1974 essay for *Screen*, 'Realism and the Cinema: Notes on some Brechtian theses', and the response from Colin McArthur in the same journal. As John Caughie notes, these original debates reduced their respective realist positions to 'polarities' (Caughie 2000: 108), and we might argue that this approach similarly underpins Nwonka's rhetorical strategy: Loachian social realism as politically committed versus new realism as sentimentalising and escapist. Indeed, MacCabe's argument is reliant on a homogenised definition of 'the classical realist text' where 'there is a hierarchy amongst the discourses which compose the text and this hierarchy is defined in terms of an empirical notion of truth' (MacCabe 1974: 8), and as Deborah Knight puts it, '[W]hat seems to be meant by "empirical" has to do with the idea that what we see is what is true' (Knight 1997: 68). As we have already suggested, the new realist films are defined by the disruption of these hierarchies through the productive plotting of multiple layers and accounts of reality within the same text.

Critiques of realist practice tend, as Knight puts it, to rely on an assumption that 'spectators must accept "the truth" of whatever the camera observes and represents to them', a 'gross over-simplification' that ignores 'the various ways that visual narrations convey information, the different audience-text relationships these narrations make possible, and the importance of the audience's pre-understanding of various story structures and generic conventions' (Knight 1997: 72). MacCabe's critique, in particular, is of course reliant on the notion that the realist text is insufficiently capable of registering contradiction, an argument that finds parallels in Nwonka's criticism of the empathy-evoking qualities of new realism and its apparent effacement of politics. To build on what Knight says, these arguments are further united by an assumption that the viewer, as constructed by realism, is passive. As John Caughie's response to the realism debate suggests, however, this homogenous coding of the specta-tor ignores that '[v]iewers, as well as being textual subjects, are also social subjects, individuals with their own social histories and their own experience of contradiction and injustice and their own utopian imaginings' (Caughie 2000: 108). For Caughie, evoking sentiment and empathy in the realist text need not be a barrier to political engagement: 'but neither does being moved to tears *necessarily* signify a reactionary and debilitating sentimentality; it may represent, in the heart of domesticity, the sudden painful glimpse of the experi-ence of injustice in the world outside' (Ibid.: 108).

MacCabe's use of Bertolt Brecht as an intellectual touchstone is felt in Nwonka's critique of new realism's emotional emphases. As Murray Smith puts it, '[F]or the Brechtian tradition, emotional responses to fiction of an "empathic" kind lock us into the perspective of individual characters, blocking a more interrogatory relationship with characters and narrative as a whole', so that, for Smith, the view that 'empathic emotions are an instrument of subjection' is 'reductive and ill conceived' (Smith 1995: 54). To return to Kuhn's exploration of the multiple realisms of *Ratcatcher*, I want to suggest in this book that new realism, precisely because of the elements that Nwonka criticises, is able to marry critical reflection with emotional response and that, in line with Smith's implication, the two are symbiotically linked. New real-ism's emphasis on landscape and its poetic encounters with place, its attempts to emphasise and accent the representation of perceptual experience, and its willingness to explore its characters' subjectivities, are all elements which actively work against a sense of the viewer's passivity. As Ian Aitken argues, one of the legacies of *Screen* theory's emphasis on 'deep' or 'innate' or 'self-regulating' internal structures is the sense of 'depleted conceptions of agency' in theorising the relationships between a viewer and the realist text (Aitken 2006: 214). The 'pronounced degree of essentialism' (Ibid.: 214) that characterises many of the critiques of realism risks homogenising both the mode (realism as fixed, static, ahistorical) and the viewer (passive, politically resistant, prone to blind emotion). I want to suggest that not only should we conceive viewers as inherently dynamic and active but that new realist texts call upon and make demands of the activities of its viewers in particular ways. The process of dyna-mism is enacted through the realist text's appeal to interpretative resources that are drawn from the viewer's own realities. As Hallam and Marshment put it, '[re]alism articulates a relationship between the conscious, perceiving individual and the social world, activating a mental *mise en scène* of memory, recognition and perceptual familiarity' (Hallam and Marshment 2000: 125), and, in seeking to place heightened, poetic emphasis on the familiar, in often non-prescriptive and indeterminate ways, the films of new realism work to further the sense of realism as an exchange between text and spectator which is 'interactive and in process' (Ibid.: 125). In his own account of new realism, exploring the term as applicable to a tendency in global cinema, Thomas Elsaesser conceptualises this relationship as one of 'contracturalism', where

> an audience is neither master nor dupe, but that spectators are partners in negotiated conventions, which make the social field, or indeed the visual field, into an arena where contracts can be entered, where there are conditions and conditionality, specifying what are the rules of the game, or indicating that a re-negotiation of the rules of the game is required. (Elsaeasser 2009: 7)

To return to Nwonka's important critique of new realism, we might find further theoretical affinities in the work of Mark Fisher. Fisher's highly influential concept of 'capitalist realism', which describes the 'the deep embedding in a world – or set of worlds – in which capitalism is massively naturalised', reveals the ways in which 'especially since 2008, that the (essentially 1990s) idea of the post-political and the post-ideological was always a cover for neoliberal hegemony' (Fisher and Gilbert 2013: 90). Fisher's term 'consolidates ... the idea that we are in the era of the post-political – that the big ideological conflicts are over, and the issues that remain largely concern who is to administrate the new consensus' (Ibid.: 90), and thus aligns with Nwonka's examination of an apparently apolitical 'realist' film tradition. Indeed, the very notion of realist art is particularly pertinent to Fisher's work: '[w]hat counts as "realistic", what seems possible at any point in the social field, is defined by a series of political determinations', so that, in this way, '[e]mancipatory politics must always destroy the appearance of a "natural order"' (Fisher 2009: 17). Fisher, building on the Althusserian formulations of ideology and hegemony that were so fundamental to the dominant critiques of realism in the 1970s, invites scepticism of cultural forms which seek to naturalise and form a consensus around an essential and fixed notion of reality. Paul Dave, however, whose work powerfully develops Fisher's to examine the place of realism in contemporary political discourses, offers a way of redeeming the mode as a mechanism for actively encountering, understanding and engaging with the neo-liberal present. Building on Elsaesser's work to situate it in the British context, Dave argues that the 'epistemological scepticism' that defined a 'philosophical position that insists that all representations are culturally coded and do not reflect external realities . . . is now clearly waning' and that key texts of contemporary British realism which, as we will see, offer more complex and nuanced accounts of reality in its multiple articulations, negotiate a position with the spectator in which 'our apprehension of reality becomes much more complex than it could ever be under constructivist scepticism, but so too does our sense of our own essential nature' (Dave 2017: 123).

To return to Thomas Elsaesser's wider examination of an 'ontological turn' in global cinematic realisms, particular features are identified as enabling a more productively fragmented approach to the presentation of reality, as Elsaesser puts it. The films emphasise 'indeterminate or non-linear temporalities and privilege memory over chronology' and

> make sense/perception a major issue [. . .] by extending perception beyond the visual register, in order to expose or engage the body as a total perceptual surface, while deploying other senses/ perceptions – notably touch and hearing – as at least equally relevant to the cinematic experience. (Elsaesser 2009: 4)

Elsaesser sees film as a key site in a wider re-evaluation of the resources for framing and negotiating the very experience as reality:

> [T]he new realism, if expressing the recognition that not everything is constructed, finds its manifestation in the humanities in general, but especially in film studies around a revival of interest and reinvestment in 'the body', 'the senses', skin, tactility, touch, and the haptic, to which corresponds in philosophy and evolutionary neuroscience the idea of the 'embodied mind'. (Ibid.: 7)

As I have already suggested, and as this book will go on to evidence, one of the key tenets of the new realist tradition in Britain is a willingness to foreground precisely the phenomenological dimensions that Elsaesser emphasises – these are films that actively render the experiences of reality to effect a visceral interaction with the spectator, one which calls upon her or his own perceptual map of references. Thus, the films deliver affective impact through the representation of bodily encounters and experiences of familiar environments, interactions and landscapes, which necessarily invite dynamic viewing relationships. The apparent sense of a 'constructed' single reality, which locks in passive encounters between spectator and film and fails to register the complexities and multiplicities of contemporary life, is disrupted by this necessarily fragmented and indeterminate emphasis on the body and on the senses. Fredric Jameson similarly notes this turn towards affect in realism more broadly, arguing that the 'contemporary or postmodern "perpetual present" is better characterised as a "reduction to the body"' (Jameson 2013: 26), wherein the representation and rendering of affect within the text works to 'activate the body' (Ibid.: 128) outside of it, something that is particularly pertinent in the realm of realist cinema, with its, as Elsaesser suggests, appeal to our sensory realms. For Jameson, affect is able to strike at a more fundamental realist encounter because it operates outside of 'name and nomination' (Ibid.: 128) – it is not subordinated to symbolic, allegorical or narrative 'effect', it does not 'mean something' within the text, and it can instead operate above and beyond its parameters because it is non-prescriptive. In more practical terms put forward by Joe Shapiro in his review of Jameson's book, '[t]he impulse of affect [. . .] entails the representation of bodily sensation in language, scenic description rather than narrative plotting, and the appearance within narrative fiction of a kind of eternal present of non-individuated, impersonal consciousness' (Shapiro 2015: 132). The filmic analogies are obvious in the 'poetic' dimensions of realist practice that we have already begun to identify in new realist films – not only an emphasis on the representation of experience as an end in and of itself, but a connected meditative engagement with space and place which is enabled by a lingering emphasis on devices which serve to accent and move the motifs beyond their narrative function.

Presenting these elements within a theoretical re-assessment of realism invites a recovery of some of the foundational thinkers of realist film theory, such as André Bazin and Siegfried Kracauer, amongst others, whose examination of the capacity of realist cinema to effect an active engagement with the spectator's own realities was overtaken by the theoretical debates of the 1970s. As Lúcia Nagib puts it, Bazin's 'realist politics concerned doubt, or, in his words, "ambiguity of expression" as enabled by the surplus of time and space contained in the long take/long-shot combination', thus 'active spectatorship' and 'spectatorial agency and participation' are enabled and not restricted by realist poetics (Nagib 2016: 28). Bazin's well-known advocacy for depth of focus centres around bringing the 'spectator into a relation with the image closer to that which he enjoys with reality', which in turn enables a 'more active mental attitude on the part of the spectator and a more positive contribution on his part to the action in progress' (Bazin 2010: 101). Meaning making is thus collaborative and, for Bazin, realism is theorised not merely in terms of offering a representation of reality but as a reflection upon it, 'not to produce a spectacle which appears real, but rather to turn reality into a spectacle' (Bazin 2005: 67). For Kracauer,

> [f]ilms tend to explore this texture of everyday life, whose composition varies according to place, people and time. So they help us not only to appreciate our given material environment but to extend it in all its directions. They virtually make the world our home. (Kracauer 1960: 304)

Kracauer describes cinema's capacity to enable the apprehension of 'physical reality in its concreteness' (Ibid.: 165), wherein 'small units' are 'free to range over all orbits imaginable' (Ibid.: 303). For Kracauer, '[n]o doubt these are intended to advance the story to which they belong but they also 'affect[s] us strongly, or even primarily, as just a moment of visible reality, surrounded, as it were, by a fringe of indeterminate visible meanings' (Ibid.: 303). Realism is thus here theorised not as a set of cinematic conventions but as the binding philosophical mechanism of a dialogue between spectator, film and everyday life. In these terms, realism invites critical reflection, rather than absorbing it. As Ian Aitken puts it, Kracauer situated his 'redemption' of realism in precisely this way: 'bringing the individual into a closer proximity with a physical reality currently obscured by the forces of modernity' (Aitken 2006: 159). Clearly for Bazin, and for Kracauer too, in order for this heightened engagement with the spectator's own realities to occur, realist texts should pursue particular textual strategies. As Aitken puts it: 'Kracauer argues that the way to escape from the "spiritual nakedness" of this debilitating modern condition is through transcending our abstract relation to our own experience of the world, and experiencing the world in its phenomenological richness' (Ibid.: 165). This assertion of cinema's capacity to evoke a heightened, sensory dialogue with the spectator finds application, of course, in new realism's tendency towards a conspicuous evocation of physical perception and feeling.

We should also consider here Bazin's and Kracauer's shared belief in a non-instrumental and indeterminate realist aesthetic. As Aitken argues, '[a]t the heart of Kracauer's conception of cinematic realism is the conviction that, at the level of form, film should allow images of the world a degree of autonomous existence from the controlling drive of narrative, action and plot' (Ibid.: 168). Thus, many of the elements of new realist poetics that we have already begun to sketch out – its lingering and non-prescriptive emphasis on landscape, for example – should also be understood as actualising the philosophical pronouncements of realist film theory. This is useful to us because it points to a way of conceptualising realist form and practice beyond some of the more rigidly theorised, and ahistorical paradigms that I have summarised in this introduction, in the hope that we might begin to nuance and broaden our understandings of the relationships between film and reality in contemporary Britain.

A New Tradition

The rest of this book is divided into five chapters, with each covering a specific realist film-maker who has been active in the contemporary period. This is not to suggest that new realism is limited to the output of a closed set of practitioners but rather that it is more productive to devote concerted scholarly attention to directors whose films have consistently reflected the features that I have highlighted in this introduction. For that reason, there is no space for the likes of Pawel Pawlikowski, nor Lynne Ramsay, mentioned earlier. This is not to underplay their formative role in articulating a new space for realism in the contemporary period, but it instead reflects that, since *My Summer of Love* (Pawlikowski, 2004) and *Morvern Callar* (Ramsay, 2002), both film-makers have pursued projects away from their initial concern with British landscapes. Indeed, it is for this reason that Steve McQueen, despite his desire to put an 'audience in a situation that feels like reality' (Gritten 2012), is also omitted. Andrew Haigh, whose film *Weekend* (2011) can be seen as an exemplar of new realism, has in recent years expanded his oeuvre, taking in American television drama with *Looking* and the American-set film *Lean on Pete* (2017). The absence of a chapter on Haigh is not to dismiss consideration of television or of films located outside of Britain, but to do justice to the diversity of his output would be to dilute the focus on new realism as a specific tradition. There are also a number of individual films such as *Catch Me Daddy* (Daniel Wolfe, 2015), *Control* (Anton Corbijn, 2007), the already discussed *The Unloved*, *The Goob* (Guy Myhill, 2014), and Paddy Considine's directorial debut *Tyrannosaur* (2011) that might also be productively located within a wider new realist tradition, but these films do not constitute a consistent body of work on the part of their directors and/or an exclusive focus on British realist themes and aesthetics.

Instead, I have chosen to focus on film-makers who have maintained a concerted emphasis on the features and fundamental components of new realism, with the case study approach enabling both a discussion of the specific characteristics of their oeuvres and a broader examination of the features that bind and connect their films to a wider tradition. Chapter 1 considers the work of Duane Hopkins, who, despite a limited output of just two feature films between 2008 and 2014 is, I argue, a foundational film-maker within new realism. The chapter explores in particular the ways in which Hopkins's work is structured by a conspicuously constructed, lyrical examination of everyday practices, landscapes and objects to invite a poetic reflection on and elevation of such quotidian material.

This thread continues into a consideration of the work of Joanna Hogg in Chapter 2, whose films are similarly structured around everyday processes and routines. Hogg's work is also particularly attentive to constructing a perceptual verisimilitude through both immersive sound design and a tableau-like approach to *mise en scène* that foregrounds a sense of spectatorial complicity. These elements, which combine to foster an often intense intimacy, point to the ways in which new realism can be understood to convey an experience of reality, and are also felt in the work of Andrea Arnold. Although similarly sensorially rich, unlike Hogg's, Arnold's films, discussed in Chapter 3, are imbued with restless, participatory energy with the camera closely aligned with her subjects to build an embodied sense of identification. But just as in the films of her contemporaries, Arnold's meticulous approach to everyday imagery both foregrounds a sense of a highly textured and familiar world and, through differing modes of emphasis, renders such material as defamiliarised and thus, poetic. This is particularly apparent in Arnold's highly dynamic exploration of landscape, place and space, and it is this feature, as mentioned already, which can be understood as a defining tenet of new realism.

In Chapter 4, I introduce the work of Shane Meadows, whose highly collaborative, semi-autobiographical films, with their reliance on untrained actors and stylised elevation of everyday spaces, can be authentically located within the new realist tradition. However, the chapter also examines the uniquely, at least in terms of new realism, non-specific, and thus universal approach that Meadows takes to his use of location, and, in addition, considers the effects of television drama and seriality on filmic content. While Clio Barnard's films are similarly invested in a concerted examination of the relationships between environment and identity, unlike Meadows's work, they are engaged in highly place-specific narratives. Barnard's three films to date, discussed in Chapter 5, are conjoined by a self-conscious examination of realist methodology and tradition. Each film operates under superficially distinctive auspices, yet they share examinations of landscape which are both visually realistic and revelatory in their uncovering of the political, economic and emotional forces that shape and are reflected by these locations. When combined, then, these films have formed a tradition that acts against the designation of Loachian social realism as the definitive realist mode.

1. DUANE HOPKINS

When I began the process of attempting to trace a new turn in British realist cinema some seven years ago (Forrest 2010), Duane Hopkins's film *Better Things* (2008), with its loose, associative narrative structure, its heavily accented approach to its rural setting, its stylised but no less ethical approach to its isolated working-class subjects, and its melding of subjective and more distanced painterly perspectives and compositions, seemed an ideal case study. In the intervening years Hopkins, along with his production partner Samm Haillay, has returned to feature films with *Bypass* (2014), a film which marks a departure from his debut, but which nevertheless illustrates a continuing commitment to a heightened mode of realist practice. Hopkins might therefore be regarded as the least prolific but perhaps the most aesthetically consistent film-maker under discussion here, and as such his place in this book is justified as a foundational exemplar of contemporary British cinema's evolution of the realist mode. This chapter will look to anatomise the poetics of Hopkins's cinema and, in the process, gesture towards a fuller understanding of the specific tools and textual characteristics that generate both Hopkins's and more broadly British realism's lyrical impulse.

Across both *Better Things* and *Bypass*, Hopkins's approach to space, place and landscape is critical to generating meaning that is at once universal and tethered to a specific engagement with the socio-political realm. Accordingly, an emphasis on cultural geography will underpin my approach to both films. Moreover, I want to look in particular at the ways in which Hopkins's realist project is partly defined by a stylised and heavily structured approach to a quotidian *mise en scène*. This creates a kind of lyrical rhythm that both transforms and recalibrates everyday gestures, objects and landscapes, rendering them poetic. With this in mind, I want to return to the realist film theory of Siegfried Kracauer, which provides a productive starting point:

> Film renders visible what we did not, or perhaps even could not, see before its advent. It effectively assists us in discovering the material world with its psychophysical correspondences. We literally redeem this world from its dormant state, its state of virtual nonexistence, by endeavoring to experience it through the camera. [. . .] The cinema can be defined as a medium particularly equipped to promote the redemption of physical reality. Its imagery permits us, for the first time, to take away with us the objects and occurrences that comprise the flow of material life. (Kracauer 1960: 300)

As I will go on to show, Hopkins's films' focus on materiality manifests itself in highly structured ways, often in the form of repetitious, rhythmic patterns of recurring quotidian imagery that transcend the demands of narrative communication. I want to approach this in a specific manner, to seek to identify and reflect upon some of the significant and precise components of Hopkins's style. For example, in *Better Things*, some 73 of the film's 852 shots comprise images of characters staring (often silently) out of windows – this is some 8.5 per cent of a narrative film that is devoted solely to static portraits of protagonists engaged in a common, quotidian gesture. This taken-for-granted activity is therefore made poetic by its lingering, repeated emphasis. In *Bypass*, 117 out of the film's 1,601 shots comprise compositions in which the camera rests on common, inescapably domestic reflective surfaces (windows, televisions, picture frames, mirrors) to fragment the representation of a character or characters on screen – thus, some 7.3 per cent of the film is made up of diegetically centred visual distortions generated from seemingly innocuous materials of domestic experience. I will spend more time later reflecting on the thematic possibilities of these leitmotifs, but first I want to consider the ways in which these devices, alongside others in Hopkins's stylistic arsenal – in line with Kracauer's theoretical project – might be seen to 'denaturalise spectators' normal experience of the world in order to refamiliarise them with content they have lost' (Wils 2016: 69), and to, in the process, 'turn our attention back to immediate experience and the everyday' (Aitken 2001: 176).

In terms of new realism, then, what I want to argue is that Hopkins's interest in the aesthetics of actuality is defined by a desire to transform what we might call realist materials – that is, those visually familiar tenets that underpin our everyday existence – into sources of affective meaning, and to, in the process, direct us towards a fine grain appreciation of the poetic possibilities of ours and others' daily experiences.

Hopkins is an eloquent advocate of his own work and of the manner in which his films depart from and remodel realist traditions. For example, ahead of the release of *Bypass* he admitted a desire to make 'realist elements very cinematic' (Haillay and Hopkins 2014) and in interviews around the release of *Better Things* showed a willingness to identify where he felt the film moved beyond conventional 'social realism':

> I wanted to take on social realist elements, or what you'd consider social realist elements, which is kind of location shooting, working-class characters, problematic things like drug use, which would normally be explored in a film in terms of class or social economics or social strata or whether or not it's a problem for society – all these kinds of political elements. I wanted to de-politicise these and look at them more psychologically and from a more lyrical, hyper-real point-of-view.
> [...]
> It's not just a recording of a naturalistic performance saying this kind of naturalistic dialogue. It becomes something else. It aspires to something which is bigger, which is more sublime than just the straightforward stuff. (Anonymous 2008)

I will return to the political dimension of Hopkins's films later in this chapter but for now it is worth focusing on the dominant feature of his comments here, that is the desire to a move beyond the 'straightforward' and towards a lyrical 'something else'. Keeping this in mind, we return again to Kracauer and his call for a realist practice that is not merely directed towards the dispassionate recording of material reality but instead affects a poetic distance from it. As Ian Aitken argues:

> Kracauer does not call for a form of cinematic realism which would merely 'record' physical reality in some *cinéma-vérité*-like fashion. On the contrary, he argues that film technique should be intentionally deployed in order to portray both perceptual physical reality *and* the underlying characteristics of the *Lebenswelt*. One consequence of the need to portray the latter of these two aspects of the *Lebenswelt* is that film form may be used in a formative and modernist manner, in order to portray something which exists beyond the immediately empirical. (Aitken 2006: 167)

Aitken's evocation of the '*lebenswelt*', literally the 'living world', as a framework for understanding and representing the lived, material experiences of life, helps to orient Kracauer's theory towards a realist project that elevates these elements – accenting them towards, as Hopkins puts it, 'something which is bigger' than the 'recording . . . of performance' (Anonymous 2008). For example, in *Better Things*, Hopkins's persistent deployment of the window gazing leitmotif, and other recurrent emphases on hands, frosted glass and artificially rendered landscapes (on canvas, plates, curtains) establishes within mundane gestures and images a kind of everyday poetics, made all the more vital and transformative by their rhythmic repetition. To be clear, repetition here enables a rejection of narrative instrumentalism. In *Bypass*, we think not only of the repeated reflected images already mentioned, but of the recurring shots of characters through doorways and caught between thresholds – meaning that human figures vie for primacy with inanimate domestic objects within the *mise en scène* – and, as in *Better Things*, of frequent close shots of hand holding. The recurrence of these motifs enables them to operate as autonomous elements of quotidian imagery not merely as diegetic accoutrement. To return to Aitken on Kracauer:

> Kracauer argued that, whilst the film-maker must give each scene in a film a dominant meaning relevant to the plot, he or she must also strive to give signification a degree of ambiguity, so that 'a considerable degree of indeterminacy is retained', and the film is able to generate 'free hovering images of reality'. (Aitken 2001: 173)

Thus while a shot of Tim in *Bypass* selling stolen goods in a pub tells us something narrationally significant about his burgeoning criminal career, the presentation of this short, one-shot scene through a reflective window – thus distorting the viewer's perspective on the protagonist and the space in which he operates – works also to disturb and defamiliarise our comprehension of a common 'image of reality'.

While it might be suggested that such stylisation of 'reality' – Hopkins's 'cinematic social realism' – brings with it ethical and socio-political implications, we must keep in mind the foundational centrality to new realism of what I have previously termed 'image-led narration' (Forrest 2013: 37). This can be defined as an approach to the generation of narrative which is driven by a particular image or set of images, meaning that a thematic agenda emerges from a pointedly visual starting point, rather than the other way around. This subsequently generates more oblique but arguably more inclusive narrative strategies, as Hopkins himself describes:

> The first thing is that I noticed with my writing that I was more inspired by images. It would be an image I felt compelled to create and that I wanted to see on the screen. Or it would be a single character saying a certain line. Or it would be a room and a certain atmosphere that I

wanted to make as an image. So it was about having that image and how I built a scene from that image, or how I constructed something which allowed me to make that image, and allows that image to be as open and as meaningful as it can be. (Anonymous 2008)

The notion that such images operate as 'open' and 'meaningful', that they are in some way freer because they dictate narrative loosely rather than acting as the servants of plot, returns us again to Kracauer's notion of indeterminacy and the sense in which the stylised textures of actuality found in Hopkins's work create meaning from their re-imagination of hitherto suppressed or ignored elements of everyday reality. In this sense, the image operating as catalyst to narration – a figure staring out of a window for example, or the face of a man in a pub reflected through glass – does not prescribe one meaning but should instead initiate a process whereby multiple points of contemplation and inter-action are incited in the viewer. This approach is not specific to Hopkins. For example, Andrea Arnold has described how '[u]sually what starts driving me is an image I have that won't go away' (Kouguell 2016) and Lynne Ramsay noted of *Ratcatcher* (1999): 'I wanted to make a film that was driven by emotion and images rather than narrative' (Liese 1999: 17). Ramsay's lingering, textured approach to quotidian detail has similarly invited Kracauer-inspired readings of her films. Tina Kendall's examination of *Ratcatcher*, for example, offers up some possible resources for an examination of similar areas of Hopkins's work:

> Such scenes foreground the sensuous qualities of things over their instru-mentality, and the long takes can similarly be said to undermine any objective quest for certainty in things, since they supply few clues to tell us where the meaning of these images resides. They seem to affirm Kracauer's contention that film pictures 'what is just there', refusing, in its thinglike depiction of the material world, to reproduce hierarchies between subjects and objects. (Kendall 2010: 184)

We might think of 'instrumentality' here both in the context of its use value in profilmic plot terms of these quotidian details, fragments, and gestures and in terms of their utility in everyday life. In moving beyond function, we uncover once again a form of poetics which is firmly rooted in the familiar and which is consequently reliant on a symbiosis between the diegetic representation of lived 'reality' and the non-diegetic experience of it.

Kendall's consideration of the 'sensuous qualities' of such aesthetic approaches suggests an affinity with an increasing turn towards the sensory in studies of realism – again, partly inspired by renewed engagements with realist theorists such as Kracauer and André Bazin. Indeed, Tiago de Luca's book

Realism of the Senses describes how sensory realist films are '[f]ascinated by landscapes and cityscapes, bodies and faces, animate and inanimate matter', and 'are driven by a materialist impetus through which the facticity of things and beings take precedence over representational categories and functions' (de Luca 2014: 12). One immediately thinks of the landscape shots in *Better Things* – both those showing natural imagery and those involving houses and cars in isolated rural settings – and of the leitmotifs already discussed in both films. Similarly, in the analyses of their case study films, both de Luca and Kendall are united by the view that such objects and iconographies exist neither as plot instruments nor as specific symbolic functionaries, but as components of a wider process of rendering heightened and lyrical that which is often overlooked in everyday life. While de Luca's work focuses largely on those films that rely on the long take to affect sensory engagement, we might suggest that in Hopkins's work an analogous poetic emphasis is arrived at through the persistent deployment of the kind of imagery I have already described.

Tiago de Luca further connects this non-instrumental tendency in contemporary realism to Kracauer by evoking the redemptive potential of such contemplative, poetic works 'in an age in which a more direct experience of material reality is increasingly replaced by technologically mediated communication models and ways of being that favour information and simulation at the expense of physical experience' (de Luca 2014: 234). In this sense Kracauer's theorisation of cinema's relationship with the *lebenswelt* takes on new currency in an age of fragmented and privatised media consumption where the possibility for affecting a mode of conscious interaction between the experience of physical reality and its representation is increasingly remote. Thus, films that elevate the processes and iconographies of daily life as central to their meaning making, work to, in Kracauer's words, reveal 'otherwise hidden provinces' of 'physical reality' (Kracauer 1960: 158).

I have begun to suggest how these concepts might function in relation to Hopkins's use of the leitmotif, but I want now to consider briefly Hopkins's treatment of external space and landscape to identify a linked tenet of his realist practice. *Bypass* and *Better Things* in particular make conspicuous use of non-specific urban and rural landscapes respectively to both punctuate and contextualise their protagonists' experiences and operate to effect contemplative encounters with the viewer. Indeed, just as the devices already discussed work to both reflect and poeticise our own ways of being in the world, so too the lyrically marked mundane spaces of Hopkins's films make cinematic our environments and habitats. For example, the opening twelve shots of *Better Things*, although woven together by Gail's voice-over, contain six static images of distinctive external landscapes, moving from a striking long shot of trees against a dark cloud to a shot of a garden outside a modest 1970s house, before a seventh shot moves into the home. The frequency and staidness of the images establishes a rhythm of mundane imagery that anticipates Hopkins's later use of the leitmotif. These are relentlessly familiar and purposefully generic national landscapes; bereft of place-specific narratives they are instead deployed for their looser articulation as markers of rural England (disconnected from spectacular heritage representation), designed to evoke universal recognition and to establish the conditions for the process of exchange between the geographies of physical reality and their mediated presence on screen. As Tim Edensor argues:

> I insist that by far the most common spatial experience is that of everyday environments, however, where familiar space forms an unquestioned backdrop to daily tasks, pleasures and routine movement. [...] the mundane, habitual world is the bedrock upon which a sense of national identity is reproduced in daily life and in the everyday consumption of media. This everyday space is the setting in which quotidian manoeuvres and modes of dwelling are unreflexively carried out [...] in everyday space, familiar things, routes and fixtures surround us and we make our home there by the repetitive performance of habitual enactions, by customary, routine engagement. (Edensor 2015: 62)

The repeatedly foregrounded 'everyday space' of Hopkins's films – composed of gestures, landscapes, housing and objects – incubates the heightened, lyrical approach to his subjects within a recognisable framework. Disconnected from their utility as mere narrative accompaniment or mechanisms of delivery, these images operate to reflect and poetically re-imagine the terrain of our own experiences, as Edensor continues:

> Such recurrent images are part of the production of the imaginary geographies of the nation – and produce intertextuality, or *interspatiality*, in that they conjure up spaces that are familiar to the national viewer. The state functions, religious practices and civic rituals, the more official dimensions of the national, are supplemented by the dense abundance of these more mundane material, spatial, sensual and symbolic elements that populate television and film sets. (Ibid.: 72)

The process of interspatiality that operates in the consumption of realist texts is therefore critical to their resonance and specific appeal. The poetics of the familiar trigger a symbiotic exchange between representation and experience. To use Hallam and Roberts's phrase 'moving images' become 'complicit in the cinematisation' of 'everyday landscapes' (Hallam and Roberts 2014: 9). In this sense, then, Giuliana Bruno's description of the relationship between film, the body and architecture is relevant too, whereby 'a phantasmatic structure of lived space and lived narrative; a narrativised space that is intersubjective' (Bruno 2001: 65) is initiated between viewer, environment and text. This emphasis on the possible affective dimension of rendering familiar landscapes and routines on screen returns us again to Kracauer. In drawing on Proust's *Remembrance of Things Past*, Kracauer points to cinema's ability to conjure up, through engagement with the representation of physical reality, 'overpowering images of things external' which in turn act as stimuli to effect new encounters with our own environment(s):

> The generic term 'psychophysical correspondences' covers all these more or less fluid interrelations between the physical word and the psychological dimension in the broadest sense of the word – a dimension which borders on that physical universe and is still intimately connected with it. (Kracauer 1960: 70)

And it is here, having made some suggestions for the ways in which we might begin to theorise and contextualise Hopkins's approach to cinematic realism, that I want to turn more specifically to his films, beginning with *Better Things*.

BETTER THINGS (2008)

Better Things is set in the Cotswolds area of South Central England. It follows the loosely interlinked experiences of ten characters over a period of days. Rob (Liam McIlfatrick) is a heroin addict who is grieving after the drug-related death of his partner Tess (Emma Cooper) and who himself dies of a drug overdose at the conclusion (Liam McIlfatrick tragically died before the film was released). A young couple, David (Che Corr) and Sarah (Tara Ballard): David is friends with Rob and is also a heroin addict and Sarah has recently moved away in an attempt to escape the drug culture of the town – again, Hopkins cast both actors for their experiences, with Corr and Ballard having 'both recently kicked heroin' and 'in the process of ending their relationship, having decided this was necessary to confront their mutual dependency' when cast (Anonymous 2008). Gail (Rachel McIntyre), an agoraphobic young woman with a liking for romance novels – similarly McIntyre was cast for 'experiences' of 'depression' and 'self-image issues . . . and her ability to draw on them, rather than her formal acting training' (Ibid. 2008). Gail's grandmother Nan Wilson (Patricia Loveland), who begins the film in hospital before returning to live with Gail and her parents and eventually dying, although not before she coaxes Gail out of the house. Mrs Gladwin (Betty Bench) and Mr Gladwin (Frank Bench) – Mr Gladwin has been in the same hospital as Nan and returns home to his wife in the middle of the film, where an unspoken issue hangs over their relationship, although by the film's conclusion they seem to have overcome their troubles (the actors had themselves been married to each other for more than sixty years). Finally, Rachel (Megan Palmer) and Larry (Kurt Taylor), a pair of teenagers whose relationship has ended – Larry is angry that Rachel has a new boyfriend, but by the film's end there is a hint of reconciliation between the pair.

With all of the aforementioned characters being played by non-professionals drawing on their own experiences to portray their roles with authentic depth, *Better Things* sits alongside recent realist traditions (Arnold, Hogg, Meadows) and more established practices (Ken Loach, Italian Neo-Realism). However, Hopkins's approach to casting also further illuminates the distinctive elements of his practice:

> I look for people from a photographic and experience viewpoint. You have to be interested in photographing them first, then their experiences give you a basis from which you can direct them, using what you know they have been through to provoke and help them. Then you try to use the camera like a microscope. (Anonymous 2008)

For Hopkins, then, the cast's individual and collective experiences have both thematic and aesthetic value. This emphasis on the visual again draws us towards the sense in which Hopkins's loose, image-led approach privileges a more ambiguous mode of narration which is built around composition and editing rather than dialogue, as Hopkins himself states: 'I never want my films to be just story or plot I want something more incongruous that evokes rather than explains' (Anonymous 2008). Indeed, I wish to suggest that this narrational sparseness is an intrinsic element of Hopkins's poetics, drawing attention away from the story elements and towards 'indeterminate' and 'free hovering' imagery (Aitken 2001: 173).

In my previous work on Hopkins (Forrest 2010) I sought to contrast *Better Things* with Ken Loach's *Riff-Raff* (1991), a paradigmatic example of social realism. I made this comparison on the basis of both films' uses of dialogue, calculating that '[w]ithin 95 minutes, the delivery of audible dialogue accounts for 61.52 minutes of *Riff-Raff*, which translates to 65 per cent of the film. However, *Better Things*, at 89 minutes, consists of just 14.35 minutes of audible dialogue, or 16.1 per cent' (Ibid.: 38). Reviewing these statistics alongside the aforementioned data (8.5 per cent of the film comprises shots of characters staring silently out of windows) it becomes clear that the minimal approach to dialogue in turn re-engages a more visceral but productively ambiguous emphasis on the self-contained image, particularly when considering its broad narrative dispersal and minimal plot. Indeed, these elements direct meaning towards the editing and composition of the non-verbal images, rendering the rhythm and structure of the film as poetic rather than functional.

To illustrate this further, I want to point to specific evidence of Hopkins's image-led approach. After the aforementioned opening scene involving Gail and the repeated landscape shots, the action moves to Tess's funeral and its immediate aftermath, before a fade to black reveals the film's title. After this we are introduced to the film's other characters, with a relatively quick succession of shots. First, we see a close shot of Sarah on a train looking pensively out of a window. Hopkins then cuts to a wider, medium-close shot showing her alone at a train table; she is still staring out of the window but this time her face is reflected back against the houses and trees that speed by. We then see Mrs Gladwin in the supermarket, and in a four-shot sequence Hopkins shows her browsing the aisles of the empty shop before picking up a cassette tape and placing it in her basket. This tape goes on to act as a crucial leitmotif for the Gladwins' relationship. It is wrapped as a gift for Mr Gladwin but remains unopened for much of the film, with two shots at separate points showing the unopened present and thus marking the continuation of their silent hostilities – when the couple reconcile, Hopkins rests on an image of the gift unwrapped, concluding the Gladwin's narrative in an image-led fashion. After the supermarket, we then move to Mr Gladwin's hospital ward, where he is looking out of a window and the next shot shows the object of his gaze to be Nan Wilson. Momentarily she too looks out of her window, then back at Mr Gladwin, and this pattern is then repeated over the next three shots, albeit from different angles and concluding with a shot of Mr Gladwin returning to his paper. The next scene reintroduces us to Gail, and in a ninety second sequence we see twelve shots, beginning with Gail in her bedroom, before she realises that Nan is arriving at the house. The scene concludes with a close shot of Gail facing the camera but not before we see an image of Gail staring out of a window. The final shots of the sequence introduce us to Larry and Rachel; Larry is with his friend, Joel (Mike Randle), in a park but on he is on the phone. We then move to a scene of Rachel and her friend, Julie (Katie Samuels), and it is clear that Larry is phoning her, and for most of the scene, despite being engaged in conversation, Rachel is staring out of the window – the source of her distraction is shown to be her new boyfriend, Mike (Michael Socha), who is arriving to pick her up. The sequence ends with a return to Larry and his friend.

This passage lasts around four minutes and contains forty shots. Dialogue is minimal, operating briefly in the Gail scene and in the exchange between Rachel and Julie. Arguably, though, there is much narrative work done here: the source of the characters' malaises and the nature of their relationships are established with varying degrees of coverage. However, what is more apparent is the 'creation of a certain atmosphere' (Anonymous 2008), to use Hopkins's words, and it is one which is established through minimal dialogue. This, in turn, emphasises other less narrationally instrumental aural elements, to generate a heightened focus on the unspoken, incommunicable sadness of his key protagonists, almost all of whom are shown staring into space, more specifically out of windows, and lost in 'unspecified' contemplation (even when characters are looking at something specific their listless expressions dominate) – nine out of the forty shots are window shots, with the fifth to the thirteenth shots of the film coming in this sequence. Thus the film's most conspicuous leitmotif is here established as both a tool of universal meaning that speaks to the film's themes of alienation and the pain of love while also operating at the level of structure – fostering a loose connectivity between the multiple characters symbolically rather than linearly. Hopkins speaks of a desire in the film:

> To edit in a way that created sequences, linking characters and their narratives. The drama in *Better Things* comes from a gradual build up of scenes that relate to, and compliment each other thematically and build an impression of an area, it's [*sic*] inhabitants and their individual stories through these sequences. (Anonymous 2008)

This connectivity is thus thematic and, I would also argue, driven by paralleled imagery. As Jonathan Romney suggests of Hopkins: 'he and editor Chris Barwell offer extended chains of discrete images for us to order associatively, as we would with images in poetry, rather than to construct narrative information', and it is this analogy to written poetry that I wish to emphasise here (Romney 2009). Hopkins effectively establishes a rhyming pattern, using the linked deployment of universal, quotidian images as the film's primary structuring device, affecting in the process a sense of interspatial resonance grounded in, as I have already suggested, the lyrical transformation of mundane images, gestures and landscapes.

1.1   Window shots as rhymes in *Better Things*.

As the film reaches its final stages, Hopkins's associative, patterned approach to poetic rhythm becomes ever more evident. After Larry, consumed by love-struck rage, scrapes his fist against a wall, Hopkins rests on his shaking, injured knuckles, a match cut takes us to the image of the injured hand as Larry appears to lie in bed, with a third shot of Larry resting his head on a pillow and staring sadly into space. We then move to a close shot of Mrs Gladwin in bed, eyes open, staring into space – the shots of the beds act as the visual bridge here, with the thematic continuity emerging from both Mrs Gladwin's and Larry's empty hope that their love be reciprocated by their respective partners. After repeated spatially matched shots of Mr and Mrs Gladwin awake but not communicating, the bed is now established as a fugue within the sequence, extending as it does to Nan Wilson, who is getting out of her bed in the next scene. This creates a feeling of panic for the agoraphobic Gail who is supposed to be caring for her grandmother, but ultimately Gail joins Nan outside, seemingly conquering her own fear of the outside world. The two then come inside and converse, with Nan reflecting on the life of her late husband. Their dialogue is framed with single, close shots of either Nan or Gail side on with the final shot in the scene graphically matching a shot of Mr Gladwin in the next one, as the Gladwins, like Nan and Gail before them, begin to communicate in a meaningful fashion for the first time in the film – a shot of the empty wrapping and the sound of the tape being inserted into the machine confirms their reconciliation, and the tone of symbolic release and redemption is palpable. The music, Schubert's Piano Trio in E flat, is sourced diegetically as the tape goes into the machine, before then soundtracking non-diegetically a slow-motion montage of all the film's characters (Sarah alone in a club; David taking drugs; the Gladwins embracing; a shot of Gail reading her grandfather's epitaph; Rob staring at the ceiling; the sequence ending with Nan's dead body being found by Gail's mother). Thus in these interlinked scenes Hopkins evolves another visual rhyming pattern, using paralleled bed scenes (the scenes are also united by repeated close shots of hands, another leitmotif throughout the film) to structure a thematic connection around a tone of emotional repression which fades into one of release and resolution. Crucially then, this sequence also works to set up the concluding passages of the film, as each of the characters begins to experience some degree of catharsis.

While the dominant motifs in these poetically charged sequences see characters interacting with their environments and with each other, another critical tenet of Hopkins's realist practice emerges from a treatment of external landscape that is perhaps more autonomous. I have already discussed the film's opening sequence in relation to the frequency of the landscape shots, but it is worth returning to it here to consider in more detail Hopkins's painterly approach to rural space. The film opens in darkness with the sound of

1.2   Another rhyming pattern.

wind growing more and more heavily until a silent image of what Hopkins's screenplay describes as:

> A beautiful image of two trees stood steadfastly together. The composition is reminiscent of classical landscape painting. The light is of very early morning, daybreak. In extreme slow motion we watch the wind move through the trees, causing their surface to move like a wave. (Hopkins 2008)

There is much to discuss here, but for now I want to focus on the primary effect of divorcing the image from the sound. In the next shot Gail's voice-over begins (a quotation from *Passion and the Past* by Miranda Lee which is also used at the film's conclusion) and all natural sound is suppressed as Gail's voice narrates over the static shots of landscapes mentioned earlier. As Stella Hockenhull argues 'the visual does not here prevail over the aural, Hopkins providing equal weight to the relationship between the two' (Hockenhull 2014: 75), and in doing this Hopkins once more disturbs our comprehension of the familiar, this time through a manipulation in sound design. Thus, while the image itself at first appears like a 'classical landscape painting' it is one that is given visceral depth by the slow motion and the interplay between silence and overbearing wind. The effect is therefore to create a deconstructed landscape shot that lays bare its constituent elements and immediately denies comprehension of the image on purely pictorial terms. As Paul Newland argues in his book on British rural cinema: 'The picturesque essentially sets up a picture frame between the observer and the landscape. Viewers of the picturesque landscapes are not embedded in these landscapes, then. They stand apart, as observers' (Newland 2016: 9). In this sense, Hopkins's heightened emphasis on sound and movement in and of the landscape reveals the otherwise hidden textures of the pictorial, and moves through the 'picture frame' to disrupt notions of external spaces as static and fixed, in keeping with the ambiguous nature of other modes of imagery in the film.

To go further, it is possible to suggest that Hopkins's approach to the treatment of landscape represents a conscious critique of the kinds of picturesque rural iconographies that, as Newland implies, operate conservatively in other cultural representations of the rural. For example, early on in the film Jon (Freddie Cunliffe) and Rob drive to a remote country lane to smoke heroin. In the first interior shot of the stationary car, a close composition of Rob has him staring directly at the camera and then moving his head towards the window. The sounds of birds and the loud, harsh wind are artificially conspicuous. In the next shot, a side on composition of Rob, we hear the sounds of foil as he prepares the heroin to be smoked, reasserting the aural coherence with the internal sound (foil) now more conspicuous than the external (wind, birds). Yet this sense of continuity between sound and image is brought into doubt in the next shot, an arresting landscape image of a stark, early evening view, with dark clouds moving at the top of the frame – here the sound of foil is present but the wind and birds are not. The two then discuss Jon's granddad (Mr Gladwin) via a conventional exchange of shots, while the sound of the outside gradually increases until another external landscape shot, this time soundtracked by the wind *and* the foil. As Jon begins to smoke, the sound of the wind increases until a return to the front-on shot of Rob. The sound of the wind is so prominent now that it is almost as though Rob is outside. The scene concludes with two static external shots, one from behind, the other from the front with the second slightly wider, showing the trees blowing in the strong wind. At no point is the layered landscape (sound and moving image) operating here at a purely pictorial level, it is instead shown to be interactive; both working with the viewer at a sensory level – in Edensor's words 'evoking the mundane textures, smells, sounds and sights of familiar spaces' (Edensor 2015: 62) – and with the characters, as it literally penetrates their diegetic space. Indeed, the next shot is a painted landscape at winter, consuming the frame entirely with a scene not unlike those seen in the moving image compositions that have preceded it. On one level this is another image-led fugue – Jon and Rob's scene connects to a scene of Mr Gladwin (the picture is in the hospital, Jon and Rob were talking about him) – yet on the other, the static artificially rendered landscape itself is offered up for scrutiny, contrasted as it is with the more organic, free-flowing images of nature that have preceded it. As mentioned earlier, similarly constructed and idealised versions of the landscape operate within the film, usually in relation to Gail: an image of birds on a plate from which she eats, a crochet birdhouse which contrasts with a shot of the same object outside her window, and flowers on a closed curtain with the outside light gently shining through to her darkened room. Just as with Mr Gladwin's literally frozen landscape painting, these images juxtapose with the film's conjoined aural and visual leitmotif of the wind, with Gail's introduction, her aforementioned moment of redemption with Nan, and the sense of release as she walks through the landscape at the film's conclusion all moments characterised by the conspicuous sound of gales (perhaps the source of her name) and of the subsequent movement of leaves and trees.

Immobile, conspicuously constructed images of nature are therefore contrasted and ultimately overwhelmed by arresting representations of the landscape as textured and unfixed. As Catherine Fowler and Gillian Helfield argue, in order to critique cinematic representations of the rural and to unmoor them from their pictorial, heritage inflections, we must read the

> ... landscape ... as a text in its own right ... not subordinated to character and plot development but a discursive terrain with the same weight and requiring the same attention as other discourses that structure and move the text [as it becomes] a site where the dynamic of history can be read. (Fowler and Helfield 2006: 6)

Hopkins's treatment of rural space in *Better Things* aids this process because it resists easy narrative instrumentalism and monolithic symbolism with a rich sensory emphasis suggesting a sense of non-diegetic perpetuity – of existence *outside* the text. This sense of indeterminacy brings us back to Kracauer. While Kracauer concerned himself largely with representations of the city, his arguments suggesting that the articulation of physical reality might see the 'flow of life ... assert itself' (Kracauer 1960: 72) can also be understood in the context of the rural, particularly in Hopkins's elliptical, multi-narrative film where human characters and their loosely told narratives work alongside mundane, but poetically charged, textured landscapes. As Kracauer says of the 'indeterminate figures' of the city, '[e]ach has a story, yet the story is not given. Instead an incessant flow of possibilities and near-intangible meanings appears' (1960: 72).

Applying the notion of indeterminacy to questions of space brings us to Doreen Massey, whose theorisations of the spatial and the temporal chime with Hopkins's approach, with the resistance of a conception of 'space as a static slice through time, as representation, as a closed system' and instead pointing to the 'coeval multiplicity of other trajectories' (Massey 2005: 59). In *Better Things*, this manifests itself in the film's elliptical narratives, its rhythmic everyday poetics, and in its landscapes, which, as we have seen, are presented as continuous, autonomous entities. As Massey continues: 'Conceptualising space as open, and multiple and relational, unfinished and always becoming,

1.3   The non-diegetic perpetuity of the mundane.

is a prerequisite for history to be open and thus a prerequisite, too, for the possibility of politics' (Ibid.: 59).

Thinking through Hopkins's poetics in this way therefore takes us to a reconsideration of the politics of his film, as he argues '[t]he setting is rural England. A very under-used area cinematically, but it was absolutely my intention to make something universal, not specific to where it was filmed' (Anonymous 2008). Hopkins's meditative but loose portrayal of his human subjects, their environments, objects and landscapes is designed to foster a sense of malleability, enabling the accommodation of multiple and coexisting narratives, memories and histories.

BYPASS (2014)

Bypass is focused on the struggles of Tim (George MacKay), a young man who is forced into criminal activity (selling stolen goods) in order to support his teenage sister Helen (Lara Peake) following their mother's death (Arabella Arnott). Tim's and Helen's brother Greg (Ben Dilloway) has been released from prison and has renounced his former life as a burglar. The siblings' father (Scott McGrath) is absent but is a haunting presence in shared flashbacks, while their grandfather (Donald Sumpter) remains as a reminder of lost industrial pasts of secure employment and cohesive communities. Throughout the film Tim struggles with an unnamed medical condition and eventually suffers a violent fit. Tim's girlfriend, Lilly (Charlotte Spencer), provides a beacon of hope and the film concludes with her giving birth, signalling an apparently positive future ahead for the young family, but not before Greg is drawn back into crime to help his brother pay off his debts.

It is clear from this brief synopsis that *Bypass* is, superficially at least, markedly different from *Better Things* – the focus on one family, the casting of professional, recognised actors, and perhaps most obviously the integration of genre elements, with Hopkins and producer Haillay labelling the film a 'thriller with a conscience' (Haillay and Hopkins 2014). I will discuss the relationship between the film's structure and its realist practice later, but it is important, too, to acknowledge the scale of aesthetic departure from *Better Things*. Indeed, the later film has an average shot length of 3.7 seconds, with a median shot length of 2.9 seconds, with *Better Things* coming in at 6 and 5.1 seconds respectively. These data should also be appreciated in the context of *Better Things*'s contemplative, painterly style, as already discussed, where camera movement is rare and where the film format brings out the photographic textures of its subjects. In contrast, *Bypass* is shot on digital and is characterised by a heavily conspicuous handheld style with an intensely shallow focal depth. As Hopkins states:

> I wanted to change the ingredients from my previous film. To work with digital not film, to work handheld but not mimic other handheld styles I've seen. I wanted the feel to be organic, the feeling that at any point the camera itself could react in order to remain close to the characters. I needed to feel the camera's presence, not just be a bystander recording objectively. (Haillay and Hopkins 2014)

Yet, despite the marked distinctions in Hopkins's aesthetic and narrational approach it is possible to identify poetic continuities across both films. For example, I have already discussed the importance of the leitmotif or poetic signature in *Bypass* in the form of the reflective surfaces, images of which occur 117 times (7.3 per cent) across the film's 1,601 shots, and it is necessary now to consider this device in further detail. These compositions quite literally transform everyday objects (televisions, mirrors, picture frames) by taking them beyond their primary functions to distort and fragment the presentation of space and character. Although fleeting, these images are frequent enough, in Kracauer's words, to see the film 'caress one single object long enough to make us imagine its unlimited aspects' and to suspend 'dramatic action', suggesting 'geographical and causal endlessness' in much the same way as the window shots operate in *Better Things* (Kracauer 1960: 66).

The shots are first used in the opening sequence. It is Grandfather's birthday and he is being joined by Greg and some of his friends in a pub – this takes place a year before the main action begins and therefore before Greg's sentencing and imprisonment. There is no conventional establishing shot and instead the camera rests closely on two pictures on the left. Empty chairs and tables are reflected onto the left frame and made visible while in the right frame Greg, moving through the doorway, comes into and then gently back out of focus, with the shallow depth emphasising fleetingly the picture – which is revealed to be a portrait of the young Queen Elizabeth II – as Greg exits the shot. In the next shot the bottom corner of a picture frame offers a glimpse of Greg from behind, before the camera moves to rest on a mirror with the gold logo of a brewery obscuring slightly another reflection of Greg as he orders a drink. He turns to his side and a point-of-view shot though a serving hatch shows a group of elderly men in the snug, raising their glasses in unison and laughing. Next, a series of short handheld close shots frame Greg sitting with the old men and Grandfather – they are reminiscing about Greg's grandfather's grand-father, 'a forge worker' and an exceptional footballer. The scene moves into slow motion as Greg's grandfather bows his head in a moment of contempla-tion and the non-diegetic dialogue – 'you were a lot like him' – begins, before being sourced diegetically in the next scene as Greg helps his grandfather move out of his flat. The pair discuss and then pack away a photograph of Greg's great-great-grandfather in his football kit and we learn 'that injuries got to him just like you'. Grandfather then explains how he had got his apprenticeship through the men in his family and that he had got an apprenticeship for Greg's own father in the same way. Then, a medium two-shot – the first conventional composition of the two scenes – shows the pair in the empty flat. Grandfather speaks: 'That's it, then.' He is of course talking about their immediate task, but his words also reflect the film's wider purpose – as an elegy of industrial masculinity and working-class community.

This sequence tells us much about the precise components of the film's lyricism – its core characters, Greg first, and then Tim, are presented through-out in a conspicuously fragmented manner as Hopkins once again renders, in his words, 'hyper-real' his quotidian locations, fostering here a pervasive sense of rupture. This reflects the film's overarching treatment of loss. Indeed, Greg's fragmented presentation in the pub scene, with the mirrors and picture frames denying his presence within a wider, more cohesive backdrop of working-class nostalgia – made manifest through the *mise en scène* and the dialogue (the communal iconography of the pub, the image of the young queen, memories of work and sport) – also reflect this sense of mourning: Greg, the criminal by economic necessity, has no place in this lost world. As Hopkins says: 'Their work had given them stability. Shape and coherent narrative to their lives' (Horne 2014), and it therefore makes sense that Hopkins should represent the uncertain post-industrial trajectories of Tim and Greg without shape and coherence.

Hopkins's distorted but no less lyrical approach to everyday spaces and practices in *Bypass* contributes to the creation of an underlying tone of public and private grief, which is both political and emotional. For example, in a later scene in which Tim goes to the toilet and then examines a mark on his hand (a sign of his worsening illness) four out of the six shots are close compositions reflected off multiple bathroom mirrors, before a bang on the door signals that the bailiffs are outside (again Hopkins frames this action through two 'reflective' shots). As Tim waits silently, so as not to make his presence known, he stares at what was once his mother's bed, now stripped to its mattress. The first shot is again reflected through a mirror, before a shot back to Tim's grief-stricken face and then another close shot of the mirror, but this time his mother's feet are visible. Another knock at the door brings an end to this ghostly flashback. In a later scene we return to the mattress, and the ghostly presence of the mother is once again activated, the feet in the mirror shot is repeated, albeit from a different angle, and the scene ends with a series of close shots of Tim's hands as he finds one of his mother's hairs on the mattress – a last material trace of her presence. Here, the shallow focal depth effects a fine grain appreciation of the physical textures of Tim's grief. The scene then dissolves and Tim wakes up to find the heating on. He berates his sister, Helen, but the bailiffs knock again, interrupting his ire. Helen tells him she needs money for food and again Hopkins makes use of the mirror in Tim's and Helen's dead mother's empty room to refract and fragment Tim's presence in the shot. The replication of the two scenes is significant in furthering the film's formal pattern: two matched scenes combining an aestheticised and subsequently dream-like representation of personal grief interrupted by the pressures and economic realities of Tim's new-found responsibility as guardian and breadwinner.

Thus, *Bypass* shares with *Better Things* a rhythmic, poetic transformation of everyday space but against a more focused and politically explicit backdrop of economic austerity. Indeed, to return to the question of space across both films, Hopkins combines the avowed universalism of landscape in his earlier film with a new confidence in the political potentials of such an approach:

> These main industries afforded a rich sense of identity and masculinity, the men were able to provide for their families. To feel secure with their place in the world. I like my locations to be non-specific which is why I never commit to accents. I want the film to be about an idea, not a specific geographical place. I hope I haven't described a specific area or region in BYPASS but many regions. (Horne 2014)

Thus, the inclusive treatment of space – *Bypass* is filmed around Gateshead but none of the characters have North Eastern accents and the location would only be recognisable to those viewers with specific knowledge of it – reflects the broad geographical instabilities of de-industrialisation, and this strategy in turn has the effect of widening the film's socio-political reach to represent what Hopkins calls 'an England within an England' (Hopkins 2015).

Thinking through space in these terms opens up another justification for the film's frenetic, fragmented and claustrophobic use of reflected close shots and shallow focal depth because these techniques conspicuously deny the presentation of external environments and direct viewer attention to a more subjective and viscerally affective presentation of character. Certainly, the painterly, meditative treatment of landscape that pervades *Better Things* is absent here. Indeed, in her discussion of the earlier film Stella Hockenhull reads Hopkins's treatment of landscape in line with Romantic traditions in painting and notes the cinematic use of the *Rückenfigur* (Hockenhull 2014: 75) motif, particularly in relation to Gail – a composition showing a character from behind, comprehending a view. Indeed, the film's penultimate scene, showing Gail walking through and seemingly mastering the external spaces that once crippled her, uses the device conspicuously. The landscape is shown with spectacular depth and width as Gail walks forward and the shot captures the trees in the foreground, the vast field in the middle of the frame and the blue skies and white clouds beyond. Tellingly, in *Bypass* this device is repeated but manipulated. The film's second shot shows a *Rückenfigur* of sorts as Greg walks through an edgeland space, shot from behind. Here the handheld camera moves with the protagonist rather than remaining still, taking in his environment as he experiences it, and the shallow focal depth denies space beyond the immediate movements of his body – the view beyond Greg is subsequently reduced to a blurred wall of lights against the night sky. The inverted *Rückenfigur* device is used repeatedly in the film to frame both Greg and Tim, and, tellingly, their father, who is glimpsed in recurring flashback. Its connotations of mastery and the sense of a sublime coming to consciousness are thus reversed, as the environment appears instead to subsume its subjects. The effect of denying 'off-screen space' in this way means, in the words of Paul Dave, that we are 'primed to expect danger', with 'this shot suggesting an uncomfortable sense of imminence' which, more broadly, reflects the film's illustration of the 'breakdown of the individual's relationship to the everyday and the social' (Dave 2017: 130).

The intensely focused, granular treatment of the film's human characters therefore makes clear any moments in which their experiences are contextualised visually against a wider backdrop. For example, after an early montage sequence in which Tim is shown selling stolen goods in a variety of places, a sequence once more underpinned by the frequent use of reflective surfaces (fifteen shots), handheld and close composition, Tim meets Lilly from work and they ride on his bike. The tone changes as the ambient music becomes uplifting. The pair, now stationary, enter into dialogue, discussing Tim's illness and his grandfather's birthday. The conversation is framed by an alternating exchange of close shots of Tim's and Lilly's faces as they speak. The shallow focal depth brings into sharp focus their skin, eyes and mouths. Quite suddenly, Hopkins moves to an uncharacteristically deep, low-angled medium shot, showing in the background a network of concrete bridges: in other words, a bypass. Later the bypass space returns with a long shot of Tim and Greg as they reminisce about their childhood. Greg asks Tim if he knows 'what a foundry is?', telling him before he can answer: 'It's where they used to make steel. It's like what them bridges are made from. Where our family used to work. Grandad told me that. Now I clean shit.' As the final line of dialogue is delivered Hopkins frames the two in a rare long shot with an urban vista beyond them. Once more the personal and political are converged through space, both its denial and its fleeting external representation. In these scenes the titular 'bypass' quite clearly becomes a significant component of Hopkins's poetics, as his reflections on the word confirm:

> I like the word. The images it conjures, its associations. Concrete. The 1950s/60s/70s. New town planning. Modern post war estates. The new social project. High employment. The hope of a new society. An architecture which is now crumbling because the idea crumbled. The idea of being on the margins, in the edges, of travelling around the outskirts. The word's meaning in a geographical sense related to the type of small city that the film is set in. The word also has possible double meanings in the context of the story and drama, either medically or, for example, the loss of opportunity – the bypassing of a generation. (Haillay and Hopkins 2014)

In one sense, then, the bypass functions on the level of interspatiality – its mundane familiarity and its placement within an already generic, undefined space furthering its universal potential. More broadly, however, Hopkins considers the structure for its symbolic presence within the post-war imagination. The sense of interspatiality is thus deepened as the ubiquity of concrete in national landscapes is recast as the tragic traces of failed utopia – a point made explicit by Greg. This sense of architectural haunting again connects the personal and the private, weaving Greg's and Tim's recurring memories of their lost parents within the textures of the film's wider political elegy. Paul Dave's work on *Bypass* (2017) has drawn on Mark Fisher's notion of 'capitalist realism' – 'the widespread sense that not only is capitalism the only viable and economic system, but also that it is now impossible even to imagine a coherent alternative to it' (Fisher 2009: 2) – as a framework for examining its mournful narration of neo-liberalism corroding effects, but Fisher's later work on hauntology also is relevant to the film:

> What's at stake in 21st century hauntology is not the disappearance of a particular object. What has vanished is a tendency, a virtual trajectory.

One name for this tendency is popular modernism. The cultural ecology that I referred to above – the music press and the more challenging parts of public service broadcasting – were part of a UK popular modernism, as were postpunk, brutalist architecture, Penguin paperbacks and the BBC Radiophonic Workshop. In popular modernism, the elitist project of modernism was retrospectively vindicated. (Fisher 2014: 22–3)

The residual traces of 'popular modernism' then, which for Hopkins manifest themselves in the film's abstract but nevertheless conspicuous treatment of architecture, should be understood in relation to the film's attempt to reflect the 'ghost towns' of Britain today, 'places that constitute our country as much as the places of economy' (Haillay and Hopkins 2014). Taken alongside the film's overarching tone of fragmentation, these glimpses of external space can be seen as attempts to render in necessarily universal terms the film's political concerns – making visible those spatial narratives that for Hopkins are forgotten.

With this in mind, Hopkins and his producer Samm Haillay were both clear in their press interviews around *Bypass* that their intention was to make an explicitly political film. Haillay even partly justified the decision to take the film's distribution 'in house' – with select theatrical screenings followed by a VOD (video on demand) only release – in line with its contemporary themes: 'Given the themes in *Bypass*, we were keen to get the film out before the UK General Election on May 7 [2015] and take advantage of the political agenda across the media' (Haillay 2015). This is yet another example of the self-contextualisation of the film's politics. I have so far indicated some of the ways in which *Bypass* functions on a poetic level to imagine in contemplative terms these political themes, but for Hopkins the film's political commitment is also bound up with its generic elements:

It is within this environment – the backdrop of austerity – that I wanted to set an individual emotional story. About a family, its history and its future. I wanted to take these contemporary themes and reconfigure them as a stage on which to set a completely modern thriller. A thriller with a conscience. (Hopkins 2015)

Austerity is thus imagined as a framing device, but, as if anticipating criticism of the mutual exclusivity of genre and political engagement, Hopkins asserts the ethical dimension of his practice too. However, these thriller elements are evident in *Bypass* and they are most amplified when debt-ridden Tim is forced to ask Greg to renege on his 'straight' post-prison life and return to the criminal world. Inevitably the theft goes wrong and the pair is chased by the police. The action stays with Tim as the brothers break off from each other and run from their stolen car. Tim is shown to return home in the morning, having presumably escaped from his pursuers. He finds that the bailiffs have finally repossessed his furniture, engages in a reconciliatory, emotional conversation with his sister, and is then reunited with Lilly. The film then returns to its dream-like aesthetic and we are shown Tim moving out of consciousness, his illness finally catching up with him. A montage begins and he is being operated on, the ghostly presence of his dead mother adding to the sense of genre disruption. Tim appears to recover and there is another time leap, as we move to Lilly giving birth. The montage is played in slow motion alongside the now familiar uplifting ambient music. Tim is visited by what appears to be the ghost of his father, he chases him down the hospital corridor, returns to Lilly and his new child and the film ends with a shot of Tim's smiling face. Thus, Hopkins leaves two major plot threads unresolved: we never learn of Greg's fate, or how Tim has managed to pay off his debts, as the causal lines of the film's thriller elements are overwhelmed by its ethereal ending. For Paul Dave, this is justified, partly at least, on the basis that the film's politics requires the construction of narrative 'worlds that defy known realities', that 'the enigma of the contemporary neoliberal real' cannot be confined 'within available frameworks' (Dave 2017: 127). For many critics, though, this melding and subsequent disruption of genre elements is a source of frustration:

> Finally, in one last coup de grace for our engagement, the film totally sells out on its threadbare story, and its hopeful classification (per our press notes) as a thriller, by employing another one of those oh-so convenient time jumps and cutting more or less directly from Tim's moment of probable defeat [. . .] to several months later and an improbably happy, hopeful ending. Having weathered this would-be kitchen sink drama's insistence on throwing every depressing plot turn at its unfortunate protagonist, we never even get the catharsis of seeing how he extricates himself. (Kiang 2014)

Jessica Kiang's biting review arguably speaks to the complexities of Hopkins's attempts to make a 'thriller with a conscience' and consequently illustrates the historical challenges of melding poetic realist subject matter with genre elements. If *Bypass* was to satisfy its expectations of closure and catharsis, the resonance of its socio-political subject matter would be similarly curtailed. As John Hill argues in his seminal examination of the 'social problem' film:

> [I]n the case of the British films under discussion, it is conventionally the actions or ambitions of an individual which precipitate the plot; the counter-actions of other individuals which provide the 'corrective action' and, thus, the establishment of a new equilibrium.

[...]
It is also this stress on the individual which helps conform the ideology of containment characteristic of the narrative drive towards resolution. (Hill 1986: 56)

Thus, the pursuit of order and 'equilibrium' risks naturalising and containing the film's complex, nuanced subject matter. In the case of *Bypass*, while Tim and Lilly's apparent salvation does seem all too conclusive, its elliptical almost hallucinatory presentation is entirely consistent with the tone of fragmentation and the poetically charged sense of rupture that pervades the film. Indeed, moments of tension that appear superficially 'thriller' like are throughout undercut by its defamiliarising lyrical tone. For example, the first chase scene of the film, as Greg attempts to evade the police, is interrupted by a slow motion flashback to a childhood scene involving his father, with the mournful convergence of personal and communal histories keeping in check the cold functionality of the film's genre elements.

Thus, as in *Better Things*, *Bypass* is a film where the creation of what Hopkins calls an 'atmosphere' (Anonymous 2008), that is a tonal, affective register which conveys something of the ambiguous but no less empathy inducing experience of everyday life, is front and centre, working to overwhelm the instrumental and linear structures of plot and character. What we have seen in this chapter, then, is a more precise illustration of the specific nature of Hopkins's aesthetic strategies: those devices and formal patterns that come to form a poetics of realism.

2. JOANNA HOGG

Joanna Hogg's three films to date underline the extent to which new realism has departed from the established traditions of the realist mode. Her first feature, *Unrelated* (2007), follows Anna (Kathryn Worth), a childless forty-something experiencing difficulties within her long-term relationship, to Tuscany on holiday with friends. While there she loosens her association with childhood friend Verena, known as V (Mary Roscoe), V's husband, Charlie (Michael Hadley) and cousin, George (David Rintoul) and instead gravitates towards 'the young' relatives, a group led by Oakley (Tom Hiddleston), a charming ex-Etonian whom Anna attempts and fails to seduce. Oakley's rejection of Anna triggers a series of events that culminate in her leaving the holiday home and revealing her infertility to V in an emotionally fraught scene. The film ends with her appearing to be on the way to repairing her relationship with her estranged partner, Alex.

Hogg's second film *Archipelago* (2010) again concerns itself with a bourgeois family holiday, set on Tresco on the Isles of Scilly. Patricia (Kate Fahy) and her two children, Edward (Tom Hiddleston) and Cynthia (Lydia Leonard), come together for a week in a holiday home familiar from childhood trips to the island to say goodbye to Edward as he leaves his job in the City to work as a sexual health worker in an unnamed African country. The family is joined by Christopher (Christopher Baker), a landscape painter and teacher to Patricia, and Rose (Amy Lloyd) – both are played by non-professional actors who work as a painter and a cook, respectively. While at the house, Edward's career change functions as the stimulus for a series of increasingly fraught arguments which reveal that all three members of the family are experiencing profound unhappiness. This sense of pervasive gloom is also driven by the absence throughout of the family patriarch, Will, a figure who is only referred to through nostalgic anecdotes and repeated phone conversations (a device used in *Unrelated* with Anna's conversations with Alex, and to a lesser extent in *Exhibition*).

Exhibition (2013) follows ten days in the lives of long-term couple, D and H, again played non-professionals: Viv Albertine, formerly of the post-punk band The Slits, and Liam Gillick, a former Turner Prize nominee and working artist. The couple have taken the decision to sell their unique modernist home in West London. The film hints at unspoken issues in their relationship and the experience of a possible traumatic event and documents their unfulfilling sexual encounters and general frustrations with one another as they work on their respective projects and deal with the pain of selling their home. By the film's ending, the couple appear to have rediscovered a sense of physical and emotional intimacy, and D seems to have turned a corner professionally having been offered a major exhibition.

Highly privileged protagonists facing existential crises within often opulent and exclusive settings are obviously not narrative scenarios typical of the British realist tradition. And yet, these are films that reflect many of the characteristics of new realism: through their commitment to perceptual verisimilitude, particularly their conspicuous emphasis on atmospheric sound and an intense focus on tableau staging; their resultant emphasis on image-led narration with domestic *mise en scène* driving symbolic articulations of isolation and emotionally alienated protagonists; their use of non-professional actors and improvisation; and the autobiographical nature of source material. While these elements will be discussed throughout this chapter by means of analysis of Hogg's films to date, it is clear that the subject of class is particularly pertinent to our wider exploration of new realism. Indeed, by including Hogg within the wider examination of realist cinema, I am not suggesting that new realism is tone-deaf to issues of class, nor that Hogg herself is. Class is central to Hogg's work, not despite but because of its particular bourgeois concerns. New realist style enables these broader thematic emphases and binds seemingly disparate socio-political concerns across its diverse elements.

In this way, then, Hogg can be read alongside Hopkins as a film-maker who pursues a mode of poetics based on the repetition of visual and aural motifs grounded in everyday, perceptual reality. These work to convey in figurative terms the emotional states of their protagonists. This imbricated mode of symbolic delivery necessarily demands a patterned focus on routine as a structuring framework. Indeed, in my earlier work on Hogg I argued that a 'kind of rhythmic, everyday verisimilitude is developed, which subtly elicits narrative meaning through *mise en scène* staging and gesture' (Forrest 2014: 8), and it is, initially at least, through this repeated focus on quotidian markers (mealtimes, bedtimes, structured leisure activities) that Hogg's films build their affective power. As Stella Hockenhull argues, 'interior scenes in *Archipelago* are used to display the characters undertaking their routine daily activities, and to expose the family tensions' (Hockenhull 2017: 137), while François Penz's 'rhythmanalysis' of *Exhibition*, following on from Henri Lefebvre, positions the film's attentiveness to temporal rhythms and subsequent repetition of formal strategies for staging ritualised activities, as the film's anchoring mechanism:

> Within the cyclical patterning of the dawn to dusk structure, the linear everyday rhythm is situated in space and time. Over the course of the film we can observe repetitive actions taking place in rooms at pretty much fixed times – reinforced by similar camera set-ups, recurring shots with similar angles; D at her desk H in his office, the view of the bed, the skyline in the morning, views of the kitchen, shots of the staircase. This contributes to establishing the film's biosphere; it anchors and creates the baseline and its tempo. And within this beat, the rhythm of everyday life evolves and subtly varies from day to day. (Penz 2014: 91)

As we will see throughout this chapter, Penz's observations are equally applicable to Hogg's earlier films in that these formal repetitions, and the recurrence of quotidian activities, offer shape to otherwise loose narrative structures. As Hogg herself states: 'I like to make a story out of these seemingly undramatic moments, and build up a network of associations around certain ideas. I'm interested in going beyond what you might consider traditional storytelling' (Anonymous 2013a).

This sense of narrative meaning emerging from repeated motifs within everyday settings is, as we have seen in our discussion of Hopkins's work, a feature of new realism's tendency to lyrically elevate the familiar. With this in mind, I want to reflect briefly on Daniel Yacavone's work on 'world building' in narrative cinema, a critic on whom Penz also draws in his exploration of *Exhibition*:

> As we have considered, the poetic model of film-making in question entails emphasis on the transformation of the preexisting and the conventional into something novel, figurative, and aesthetically expressive in a pronounced and symbolically dense fashion. This process may be seen as roughly analogous to the poet's creative use of his or her inherited base language. (Yacavone 2015: 83)

As we will see, in Hogg's films, the repeated mealtime scenes operate as spaces of unspoken tension, and the bedtime scenes work as markers of painful self-reflection. The recurrence of these spaces and compositions not only orders an approach to everyday temporality which is rhythmically familiar; they also work, in much the same way as the window leitmotif in Hopkins's films, to discharge meaning and to make poetic the spaces and objects which are otherwise innocuous in the protagonists' (and the spectator's) worlds. With this in mind, I am arguing that the everyday poetics of new realism are able to accommodate radically differing thematic preoccupations, and that we might therefore evolve a more inclusive sense of what constitutes realist subject matter.

Hogg, Hopkins and the other film-makers explored in this book, can be united on the basis of their interest in fundamental relationships between environment and identity. For Hogg, the locations of her films are personally familiar to her – she holidayed in Tuscany and Tresco and was a friend of the architect, James Melvin, whose house is used in *Exhibition* – and it is clear that her real experiences drive the fictions which unfold within these locations on screen. For example, all Hogg's films involve a focus on childlessness, most obviously in *Unrelated*, but also in *Archipelago* when Patricia discusses with Christopher the absence of children in his life. In *Exhibition* the conspicuous absence of children is marked by a comparison with H and D's neighbours, who describe the house as 'not really a family home . . . but an artists' home', as if the two were mutually exclusive, and the film's final shot shows the new residents enjoying the home with their children in tow. Hogg herself describes how, in practical terms, 'I would be unlikely to be making the films I have been making if I had had children. I see my films as a way of creating something', and that '[t[he feelings of sadness about not having children never go away . . . I am already anticipating what life will be like not having grandchildren. And imagining the pleasure that I will not have then' (Adams 2013). Hogg's realism, therefore, emerges from a personal rather than consciously social impetus, one that establishes a melancholic tone from the outset, yet it is nevertheless reflective of a commitment to what she describes as 'an emotional truth' (Wilkinson 2008). This is not to say that Hogg's approach is in any way de-politicised, as I will go on to argue, but it is necessary to examine the means by which Hogg's films, although differing in the specific nature of their realist materials, operate in formal terms alongside her contemporaries examined elsewhere in this book.

In interviews, Hogg has explained that documentary photography, in particular a project photographing 'the dying shipbuilding industry' in the North East of the late 1970s and a concurrent sense of being 'very inspired by Ken Loach, particularly *Kes*', offered a way into her film-making aspirations – 'it was probably that project that got me into film school because they liked the social realism aspect' (O'Brien 2016). Later, Hogg would establish a successful career directing television dramas, including *London's Burning* (ITV 1988–

2002), but she has subsequently described 'those lost TV years as colourless ones from a creative point of view' (Wood and Haydyn-Smith 2015: 90). This brief reflection on Hogg's work prior to *Unrelated* is not to suggest some kind of holistic, authorial continuity through her career, but to argue instead that Hogg's realist style is catalysed by an engagement with her own milieu and that this personal impetus is bound up with the formal characteristics that define her feature films. In short, Hogg's realism emerges when she connects to and draws from those environments and narratives that are familiar to her.

While these spaces might be drawn from Hogg's own experiences and memories, their articulation is grounded in a commitment to a kind of sensory, perceptual verisimilitude that underlines her films' more universal realist credentials. As mentioned, the repeated mealtime scenes operate alongside other quotidian group rituals (walks, for example) to give shape to the more implicit, poetic elements of Hogg's films. Often, such communal activities are framed in a tableau formation and in long takes to enable a comprehensive and lingering focus on the characters within their environment and in interaction with one another. Examples of such scenes include Anna's first breakfast in *Unrelated* in which the characters move around her while she remains fixed in the centre of the table, the dinner scenes in *Archipelago* which repeatedly throw up emotionally fraught exchanges, or H and D's laboured and terse conversations during mealtimes in *Exhibition*. As Hogg argues, this is a device which is central to her observational aesthetic:

> I like seeing things from a certain distance. I'm more of an observer than a participator, so a lot of that stems from me personally, to have a safe distance between myself and what I'm looking at. I'm aware of the distancing effect it can have on some audiences, but if you look at the complete picture of something, you learn more than you do than if it's a close up. (Salovaara 2014)

It is significant that Hogg's aesthetic decision seems at least partly motivated by her own personal connection to the narrative content of her films; that the act of framing is in some way a disavowal of subjective exploration while maintaining a more enabling and holistic commitment to spectatorial comprehension, and with this in mind Hogg states:

> For me there's something powerful about just holding something in a wide frame and I think it's because the audience can create their own close-ups and medium shots out of that. You can explore the frame and then if you watch the film more than once, you find different things each time you watch it and there's just something about letting real time pass in front of your eyes that creates a sense of something. (Turner 2010)

Here, we move closer to the essence of Hogg's realism as an interlinked aesthetic and philosophical practice. Her evocation of 'real time' and the sense of her audience 'creating' through the long-held, wide and deep composition recalls André Bazin's discussion of 'depth of focus', whereby 'the spectator' comes 'into a relation with the image close to that which he enjoys with reality', with the sustained depth and duration of composition fostering 'a more active mental attitude' (Bazin 2005b: 35).

In a manner that recalls the tension Hogg herself seems to identify, for Ágnes Pethő, the tableau aesthetic is similarly evocative of a sense both of being there in the Bazinian sense, and of impartial observation:

> As a frontal long take, filmed with a more or less static camera, the tableau offers the impression of viewing a painting, a photograph in motion, or gives the viewer access to what seems like the interior of a box. (Pethő 2015: 42)

Pethő goes on to describe how such an aesthetic strategy enables 'a flexible template in film modulating in-between life and art is able to paradoxically reconcile immersion with abstraction', and in doing so she captures something of Hogg's realist approach – it is both enabling for the spectator in terms of visualising spatially the poetic and emotional formations of a scene, while simultaneously fostering a sense of perceptual authenticity. Although *Unrelated*'s average shot length (17.9 seconds) is significantly less than *Archipelago*'s (39.5 seconds) and *Exhibition*'s (30.3 seconds), the film does contain a number of long-take scenes – moreover, across all three films camera movement is minimal, further amplifying the role of the tableau. To return to Bazin, Daniel Morgan's summary of Bazin's praise for 'deep space and the long take' offers up more tools for reflecting on the realism of Hogg's framing and compositional strategies: 'these films not only provide an experience of the world of a film that replicates our habitual way of being in the world; they employ styles that emphasise it' (Morgan 2010: 112).

In a Bazinian sense the tableau offers a melding of complicit and observational modes of spectatorship and address in terms of both space and time, yet Hogg's films go beyond simply updated middle-class neo-realism. For Hogg, the 'seeing from a distance' that such compositional strategies invite enables a greater emphasis on the non-verbal elements of narrative:

> And I'm also interested in body language, so if you're cutting all the time to close-ups, you don't see how someone's whole body is reacting to something. So it's like dance – I've always been interested in how dance films in the past – musicals were often shot in wide shot, so you could see the whole of the dance. (Turner 2010)

Hogg's use of the tableau therefore draws spectatorial attention away from dialogue and towards other traditionally less obvious elements such as bodily position and movement (or the lack thereof) and, perhaps most significantly, her highly conspicuous approach to atmospheric sound. In many of these scenes it is the aural spaces in between or evoked by an absence of speech sounds that generate meaning. Moreover, Hogg's films, because of their recurring focus on isolated protagonists, necessarily contain scenes in which characters are alone – Anna in *Unrelated,* Edward, Rose and Cynthia in *Archipelago* and D in *Exhibition* – or characters are 'alone together', a feature particularly prominent in the awkward silences during group scenes in *Archipelago*. As Michael Chion argues, 'the impression of silence in a film scene does not simply come from an absence of noise. It can only be produced as a result of context and preparation' (Chion 1994: 57). Hogg's visual austerity therefore places to the foreground the more innate materials of perceptual realism: in this case, an illusion of physical immersion and sound or rather, following from Chion, the sound of silence.

To return to Pethő, the tableau form therefore operates alongside Hogg's heavily accented sound design:

> This ambience of sounds does not only announce the presence of a world outside the frame and underscore the sensory, overflowing opulence of the tableau, it also reminds the viewer of the fault line between the discursive and the non-discursive, perceptual elements of the cinematic image. In the meanwhile, the protagonists appear in abeyance, being deprived of a classical dramatic structure, they remain stuck in the rigidity of the tableau. (Pethő 2015: 56)

These symbolically rich static compositions foster a sense of sensory depth in part through sound, which both presents itself within the frame to, in Ciara Barrett's words, 'highlight the isolation of [the] protagonists in space, and . . . as a punctuational echo of their emotional states' (Barrett 2015: 12) and in a non-diegetic sense, to enable a more immersive and sensorially rich spectatorial connection to the auditory realm of perceptual experience. Tiago de Luca's work on sensory realism, building on phenomenological realist film theory, makes further connections between the kind of compositional rigour Hogg pursues and its potential to accommodate a perceptual mode of realism rooted in sound and other sensory elements:

> These cinemas are different facets of a systematic, rigid and austere style that impresses for the plastic, even painterly, beauty of its rigorously composed images. As such, they frame reality through an aesthetic gaze which itself restructures the sensory and perceptual experience of the

sensible, an aspect also observed in their ingenious use of sound. (de Luca 2014: 238–9)

The phenomenological approaches on which de Luca draws offer useful resources for understanding Hogg's particular exploration of the realist mode. Sound, as Lucy Fife Donaldson puts it

> is used within film and television to expressively communicate and develop the density of the fictional world we experience and to which we respond. Such responsiveness to the affective potential of sound is informed by phenomenological approaches that seek to understand the perception of film as shaped by our lived experience and physical interactions with the world. (Fife Donaldson 2017a: 85)

She goes on to argue that '[the] sensuous impact of sound derives from its simultaneous invisibility and tangibility – it is all around us [. . .]' (Ibid.: 86). In this sense, Hogg's pronounced focus on sound might be understood as a mechanism for fostering a more embodied, perceptually rich engagement with the text. Sound is, then, a fundamental component of Hogg's everyday poetics, working to amplify and render lyrical thematically significant elements while simultaneously evoking a deep engagement with the very experience of reality, integrating the aural and the visual through the 'immersion' and 'abstraction' of the tableau (Pethő 2015: 43).

Brandon LaBelle identifies attentiveness to sound in everyday life as 'auditory knowledge' which in turn might create 'shared spaces that belong to no single public and yet which impart a feeling for intimacy: sound is always already mine and not mine' (LaBelle 2010: xvii). LaBelle goes on, 'Auditory knowledge is non-dualistic it is based on empathy *and* divergence, allowing for careful understanding and deep involvement in the present while connecting to the dynamics of mediation, displacement, and virtuality' (Ibid.: xvii). In amplifying atmospheric or ambient sound as a prominent feature both of meaning making and of affective verisimilitude, Hogg draws on its ubiquity – we think of the near perpetual wind in *Archipelago* and the street sounds of *Exhibition* – to position it as a unit of perceptual empathy which evokes the viewer's own 'auditory knowledge' (Ibid.: xvii), to again use LaBelle's phrase. As Laura U. Marks's exploration of 'haptic visuality' emphasises, film's capacity to function 'multisensorially' (Marks 2000: 22) is critical to the embodied and embodying potential of a film text. Indeed, it is this more markedly perceptual sense of affect, defined by sound, and working alongside a highly constructed tableau-like approach to *mise en scène*, that I want to argue formalises the core of Hogg's realist approach.

UNRELATED (2007)

To begin a more concerted examination of Hogg's style, I want to first turn to *Unrelated*. In my earlier work on Hogg, I observed the ways in which the repetitions of quotidian activity cohere within and are given narrative function by a 'crisis point' (Forrest 2014: 10), or, to borrow Bordwell's useful phrase, 'boundary situation' (Bordwell 1985: 208). This occurs in *Unrelated* when Anna betrays her 'young' friends by disclosing to V that they wrote off the car of their neighbour, Elisabetta (Elisabetta Fiorentini), triggering a painful rejection of Anna by the 'young' and a wild argument between Oakley and his father. The scenes following these further inculcate visually Anna's marginalisation from the group, a social breakdown that culminates in her decision to leave the holiday home and check in to a modest, roadside hotel. Anna's removal from the group initiates a sequence which is critical to the film's emotional impact and which draws together its core motifs.

The sequence begins with a six-second low-angled shot of a field of drooping, dying sunflowers, offering a foreshadowing of the wider theme of infertility, before another six-second shot of the field, this time showing a concrete bridge, before another wider seven-second shot of the sunflowers with cranes in the distance. These shots, both aurally and visually, mark Anna's departure from the holiday home with the pervasive sound of cars and the signs of modern housing and industry (a later shot shows the roof of a Fiat factory), signalling a significant disjunction in the film's soundscape and image palette – it is important to note that the sound of cicadas and birdsong has thus far dominated the atmospheric aural dimension of the film, given that the majority of the action has taken place at the secluded house. We then see Anna arriving at the hotel and an interior shot held for some eleven seconds shows her staring out of the window, forcing our attention both on her fixed reflective gaze and on the ambient sound. A point-of-view shot then shows the rooftops of houses and commercial buildings in a further reminder of Anna's dislocation, before a cut to her sitting on her rooftop terrace re-introduces dialogue (Anna answers a call from V). Hogg then moves to a medium long shot of Anna lying on the bed staring blankly. The shot is held for eight seconds until Hogg cuts to a medium shot by the door, as V enters, announcing herself with the dismissive line, 'God, this is grim'. Hogg then re-initiates the bed composition, this time with V sitting alongside Anna, and holds it for four minutes and four seconds (easily the longest take of the film). During this time Anna reveals the truth behind her relationship woes, her empty hope that she might have been pregnant, and the desperation at her feelings of loneliness. During the course of the scene, V moves from being seated at the edge of the bed, at the opposite end to Anna, to cradling her friend maternally on her bosom – further emphasising the 'dance'-like emphasis on bodily movement and language that the long-take

2.1   'I will just be forever now on the periphery of things.'

tableau necessitates. The scene climaxes as Anna tells V through her violent sobs: 'You're surrounded by your family, you belong somewhere, I will just be forever now on the periphery of things.'

There is much to explore here. Primarily, Anna's last line seems to actualise the film's poetically charged spatial examination of her profound sense of displacement – the titular feeling of being 'unrelated' and 'peripheral'. Here, then, we see evidence of Hogg's use of the static frame and its tableau qualities to drive a mode of image-led narration which has deepened, through recurring associative compositions, our sense of Anna's solitude and separation from the group. In the early moments of the film we see Anna's growing social and sexual – as her desire for Oakley reveals itself – confidence emerge as she is gradually initiated as an honorary member of the 'young'. This is signalled most emphatically in a scene at a natural spring when Anna, having given way to V's desire to travel to the excursion with the older members of the group, is shown swimming from V, Archie and Charlie, to the young – what is significant here is that the camera moves with Anna as she makes her symbolic social choice. Given that there are only six other instances of camera movement (almost all of which involve Anna interacting with the young) the exceptional nature of this break from the film's compositional structure marks a shift in meaning. Naturally, therefore, Anna's subsequent ejection from the group is similarly marked in spatial rather than explicitly verbal terms.

Indeed, we are with Anna as she hears Jack (Henry Lloyd-Hughes) being told off by V and Charlie. The shot, static of course, rests on Anna for some forty seconds as she gingerly waits at the bottom of the stairs, listening in – the wide shot places Anna at the margins both in terms of width and depth. Hogg then cuts to a ten-second-long shot of Anna at the end of the dark corridor, before picking up her point of view for one minute and twenty-five seconds as she observes from a distance Jack being reprimanded within the door frame of the bathroom. We then have a brief close shot of Anna's concerned but impotent expression before returning to the fixed position focused on the doorway at the end of the darkened corridor, as Anna continues to listen and V and Charlie desperately reflect on the situation.

The next scene is arguably the most tableau like in the film, establishing a wide shot of the residents by the pool, fixed in silence while George and Oakley scream at each other off screen. Anna is, as we would expect, the most marginal figure – conspicuously set apart from the rest of the family (Charlie, V, Badge and Jack).

As Pethő argues:

> Such scenes of eavesdropping make us aware of the way these spaces fold into interconnected boxes that can both reveal and conceal, draw us in as complicit witnesses and shut us out [. . .] Anna's position within the group is not only an outsider, and she is not only single (and becoming painfully aware of being unmarried and childless), but she is trapped in her role conceived as an extension of the marginal role of eavesdropper, listening in at conversations most of the time, and observing how other people live their lives. (Pethő 2015: 53)

Thus, Anna's later verbal recognition that 'she is forever now on the periphery of things' is first actualised through the visual framing of her marginalisation in the repetitive, near rhythmic, inculcation of her sensory and spatial disconnectedness in the shots I have described. To further reflect on the theoretical implications of the kind of conspicuous framing in the realist text, I want to turn again to Daniel Yacavone:

> Such transformative meaning – and feeling-generating power of the act of framing, of what happens when the representation of a person, object, or event is (a) isolated, or cut off from others, and (b) made the focus of attention – or, in contrast, (c) de-emphasized within the confines of the frame or bisected – familiar to anyone who has ever used a still camera or has cropped a photograph, for example, in software programs like Photoshop [. . .]
>
> We may [. . .] point to the pronounced, often dynamic *actualization* of offscreen space in other films and cinematic styles, which, through

image, sound, or both in conjunction, more actively engages the viewer's imagination, as a familiar way in which composition/decomposition is effected. This […] involves contributions from the creative imagination of viewers or direct perception or both, simultaneously, just as it may have pronounced temporal as well as spatial dimensions. (Yacavone 2015: 87)

Yacavone then again points to the phenomenological import of framing for its ability to emphasise or downplay elements of composition that reflect our own perceptual experience of space and movement. Moreover, this, to borrow Yacavone's phrase, 'world building' quality, is given enhanced depth through the use of off-screen sound, just as we have seen in Hogg's films.

I will come back to the question of sound shortly, but to return to the hotel room scene, the stark framing and the long take centre 'the feeling-generating power' on the image of the vulnerable Anna on the bed. As mentioned, before V's arrival, Anna's visual isolation has been explicitly connected to the bed, when she is shown lying on it, alone. This is the fourth of six scenes of Anna that show her alone in her bedroom. Although the other compositions take place in the holiday home, they work within the aforementioned pattern of 'rhythmic everyday verisimilitude' to mark the passing of a day, but to also gradually embed a sense of Anna's solitude in sexual terms.

This motif emerges gradually, and in line with Anna's developing affinity with Oakley's group. For example, the first 'bed scene' shows Anna struggling to sleep because the 'young' can easily be heard outside. She closes the shutters and plunges her room into darkness. This is repeated at the end of the following day with a closer shot of Anna's restless body which dwells on her for forty-eight seconds, drawing attention to the muffled off-screen sounds of the young – again underlining Anna's isolation by foregrounding it starkly against a conspicuous soundscape. The third bedroom scene, however, marks a shift. It comes at the end of a day when Anna has been fully inducted into the 'young' group – including the pivotal swim from the old to the young mentioned earlier – and shows a wide shot of Anna's room as she inspects her naked body. The starkness of this scene is emphasised by its duration and its spatial width, and the bright light of the space is contrasted with the scene preceding it in which Anna joins the young in a barely-lit impromptu 'skinny-dipping' scene. This pool scene is significant for Hogg's privileging of Anna's point of view as she views Oakley's body, a sexualised gaze which is reversed as Anna climbs out of the pool and Hogg's camera rests on the gawping, adolescent, objectifying stares of Oakley, Archie and Jack. Anna's subsequent bodily self-examination therefore simultaneously acknowledges her burgeoning sexual desires and the vulnerabilities of her fragile self-image.

The following day, Anna and V have a heated debate about Anna's increasing privileging of the young and her apparent rejection of their own friendship. The entire conversation takes place in V's bedroom with the two shot emphasising V's presence in the foreground with her bed prominently in the background and her dressing table and mirror working to contain and marginalise Anna within the frame. Indeed, here Anna is on the 'periphery of things' once more – an adult woman, infantilised by her best friend in this markedly maternal space, a space in which Anna is not able to pass over the threshold. This 'bedroom scene' therefore anticipates the later revelation of Anna's infertility in the hotel. The next scene in this poetic pattern of symbiotic sexual and maternal marginality occurs after Oakley has rejected Anna's proposition to join her in bed – as she articulates the latent sexual tension that has been developing between the pair. In the following scene Anna lies in bed, awake and naked in a static composition held for nineteen seconds – Anna's sexual exposure is here re-emphasised physically as the subtle sounds of the 'young' – further underlining her literal and symbolic distance - are again heard alongside the perpetual buzz of the cicadas. The penultimate bedroom scene confirms Anna's estrangement from the group and comes after her return from the hotel. In an echo of the opening, she struggles to sleep because of the noise of the young as they drink by the pool. This time she comes to the window (another threshold space that further underlines her marginality) and verbally censures them: 'could you be a bit quieter please?' – here Anna is forced to play the role of secondary mother, having been rejected both as friend and as a lover. This sense of the bedroom as a site of sexual and social isolation is confirmed towards the end of the film, in its final use, as Anna is shown through her window silently observing Oakley courting another, much younger woman.

The bedroom is therefore a critical space in establishing poetic meaning through familiar, patterned imagery and thematic association, and emphasises the extent of Hogg's realist image-led narration, here fostering for Anna a visual iconography of solitude, given added depth through a pointed use of sound. In line with the previous discussion of framing, this rhythmic approach to *mise en scène* – dependent as it is on formally stark composition and minimal camera movement – draws audience attention to elements of quotidian detail that might otherwise have been overlooked. For example, to return once more to the crucial scene between V and Anna on the bed, the stark focus on the two women draws attention to their costume. Anna wears what Hogg suggests 'looks like a maternity dress', which had 'belonged to Kathryn Worth's mother' (Titze 2014), as Hogg confirms this choice of costume is designed to emphasise the connections between Anna's childlessness and her isolation from the family, describing how she wears the dress:

> When they're walking to the castle and have lunch. When she is ostracised by the group and she is eating alone. She wears the dress when she goes to

stay in the hotel on her own. What we thought was poignant about that dress was that it looked like she's pregnant but her big problem is that she can't have children. (Titze 2014)

Hogg goes on to discuss the importance throughout her work of 'details' in costume design, reinforcing the sense that a realist style which is dependent on minimal and/or inconsequential dialogue, atmospheric sound design and repetitious, tableau composition necessarily disperses its meaning making capacity beyond the obvious and immediate. For example, Hogg discusses how Anna wears 'hair ribbons that are two different colors [sic] – which is something you stop doing when you're five' (Titze 2014), with these details seemingly illustrating her enchantment with the 'young' and her desire to shed her middle-aged persona – we might also read Anna's transition from wearing a swimming costume to a bikini in this way (a 'detail' which is conspicuous in the swimming scene mentioned earlier).

This combination of symbolically significant visual 'details', made conspicuous through tableau framing and given perceptual depth through intricate sound design, is evident in a pivotal scene that takes place as the group visit Siena. In the early part of the sequence, Anna is shown nervously buying lingerie – further equating the shifts in her costume with her re-awakening sexuality. We then see an extended montage of shots featuring Anna and Oakley playfully exploring picturesque parts of the city, namely the cathedral – here two minutes and twenty-five seconds pass without dialogue, but with a persistent emphasis on atmospheric sound. The couple are then re-connected to the rest of the group, shown in a wide shot in the square, with Anna and Oakley in the foreground. They are discussing the nature of relationships and, after a range of compositions showing the pair within their environment and alongside the rest of the family, Hogg rests on a two minute and fifty-eight second two-shot that shows both characters in parallel from their chests upwards. The duration of the shot again emphasises the 'details' that Hogg describes: here, Anna wears a straw, Stetson-style hat and a pink hairtie holds in place a ponytail that sits on her shoulder, while Oakley wears a vest, creating a doubling effect alongside Anna's exposed shoulders. The close framing emphasises their shared body movements and their physical proximity provides the clearest indication yet of the desire that is apparently shared by both characters. The tone changes significantly, however, when Oakley's wish to learn more of Anna and Alex's sex life prompts the question: 'what about kids?' There then follows a pause of eight seconds – this is palpable because the conversation for so much of the scene has been free-flowing – and so our attention is drawn to the atmospheric sound of the square, evoking Chion's aforementioned 'impression' of cinematic 'silence' (Chion 1995: 57). As Anna responds 'we don't have them', an element of the previously ambient soundscape is thrown into the foreground and a baby is heard crying at the exact point of Anna's shy utterance. Here, this element of recorded reality is brought into dialogue with the foregrounded narrative components in a manner which asserts the depth of Hogg's realist poetics – its highly formalised visual and aural registers converging compositional rigour with quotidian coincidence.

As de Luca argues of long take cinema, such formal austerity can enable rather than suppress the free-flowing and non-instrumental elements of realist detail that contextualise and give scope to the more consciously narrated elements of image and sound:

> This is not to say that meaning-making patterns cannot be deduced from protracted images and/or their sequential arrangement, but simply that to reduce their surplus of materiality and concreteness of detail exclusively to narrational and representational schema does not do justice to the way they are most likely experienced, that is to say, as sensuous, non-conceptual phenomena. To what extent, moreover, can we dispense with realism as a method when the long take is clearly utilised as a means to foreground, rather than submerge, the recording power of the film medium and the profilmic event? (de Luca 2014: 24–5)

To return to Hogg, sound both constructs a cinematic world of auditory depth and authenticity and works at the narrative level to contain and convey specific meanings. This balancing of sound design as enabling a multi-dimensional, perceptual realism and as a tool of highly composed image-led narration moves to new levels in Hogg's next film.

ARCHIPELAGO (2010)

While the similarities in their respective narrative scenarios and formal details are evident from the outset – as Anton Bitel puts it, '*Archipelago* exposes the mores of Britain's vacationing *haute bourgeoisie* to an unforgivingly fixed and distant camera that leaves every awkward tension or emotional crisis with nowhere to flee' (Bitel 2015: 242) – Hogg's second film also picks up from *Unrelated*'s conceptual exploration of poor communication and alienation, albeit dispersed across the Leighton family (Cynthia, Patricia and Edward) rather than as themes focused through a sole protagonist as they are in *Unrelated*. Following from her debut then, Hogg's 'rhythmic, everyday verisimilitude' (Forrest 2014: 8) is again given shape through the temporal parameters of the holiday, the internal architecture of the house and the characters' external environment, in this case the simultaneously rich but desolate landscapes of the Isle of Tresco. As Pethő notes:

> In *Archipelago*, the tiny attic room with slanted walls assigned to the son mirrors his subdued position in the family and is in grotesque contrast with his tall stature. (Meanwhile the assertive sister takes possession of the largest room with a king size bed. [. . .]) (Pethő 2015: 42)

Just as in *Unrelated*, recurring spatial motifs create poetic associations with specific characters – we might think of the bedroom, threshold spaces or the lonely hillside shots that give visual articulation to Anna's torment in the earlier film. In addition to those mentioned by Pethő, in *Archipelago* we should point to the repeated corridor shot showing a window with a telephone on its ledge, housed within an arched doorway – it is here where Patricia on three occasions engages in increasingly exasperated and desperate phone calls with her absent husband, providing a rhythmic escalation to the emotional crisis of the family while echoing Anna's conversations with Alex in *Unrelated*. We should also recognise the importance of the dining table, with its spatial ordering of familial strife and tension and with the depth of its framing enabling the cook, Rose, to be rendered visible as a silent witness to the Leightons' crises, and the living room, where, as Anton Bitel, describes, 'a rectangular discoloration [*sic*] marks the place from which a painting (uncoincidentally, of a stormy sea) has been taken down at Patricia's request, in symbolic denial of the tempestuous chaos that is coming with the breakdown of her marriage' (Bitel 2015: 242). While I will move on to discuss Rose in more detail, it is significant that she, too, is repeatedly associated with specific spaces in the home – particularly the back door and most significantly the kitchen, both indicative of her status. These highly structured internal compositions work alongside external shots, with, as Hockenhull puts it, 'the characters appearing diminished and distant in the frame to convey their detachment' (Hockenhull 2017: 137).

Yet again, then, Hogg's visual style is defined by the compositional rigour of the tableau – crucially, these recurring motifs are offered to us often in long takes (we should remember that *Archipelago* presents us with Hogg's longest average shot length to date) with no camera movement, and with almost no close shots or medium-close set-ups – these elements work to centre attention on the image-led, non-verbal quality of narration. The combination of stillness and symbolic patterning in turn fosters a painterly quality to the *mise en scène*, with Pethő observing that the scenes involving Rose bear comparison with 'the courtyard scenes in Peter [*sic*] de Hooch's canvases [. . .] or the liminal situations of Dutch paintings displaying trades with travelling salesmen coming to the kitchen doors' (Pethő 2015: 42), while Annette Kuhn and Guy Westwell note how 'the soft greys dominating the colour palette and the *mise en scène* of quiet, sparsely-furnished rooms [. . .] suggest familiarity on the production designer's part with the world of Danish painter Vilhelm Hammershøi' (Kuhn and Westwell 2012: 332). These allusions to visual art illustrate the extent to which Hogg's compositions work both as self-contained and, when connected, associative mechanisms of meaning making, while also working to render through *mise en scène* a mirror to Patricia's and Christopher's use of painting as a means of making sense of their own landscape.

However, as we have already discussed, Hogg's realist poetics are arrived at when the tableau formation of the image is given texture through its accompaniment with a richly intricate sound design. While the visual repetitions and formalised compositions in *Unrelated* are matched by aural patterns (the sound of the cicadas, the muffled but incessant drunken chat of the 'young') and more narrationally significant diegetic sounds (the baby crying in Siena), *Archipelago*'s soundscapes are even more conspicuous. The film's aural palette is dominated by the twinned sounds of the wind and birdsong, with Hogg commenting of the latter:

I also love natural sounds. I am very aware of them in everyday life and enjoy recording them. I have a particular fondness for birdsong, though, like certain music, I can find it excruciatingly sad. In *Archipelago* I wanted to explore the idea of birdsong and communication. I liked the idea of counterpointing the awkward silences between the Leighton family with the constant chattering of birds. (Wood and Haydyn-Smith 2015: 92)

Hogg here points to two uses of 'natural sound' in the film. Firstly, the near constant, and amplified, presence of 'everyday' sounds within both the internal and external spaces of the film works to deepen its visceral, perceptual realism by anchoring it to a sensory engagement with ubiquitous sound. In addition to the 'natural' sounds of birds and the wind, we might also add those of eating and drinking (chewing, swallowing, clattering of plates and cutlery), and the more general textured sounds of furniture and bodily movement – these aural elements of everyday life are of course also developed through their repetitious deployment through the narrative's reliance on daily routines and structures. In this sense then, the film's lyrical rhythm is not only visual but aural, and our sense of Hogg's realist poetics again appeals to our own experience of reality in a perceptual, sensory as well as image-led fashion. Indeed, the constancy and conspicuousness of ubiquitous sound combines with the painterly *mise en scène* to effect an enveloping and converged engagement with the auditory and visual components of the text. Lucy Fife Donaldson usefully examines this sense of sound-enabling embodied immersion:

[. . .] sound is a physical and tactile phenomenon, it impacts the bodies of the audience. In all these ways, which are of course interrelated, sound appeals to an audience's sensory perceptions, creating an atmosphere that we respond to. This close integration of film and viewer builds on the notion of phenomenologically informed intersubjectivity of film and audience. (Fife Donaldson 2017b: 34)

Fife Donaldson's identification of the possibility for sound design to generate a sense of 'intersubjectivity' is particularly relevant to the audio-visual texture of Hogg's films and to our discussion of new realism more broadly. While Hopkins's use of ubiquitous landscapes of urban (*Bypass*) and rural (*Better Things*) Englishness might be seen to call upon the national viewer's familiarity with and experience of such spaces, Hogg's emphatic use of ubiquitous sound similarly appeals to our perceptual, innate understanding and experience of everyday senses – in isolating and amplifying these aural elements Hogg in turn poeticises them as free-flowing units of embodied meaning, providing indeterminate spaces for contemplation and inhabitation beyond the immediate diegetic realm.

To return to Hogg's comment, she also points to the role of pervasive atmospheric sound in emphasising the 'awkward silences between the Leighton family' (Wood and Haydyn Smith 2015: 92). Here we think again of the ways in which a conspicuous emphasis on ambient sound design evokes a universally recognised 'sound of silence', with its accented presence making conspicuous those familiar but implicit auditory experiences that characterise moments where human communication is lacking or absent. In this sense, then, Hogg's use of sound both calls upon and draws attention to our own quotidian, auditory encounters but is also narrativised to emphasise the experience of bitterly ill communication that eats away at the Leighton family. For example, in the final third of the film Christopher, Cynthia, Edward and Patricia each drink a Bloody Mary before a characteristically fraught dinner, which culminates in Cynthia storming out of the house. The group sit in the now familiar tableau formation in the living room and initially their small talk is jovial with Edward repeating an earlier impression of his absent father, but after this none of the characters speak for some twenty-six seconds (the entire take lasts one minute and fifty-eight seconds). In the absence of verbal communication the rising winds are made emphatic, a distant church bell is heard, the pervasive birds chatter, and the blocks of ice in the drinks crack against the walls of the glasses, this aural, off-screen movement starkly contrasting with the listless, stationary human bodies that occupy the frame. The human silence is broken when Patricia bites into her celery and Cynthia asks Christopher 'have you eaten yours?' Christopher and then Edward respond to Cynthia's enquiry before another sustained period of silence (thirty-two seconds) brings back into aural focus the chorus of birds, ice and wind, eventually broken by Rose informing the group that their food is ready. Here the sense of absence (of the father, of happier times in the house, of love and fulfilment, of communication) is enabled by the presence of atmospheric sound, which amplifies through

2.2   The 'sound of silence'.

poetic realist means – in this case, accented natural sound and the painterly long take – the film's exploration of its core themes. In essence, *Archipelago* is interested in silence, both thematically and formally, and thus sound design is critical to the film's poetics. To return to Michael Chion:

> Another way to express silence [. . .] consists in subjecting the listener to . . . noises. But I mean here the subtle kind of noises like the ticking of an alarm clock, naturally associated with calmness. These do not attract attention; they are not even audible unless other sounds (of traffic, conversation, the workplace) cease. (Chion 1994: 57)

In short, noises express and make emphatic human silence.

It is significant that Rose breaks the silence in the aforementioned scene, and an analysis of her role in the film opens up significant insight into Hogg's place within the emerging traditions of new realism. As mentioned previously, Rose is played by Amy Lloyd, a real-life cook, and this lends her performance a degree of authenticity which is complicated by her deployment alongside professional actors. As Hogg explains, the professional/non-professional divide also extended to the actors' comprehension of the wider narrative: 'Amy and Christopher knew nothing about the story except the setting, so they never knew what turns the story was going to take. The actors, on the other hand, knew the story' (Wood and Haydyn-Smith 2015: 93). While this might align Amy Lloyd with Christopher Baker as the two non-professional performers working functionally and instrumentally within an otherwise seemingly collaborative process open to creative interpretation, it is important to note the significant distinctions between the two performers. Of Baker, Hogg explains that he 'became part of *Archipelago* because he was someone I knew and not because I was looking to have an artist in the film. I was having painting classes with Christopher and found him to be a very interesting presence, so I asked him to be in the film' (O'Brien 2016), thus, in non-fictional terms, Baker emerges from Hogg's own social circle in a manner which is continued within the fictional realm as Christopher acts as painting teacher to Patricia. Lloyd, on the other hand, was identified as a cook and accordingly her marginality is rendered non-diegetically (unlike Baker, she was recruited primarily because of her labour status) and within the diegesis she literally occupies the margins and background of the other characters' (and actors') space. This sense of difference and distance, therefore, is critical to one of the film's most surprising and effective elements – its subtly sophisticated class analysis.

As David Cox writes of the characters:

> Patricia seeks salvation through creative self-indulgence, while deluding herself that the arrival of her absent husband would somehow resurrect her defunct family. Her son Edward can't help noticing the absence of any ethical basis for the lives of his kind. He toys with bewildered stabs at virtue, to understandably little effect. His sister Cynthia's rage reflects not just disgust at their collective condition but also resentment of Edward's efforts to break free from it. Meanwhile, hired mentor Christopher supplies babble designed to lend bogus credibility to all of their senseless existences. (Cox 2011)

These character profiles all suggest a particularly 'bourgeois ennui' (Pethő 2015: 46), of the kinds of crises that might emerge specifically from those individuals and groups with an abundance of social, cultural and financial capital – crises which are bound up with the film's wider examination of silence and the unspoken. Indeed, Rose's distance from but near perpetual presence at the background of the cumulative crises works to emphasise the Leightons' emotional dysfunction – while her status is marginalised within the diegetic and non-diegetic social 'worlds' of the film, her physical presence is not. As mentioned previously, she is often present at the back or side of the frame during the worst conflicts, but she is also present in some sixteen scenes that do not involve the family. In these moments she is either on her own (usually working or resting) or in dialogue with other workers (a fishermen, a hunter). Like the atmospheric sound, Rose's presence – defined as it is in contrast to the Leightons' and Christopher's – works to emphasise a sense of absence; of something missing in the central protagonists' worlds.

With this in mind, Rose's first interaction with the whole family on screen comes when she enters the living room before serving a meal. She joins the tableau composition (a wide shot of the living room, rendered statically, held for two minutes and twenty-four seconds) to check that 'everything is all right'; while Patricia and Cynthia are concise in their responses, Edward seeks to engage Rose in conversation (something which Cynthia, with her mother's endorsement, mocks). Despite her marginal position in the frame it is Rose who draws attention to the discolouration on the wall – the mark left by the absent picture, mentioned previously. It has been visible for one minute and twenty-five seconds already, but it is Rose who explicitly designates it as a mark of absence. Rose first asks about the family's history with the house, and Cynthia concludes her response with 'lots of lovely memories'. Rose then changes the subject by asking, 'did there used to be a picture on this wall?', to which Patricia replies, punctuated by the already omnipresent birdsong, 'yes, it was rather horrible, and Cynthia and Edward very kindly took it down'. In this scene, it is Rose, the outsider, who unlocks the narrative's exploration of loss and unbearable silence – it is she, a character (and an actress) who has been hired to perform a simple, perfunctory role, who makes visible the complexities that will underpin the film's excruciating analysis of familial strife.

Rose's role in holding up a mirror to the Leightons' deep emotional inarticulacy does, I want to argue, position their psychological malady within a wider social framework in ways that illuminate Hogg's role as purveyor of realism, a realism which is necessarily always – despite the director's claims otherwise – bound up in discourses of social class.

Indeed, after the first dinner, where Cynthia begins her assault on Edward's decision to quit the City for his charity role in Africa and where the dinner tableau motif is established (with Rose framed in depth coming in and out of the shot as she works and silently observes the tense scene), Hogg keeps the narrative focus on Edward. We observe him in, for *Archipelago*, an uncharacteristically cramped static shot (held for two minutes), to match Edward's cramped room as he goes to bed and then attempts to begin writing. He sighs and looks to the ceiling in frustration. Throughout, the heavy sound of the wind and the waves is pervasive. Hogg then cuts to Rose in the kitchen, clearing up after dinner. There is a notable contrast: where the previous scene was defined by restlessness, this one conveys Rose's sense of purpose as she goes about her duties, and while the atmospheric sound in Edward's room points to a sense of the uncertain external world, here the hum of the dishwasher neutralises the possibility of any of the outside seeping in. Hogg then cuts to Rose going to bed – her room appears similar to Edward's, and only now we do hear the wind and the waves, but Rose's purposeful rolling of her cigarette rhythmically marks a contrast with Edward's earlier bedroom scene.

As night passes to morning (establishing the film's temporal structure), the following scenes confirm that Hogg is establishing a pattern of association through contrasting the Leightons, specifically Edward in this case, with Rose's activities and behaviours. We pick up Rose, walking downstairs to begin her duties, and in the next shot leaving on her bike, framed through a doorway in the yard. The composition is matched in the next scene, another doorway shot, but this time we are back in Edward's claustrophobic bedroom as he moves gingerly around the space. A wider shot shows him idly exploring the assorted trinkets on the dressing table, chuckling to himself as he does so, this is then followed by an external shot as he freewheels his bike downhill – another point of visual continuity which conversely works to mark a distinction between him and Rose. Hogg then cuts to a punctuation shot of a dark cloud and we hear Christopher's voice. He is opining on the nature of landscape art: 'Abstraction is a reductive process; a way of simplifying, distilling really, so, uh, there's no such thing as, really, abstraction; there's no such thing as reality.' As Christopher attempts to convey his artistic philosophy, Hogg cuts to shots of Cynthia and Patricia listening intently. Christopher can still be heard as Hogg cuts to Rose, who is methodically cutting and preparing a bird in the kitchen. Hogg then returns to the outdoor scene and Edward has joined the party. Christopher is talking about a journey to Iceland where he slept 'out on the ice' and was mesmerised by the colours. He equates his trip with Edward's plan: 'to go somewhere and do something that I'd never ever do again.' Patricia is clearly impressed: 'Yes, a real adventure'. Hogg then closes the scene with a twenty-eight-second static take of a darkening sky, the familiar winds are joined by the distant sound of a church bell, and then a shot of a darker sky, as the sun goes down. In one sense, Hogg is establishing the rhythm of daily life on the holiday, but more significantly she is cementing Rose's role not only as silent observer of the Leightons but, through the repeated foregrounding of Rose's purposeful labour, as a marked counterpoint to their slowly increasing sense of collective anxiety, one which is bound up with distinctly middle-class trigger points – the existential crisis of a frustrated banker who seeks meaning through aid work and the landscape painter and teacher whose reflections on art and life mark him as surrogate for an absent husband and father.

This pattern of contrast is embedded further over the following days. Following Hogg's now familiar nocturnal punctuation shots, the narrative resumes with a medium side-on shot of Rose in the yard of the house. She is talking and laughing with Edward, although we do not see him until Hogg cuts to a wider shot, which shows him in pyjamas at an outdoor table, eating breakfast that Rose, standing next to her seated employer, has obviously prepared for him. During the conversation, Edward asks Rose about her family – she reveals that that her sister is called Chloe (the same name, Edward says, as his girlfriend) and that her father died in the previous year. As she shares this intimate information, Cynthia enters the frame, coming into the yard through the patio doors. Immediately Rose re-assumes her role as servant, offering to make breakfast for Cynthia and moving into the back of the frame and back to the kitchen. Cynthia conveys the news to Edward that their mother is unwell, putting the planned walk and picnic in doubt, before then turning to Rose, just visible through the kitchen window, asking her to change the picnic. Edward leaves the frame to get ready and Cynthia assumes his position at the outdoor table in the centre of the shot. Hogg then cuts to a closer shot of Cynthia, clearly exasperated as she sighs and stares in silence – the atmospheric noise of the birds and a distant helicopter further emphasising her forlorn state. She then beckons Rose – once again assuming her servile position at the back of the shot and firmly in her space (place) the kitchen – through the window, asking her to find picnic rugs. The rhythmic contrast between Edward's and then Cynthia's dialogue with Rose (and matching compositions) further deepens the film's conspicuous placement of Rose as paradoxically an implicated outsider in the Leightons' psychodrama.

Indeed, as the picnic and walk begin Rose's role is firmly functional. Although she exchanges small talk with Christopher about the weather she is largely a silent presence, on hand to serve the food as Edward discusses Africa, Cynthia directs passive aggressive barbs at her brother and Christopher gives Patricia a painting lesson, and yet the sequence ends with Rose, as she emerges from a coastal cave, alone, clambering along the rocks while the waves can be heard crashing against them in the high winds. The cave is situated in the centre of the frame so that it resembles a doorway and significantly Hogg then cuts to the first of the aforementioned phone call scenes with Patricia talking to her absent husband in a shot held at the distance in the gloomy afternoon light, shot through a doorway. Here the spatial match works to further suggest Rose's crucial place, despite her apparent marginalisation, within the film's symbolic palette.

After further punctuation shots mark the passing of time and the changing of the weather to heavy rain, we follow Edward as he joins Christopher, who is painting on a hillside looking out over the coast. Christopher discusses his work with Edward in typically vague fashion: 'I quite like that blue, that's kind of joyous'. Rose is again used to draw out a contrast in the next shot as Hogg cuts to her on a jetty in the harbour, with the prominence of the water ensuring that the blue of Christopher's painting is here actualised. The scene lasts just under two minutes and contains three shots. It involves Rose meeting a fisherman who arrives on a speedboat and learning from the fishermen how to determine the lobster's gender. Again, then, Hogg places sustained emphasis on Rose and the undertaking of her labour as a counterpoint to the Leightons' routines and practices.

This continues into the next scene as she tentatively inspects and prepares the lobsters. The scene lasts for forty-eight seconds before Hogg cuts to a close shot of the lobsters in their water. Rose's voice interrupts the sound of the water reaching its boiling point and a return to the initial composition reveals that Edward has joined her. A two-minute twenty-second take comprises Edward and Rose discussing the methods and ethics of lobster cooking, with Edward's bridging presence accentuating the sense in which Christopher's art is held in contrast with Rose's craft. The rhythmic structure is further developed as we return in the next scene to the now familiar dining room tableau – Rose and Edward are at the back of the frame (in the kitchen) and Cynthia and Patricia are in the foreground, mockingly laughing at Edward's burgeoning friendship with Rose. As he joins them, Cynthia remarks to her brother, 'You don't have to make friends with the cook, you know.' Yet Hogg's sustained emphasis on Rose up to this point has elevated her in narrative terms beyond the subjugated, ancillary role that Cynthia bestows on her. This makes Rose's recurring position at the wide margins or at the back of the repeated tableaux particularly significant in terms of the film's poetic structure. As Yacavone writes of the concept of 'weighting':

> [. . .] weighting equally pertains to how the contents of the film image [. . .] are perceptually (i.e., spatially and temporarily) foregrounded or backgrounded through staging, framing, camera movement, shot scale, and lens and focus choice (and alternation), for example, as well as editing. In all of these respects a given film can bring something to our explicit attention within the framed image, and within the represented and fictional reality of a work, that would not normally be so 'selected' [. . .] in every life-experience, or, indeed in other films. Often these are small details that while literally present and available in a perceptual environment, including one of interpersonal interactions, may "normally" be imperceptible. (Yacavone 2015: 94)

As we know, Hogg's use of recurring, long-take tableaux (alongside her intricate sound design) enables the representation of a perceptually grounded sense of the characters' worlds, and as Yacavone implies, such an approach, with enhanced capacity for depth and width of composition, might be seen to enable the 'weighting' or emphasis on details that might otherwise be missed. In the case of Rose, such an effect is emphasised because her 'weighted' but marginal emphasis inside the tableau is accented further by those moments in which she is outside it.

The following day begins with Cynthia waking, opening her curtains and returning to bed. She stares out of her window in a desolate fashion as, in contrast, another of Edward and Rose's breakfast conversations can be heard downstairs. Again, the Leightons' emotional inarticulacy is contrasted with

Rose's lucidity as she freely and eloquently discusses the death of her father with Edward: 'It's like we've come out of the coma, and that can be good, and that can be bad, because it's the realisation that he's never coming back ... that's the hardest thing really.' As Antoine Bitel remarks, it is again Rose who makes visible the film's exploration of absence:

> [...] the siblings' father Will is ... absent from what ought to be an important family get-together to mark Edward's departure to Africa – although, in an oblique strategy typical of director Joanna Hogg's writing, it is left to the hired chef Rose (Amy Lloyd) to articulate the 'coma'-like trauma of losing a father (in fact her own, who died the previous year). (Bitel 2015: 242)

The absence of the father is felt throughout the day as it unfolds. Rose plays photographer as the Leightons pose in Abbey gardens, with Cynthia telling Christopher, 'you can be dad' and then, in probably the film's most excruciating scene, Cynthia loudly complains about her meal at a restaurant and angrily belittles her brother who storms out, with Rose a passive observer. In the evening, the telephone shot is repeated, this time with Cynthia, before she passes the receiver to Patricia, whose angry tone with her husband marks a contrast from their previous exchange. The day ends as it started, with Cynthia in bed, only this time she is sobbing against the lingering soundscape of the chattering birds.

The next day begins with a close shot of Christopher painting, followed by a short sequence showing Rose beginning her duties. She and Edward are again in conversation at breakfast, before Edward visits first Cynthia and then Patricia in their respective beds, telling his mother of a nightmare involving his father: 'He was so angry.' Hogg then cuts to a repetition of the earlier shot of Edward on his bicycle drifting down the hill, with the birdsong prominent. However, rather than follow Edward into the next shot, Hogg cuts to a long shot of three men in hunting garb standing still with rifles awaiting their prey; she then cuts to a sequence of three low-angled shots in a woodland area as a group of beaters move through the space with their dogs, before a wider shot shows birds flying in multiple directions as shots are fired. After this four shot, ninety-second sequence, Hogg returns to Edward's bike ride, as he gently turns a corner past two trees in the middle of the frame, with birdsong again prominent but the sound of gun shots ominous in the distance. We then pick up what appears to be one of the men from the shoot – he is walking up the path to the Leightons' house and is carrying two dead birds alongside two of his dogs. In the next shot he knocks at the door, asking for Patricia, but Rose answers. It transpires that Patricia has ordered the birds without informing Rose. The take is held for one minute and forty seconds in a side-on shot which frames the doorway from the yard where Edward had breakfast earlier in the film. In an echo of the earlier scene at the jetty, it consists of the man, Steve, explaining to Rose how to de-feather the bird and how to remove its guts. Hogg then cuts to the familiar shot of Rose in the kitchen but now, acting on Steve's instruction, she is carefully removing the feathers and is preparing the pheasant. In customarily stark contrast, Hogg then returns to the living room tableau. Christopher is delivering a painting lesson to Cynthia and Patricia as Rose comes in and out delivering bowls of soup. Christopher's tentative edicts combine the universal and the specific, seeming to relate not only to painting but to the art of life, albeit in a somewhat trite manner: 'It's great to get this kind of degree of chaos, cos chaos gives ideas, which you may not have found if you'd tried to control it.' Edward comes into the room momentarily and then goes to the kitchen to speak to Rose. We then move to a shot of Rose smoking out of her attic window. The thirty-four-second shot contains her full body at the right of the frames, her elbow resting on the window ledge, her single bed to the left and her bedside table in the centre. The duration of the take forces attention on the details of the room and a photograph of a couple, presumably Rose's parents, is visible. As ever, the birdsong and wind are prominent but it is now more than background, or 'noise', to accentuate human silence – instead, Rose's attention seems focused on the movement of the birds. Although they are not visible to us, she gently arches her neck and moves her head to follow their sounds. Rose's head then lowers slightly and drops down as she appears lost in thought, the birdsong continuing as the shot lingers on her dejected stance. This quietly intimate moment is offered as a moment of grief. Here, the birds – ubiquitous throughout as intrinsic elements of the film's perceptual realism and as mechanisms to underline the contrasting silence of its human subjects – are re-narrativised and re-imagined as bearers of suffering. The scenes of shooting and the emphasis on the process of de-feathering assert the significance of the birds to the film's symbolic system and, almost in parallel, the fact that Rose's moment of sad reflection occurs during this sequence places her at the film's emotional centre. Again, the processes of Rose's labour are presented against the Leightons' activities: the art lessons which double as thinly veiled life coaching sessions; stunted expressions of existential angst; Edward's aimless drifts, both physically and figuratively; and the painfully tense dinnertime arguments. Indeed, in the following scene Christopher is seated with Patricia reflecting on his life as an artist, in particular discussing his childlessness (a theme across all of Hogg's films), while Patricia talks about her husband. Soon after, the Leightons (and Christopher) gather to eat the pheasant. The atmosphere is tense and another argument breaks out, with Cynthia at its centre. Tellingly the trigger for her angry departure from the table is the discovery of 'shot' in her portion of pheasant, which hurts her mouth. The bird is thus no longer abstracted as food on a plate and we are reminded of its former status as a living being, and, subsequently, as a symbol of loss – again, throughout the meal, Rose is visible at the back of the frame.

As the holiday concludes, there are more moments such as this one, most notably when Edward and Cynthia silently listen at the dinner table as Patricia has a raging argument with their father. Rose leaves early the next morning, before the end of the Leightons' stay, although her departure is not mentioned by any of the characters. In one of the film's final scenes, Edward re-hangs the contentious painting with Hogg resting on it in a two-shot succession, the second moving closer on its central image of dark, stormy waves. A kind of order is restored, then, and if Rose's presence opened a window onto a corrosive sense of absence at the heart of the family it has here been firmly closed.

Archipelago thus subtly evolves patterns of meaning within its tightly regulated quotidian rhythms. Repetitions of daily process and routines with attendant recurring tableau and visual motifs are given added perceptual richness through the intricacies of a sound design which works to communicate the film's themes and to foster an atmosphere of physical depth and intimacy. Days and nights pass, and characters embed processes and routines, enabling a structure that regulates and authenticates the film's sense of place and affect. Within these frameworks, parallels and contrasts emerge – as we have seen in our exploration of composition, sound and through an examination of Rose's position within the film – by means of which Hogg anchors her poetic examination of emotional inarticulacy and loss. Just as we identified in the work of Hopkins, a sense of the 'poetics' of new realism might be arrived at through an attentiveness to these rhyming patterns and schemes – those recurring and/or accented everyday visual and aural motifs that, while not explicit in their meaning making import, when viewed together, work to structure and articulate in lyrical terms the films' underlying concerns.

EXHIBITION (2013)

As I mentioned at the outset, *Exhibition* is similarly constructed around the passing of time, with the daily routines of H and D lending a sense of verisimilitude to a film that, in many other ways, departs from *Unrelated* and *Archipelago*. Indeed, Hogg's examination of D's dreams and fantasies, allusions to the unspoken incident and ambiguous scenes such as the one when, in a park, H inexplicably lies face down on the grass while D tries to comfort him, contribute to a sense in which the film's presentation of reality is more explicitly subjective than in the earlier films. Yet the film's use of sound follows on from *Archipelago* in positioning the aural realm as central in communicating a visceral sense of place and of physical, perceptual experience. While the dominant elements of sound design in *Archipelago* are the birds, the wind and the waves, here the intrinsic elements are the internal timbres of H's and D's modernist home and the sounds of the city beyond its walls.

For Hogg this heightened focus on the tensions between internal and external sound in the film is both about evoking something of the universal, perceptual experience of *being* in a place and of the subjective possibilities of sound as a bridge to the internal realm:

> I am hyper aware of sounds in everyday life. My ears work harder than my eyes. I am fascinated by how imagination is triggered by sound. This can also create anxiety – often an un-nameable anxiety because there is no eyewitness to these stories. It was these ideas I wanted to express inside D's head. The house is sponge-like not only visually but also aurally. A sound coming from outside the house, like a door closing or a person speaking, can appear to be coming from within the house. At night this can be frightening for D. (Sumpter 2014)

Hogg's use of 'sponge' as a metaphor is significant for a number of reasons. In a primary sense, she imagines the space as possessing a character, drawn from an absorption of its many inhabitants and their practices and processes. Indeed, not only can the house be seen (heard) to speak through the emphasis on its aural character, but the repeated, static foregrounding of rooms, doors and corridors gives the impression that it, too, has the capacity to see. Significantly, Hogg cites Gaston Bachelard as a key influence on the film:

> Books that I was reading at the time were Gaston Bachelard's *Poetics of Space* which helped me think about the house as a living organism in a way; a house that's been lived in for a number of years does become a vessel of memory and feeling. So I found reading that book very inspiring. (Williams 2014)

In this sense Hogg furthers her interest in the lyrical transformation of her everyday environments – through heavily conspicuous approaches to space and place, authentic locations which evoke physical, perceptually plausible senses of being in the world are imbued with poetic potentials. Bachelard's phenomenology of the homely, whereby 'the house' is positioned as 'one of the greatest powers of integration for the thoughts, memories and dreams of mankind' (Bachelard 2014: 6) is felt throughout the film, as material, domestic space is enmeshed with fragments of the wider environment, human emotion and the senses.

The film's first five minutes work to emphasise the home both as a space of familiarity and function and of indeterminate, multidimensional depth and figurative possibility. *Exhibition*'s arresting aurality announces itself in the title sequence. The scrapes of chairs, the sliding of drawers, footsteps on the floors, the pervasive hum of wind and cars outside and human breath are all heard before a coherent image presents itself. When it does, just one minute into the film, the large window of the house, shot from the side on, consumes some two thirds of the frame. A hooded woman (D) lies cat-like on the ledge, pushed up against the window, her reflection visible as the wind blows, the leaves on the trees sway and a church bell and then a police siren sound in the distance. D disentangles herself from her position and eventually moves from the frame, but as she does so, the sound design seems to linger first on her movements, as her clothes rub against the window, and as she pulls the hood from her head. In the next shot she moves down the spiral staircase, with her bare feet producing seemingly amplified bass tones, and we then see her entering her office and dragging open and then closing the sliding door. Again deep, low notes are produced by the action with the final bang of closure particularly emphatic. A cut to her at the desk in medium shot, back to camera, is met with the slide of her chair as she dials up her intercom. Elsewhere in the house another low, rolling sound can be heard, and as D speaks into the intercom, the source is revealed to be H in a room above her. For Hogg, the prominence of the sound is necessary for use of the house both as a mechanism for the film's perceptual verisimilitude and, as suggested, as a figurative entity:

> Those sounds, such as when Viv [D] is in her studio on the first floor and we hear Liam's [H's] chair rolling across the floor above her, are for the most part very real and very much a part of that particular space, and come from the Eames office chairs they're using. However, as a filmmaker you obviously manipulate the levels when you're doing the sound design, and I was very concerned to get the right pitch. I wanted to push the sound so that it's almost like thunder above her. (Dallas 2014)

This conscious manipulation of the space's acoustic characteristics along with the contemplative, lingering emphasis on D's pronouncedly tactile presence in and interaction with the home establish the importance of 'texture' as intrinsic to the film's meaning making. To expand on this, I want to turn briefly to Lucy Fife Donaldson's important development of embodied, phenomenological theories of spectatorship to account for 'texture':

> If engaging with the sensuousness of film has tended to involve a physical closeness, of visual proximity – looking across the surface rather than into the depth – and a material entanglement of filmic and spectatorial bodies, then there is space for attention to materiality from a bit further away, to reflect on the look and materiality of the film as a whole. Texture comes from the warp and weft of fabric – it is the result of weaving, the

composition of a made object, threads woven together. As such it encourages consideration of the interrelation of material decisions, narrative and other frameworks: how sound and image relate to one another; how style supports and contributes to narrative; how the nature of a genre (expectations around the shape of narrative, location and so on) contributes to the affective qualities of a particular film. (Fife Donaldson 2014: 6)

Fife Donaldson encourages a particular reading strategy rather than necessarily identifying an aesthetic tendency, but I would argue that Hogg's films – with their sustained emphasis on sound design as enabling a sense of acoustic depth to visually deep and wide images – lend themselves to being 'felt' and 'perceived' in 'textural' terms, and, indeed, that this is Hogg's intention. As the director states, '[w]ith *Exhibition* I wanted to push the imagescape and soundscape in a way that is not about telling a story in a straight line but is much more connected to my own perception of life' (Dallas 2014). While I will come back to the importance of Hogg's own subjectivity to the film's realism, it is important here to register again the sense that Hogg's heightened and conjoined approach to sound design and her treatment of the home as a visual entity is interpreted in spatial terms – here, as non-linear and consequently both perceptual and internal. In this way, the film's causal ambiguities also contribute to its 'textured' quality because its sensory emphasis can be seen to be privileged over an apparent recourse to narrative coherence. As Daniel Yacavone argues, a kind of spectatorial absorption can be seen to emerge in such sensorially rich texts:

> [...] what I have termed sensory-affective engagement involves the viewer's becoming notably absorbed in a film's perceptual and affective experience on a basis that is more immediate and primary than one reliant on any aspect of the fictional-representational and narrative dimension. (Yacavone 2015: 186)

We can return here to *Archipelago* as a film that, like *Exhibition*, invites such an 'affective', 'textured' engagement on the basis of its long takes and its distinctive and pervasive aural emphasis on birdsong and wind – one which seeks to situate its spectator within a perceptually plausible, embodied dialogue with place and space. In this sense Hogg's perceptual realism might be seen to involve the viewer in a kind of 'dynamic subjectivity between looker and image', to borrow from Laura U. Marks (Marks 2002: 2). Indeed, Fife Donaldson augments the phenomenological reading strategies advocated by Marks and Vivien Sobchack amongst others, to take account of sound and, in the process, to call into focus the 'textured' nature of a sensorially rich, perceptually attentive form of cinematic engagement. As I suggested at the outset, one way of situating Hogg's realist project is to understand it through the lens of such 'embodied' modes of watching (and listening). As Sobchack argues, film's capacity to draw upon spectators' experiences and ways of being in the world necessarily involves them in a complex process of experiential dialogue with the cinematic text:

> In a search for rules and principles governing cinematic expression, most of the descriptions and reflections of classical and contemporary film theory have not fully addressed the cinema as life expressing life, as experience expressing experience. Nor have they explored the mutual possession of this experience of perception and its expression by film-maker, film, and spectator – all *viewers viewing*, engaged as participants in dynamically and directionally reversible acts that reflexively and reflectively constitute the *perception of expression* and the *expression of perception*. Indeed, it is this mutual capacity for and possession of experience through common structures of embodied existence, though similar modes of being-in-the-world, that provide the *intersubjective* basis of objective cinematic communication. (Sobchack 1992: 5)

Sobchack's invitation to focus on cinema as both representing and calling upon a spectator's own 'life', 'experience' and 'perception' is particularly pertinent when considering Hogg's oeuvre, such is its emphatic privileging of a 'sensory-affective' realism that seeks to construct 'textured' aurally and visually perceptible worlds. More broadly, it is undoubtedly possible to add the affect-centred insights of these theorists to those more traditional realist and phenomenological thinkers that we have already called upon in attempting to draw conclusions from new realism's poetic engagement with everyday life.

However, we must be cautious in considering realism, as both an aesthetic process and as a historical tradition, in line with such embodied modes of viewing and comprehension, and in drawing upon the perceptual and sensory as resources for examining realist texts' dual capacity to depict and evoke an experience of the everyday to do so. Such theorisations of affect, drawn as they are from something of a universal sense of quotidian experience, risk overwhelming the necessarily complex intersections and flows of capital that form in the consumption and creation of a cinematic text. These questions are particularly critical to considering the work of Joanna Hogg, given the intensely narrow social focus of her films. Thus, to return to Hogg's use of sound in *Exhibition*, while it might be said that the film draws our attention to 'sounds in everyday life' (Sumpter 2014), it is important to acknowledge that our appreciation of these sounds is heavily filtered through the prominent emphasis on the house as a conduit of thematic meaning and embodied feeling, a house which is bound up with Hogg's own experiences and memories:

> My personal relationship to the space is key. It's one of the springboards for my imagination. My feelings surrounding a place become the foundations of the story. Once I decided on this house, then so many of the visual and aural ideas followed on from there. The sponge like nature of the house, the way it soaks from the outside so they appear to be coming from the inside. (Wood and Haydyn-Smith 2015: 99)

Hogg again uses the 'sponge' metaphor as a way of conceptualising the house's porous nature, its ability to absorb and disperse subjective feeling and memory. Thus, like the spaces in *Unrelated* and *Archipelago*, the central location is deeply personal – as mentioned previously, Hogg knew the architect James Melvin and visited the house regularly. This contextual awareness is necessary to appreciate the film's perceptual, sensory poetics – while these are fundamental to its power as a text that calls upon a sense of experiential and embodied spectatorship, the house – the arena in which these elements play out – is anything but an everyday space. Indeed, as a stunning example of Le Corbusier-inspired modernism, the location's intense architectural idiosyncrasies enable its unique visual and aural character. It is the home's very exclusivity that enables its unique capacity to reframe everyday space and sound. One might say the same for the recurring visual and aural motifs of *Unrelated* and *Archipelago*, generated as they are in locations where the sense of space and grandeur is available to only the most privileged. The question of social class therefore presents itself once more, just as it does through Rose's pivotal presence in *Archipelago*. Hogg has justifiably explained her persistent interest in middle-class characters by emphasising the personal nature of her narratives, drawn as they are from her own experiences, yet, perhaps curiously, she argues that this changed in *Exhibition*:

> But, as much as I don't like to be defined as someone who would depict a particular class of people, there's no getting away from the fact that it's true of *Unrelated*. I made it after a long time of working in other spheres. I worked in television for about 12 years and felt increasingly frustrated that I wasn't expressing my own ideas and experience of life. [...]
>
> It carried through into *Archipelago*, but with *Exhibition* I felt I wanted to move away from [the middle class] because I was a bit frustrated by being labelled [...] It's more apparent there than when I show the films in other countries. We're particularly class-obsessed, as you know. I thought: 'If I take two artists, they don't fit into any class really.' Except obviously they live in this particular house so they also get described as

middle class. It's not a theme I'm interested in, but I can't deny it has occurred through going deeply into my own experience. (Fuller 2014)

Hogg's suggestion that H and D should be viewed as socially neutral characters is disingenuous. This 'particular house' is not merely an architecturally interesting building but it is a piece of highly prized real estate in Kensington, one of the most sought after and exclusive suburbs in one of the most unequal cities in the world. In June 2015 the house was sold for £7 million. Moreover, just as in *Archipelago*, the specific nature of the crises that the characters face can be seen to arise as a result of their economic and professional circumstances. This is not to dismiss the severity of D's emotional pain – her sadness at the sale of the home and her feelings of inertia about her creative labour are entirely legitimate, but they are also highly specific to the particular circumstances of her class experience.

In this sense the house is a continual reminder of the extent of H and D's removal from the world outside, an outside that might be seen to function, like Rose's presence in *Archipelago*, to hold a contextual mirror to the highly localised crises of the protagonists within. This is one way of conceptualising the textured aurality of D's experience of the home, defined as it is by the pervasive presence of outside sounds that penetrate her internal reality. Moreover, the moment when H angrily confronts a workman who has parked in front of the house, blocking the drive, makes explicit this social divide. H, whose discussions of art and stoic, philosophical reflections on the decision to sell the home have been defined up to this point by their free-flowing eloquence, is here notably inarticulate as he manically asserts his ownership of the property: 'My bit, your bit ... it's context, right, this is everyone else's bit ... what's going on? I don't understand? This is driving me nuts ... I'm gonna put big gates up here and write fuck off along them ... fucker, fucker ... move it ... move it.' D stays alongside H trying to calm him, but his rage is palpable. This disproportionate response to an apparent 'threat' to the home reveals the extent to which H's and D's homely immersion is both emotional and innately proprietorial, and that these two elements are inextricably linked, particularly in the context of an urban economy in which vast financial capital is concentrated on the ownership of land and property.

Again then, despite Hogg's arguments to the contrary, her films can be seen to reveal in nuanced but illuminating ways hitherto unrealised perspectives on class identity in Britain. This is not simply because of the direct focus on middle-class characters and locations in her films, but because these representations make visible and audible through the expressive and explicit emphasis on the relationship between environment and experience the extent to which location determines identity. This view of class in Hogg's work goes beyond

2.3 'My bit, your bit.'

Jonathan Romney's claim that her films represent an example of 'outsider cinema':

> While portrayals of working-class life have long held the moral high ground in British cinema, and images of archaic privilege continue to do a roaring trade as television luxury goods, the upper middle class is generally considered too bland or too embarrassing to be given screen space. (Romney 2014)

This argument that by representing a specific and subsection of the middle-class Hogg addresses a kind of imbalance in British cinema takes no account of the complex intersections of cultural and financial capital that are bound up both in the industrial and representational dimensions of British screen culture, and of the arts more broadly, areas of national life that are increasingly ignoring issues of class and regional representation and which naturalise a homogenising view of British 'reality'. Issues of aesthetics *and* access should be considered in terms of the class politics of realist cinema, and while Hogg's realist focus on the middle-class is novel it must be critically contextualised within a wider politics of cultural representation in British life. This is not to say that Hogg perpetuates an ideologically conservative fetishisation of privilege in national culture – we have seen how her films draw attention to the structural contexts of her protagonists' everyday lives and how they pointedly emphasise underrepresented issues specific to women in middle age – but that our readings of her work must not miss the unspoken but defining economic forces that govern the worlds that she both constructs and depicts.

Despite the highly specific scope of Hogg's social focus, however, her films evoke a profound sense of 'being in the world', in which the lived experience of reality is depicted in spatially, temporally and sensorially authentic ways – indeed, in which the very experience of daily life is called upon as an interpretive resource for the audience, as embodied spectators. It is in this sense, then, that Hogg's films must be understood within the emerging traditions of new realism. More specifically, within the framework of everyday poetics that I have used throughout this book, Hogg's work coheres around the sense that units of lyrical meaning are constituted not only through the visual realm but also through the dimensions of sound and touch. While Hogg's 'everyday' is far from representative, her films form highly textured structures of reality which connect to and interact with indeterminate narratives outside the frame, with their images and soundscapes appealing to multiple experiences beyond the particular conditions of their subjects.

3. ANDREA ARNOLD

No film-maker defines the characteristics of new realism more clearly than Andrea Arnold. Her films to date have attracted significant and widespread critical attention and she is unquestionably at the vanguard of contemporary British cinema. Like Hopkins and Hogg, Arnold's realism can be defined by its poetic transformation of familiar, quotidian materials and details and its marked appeal to the senses, through an emphasis on perceptual, physical experience. Just as in the other new realist films we have explored so far, Arnold's work draws on our own visual and sensory appreciation of lived experience to enable empathic and embodied engagements with the people and places her films depict. By emphasising universal, experiential visual and aural reference points, and by calling on the spectator, through repetition, duration and other forms of enunciation, to dwell on these everyday phenomena, Arnold's work, in the spirit of new realism, makes lyrical that which is often ignored.

If we look at a familiar landscape or object for long enough, or if such an image is brought to our attention and we are given the tools to imagine it divorced from its practical, everyday application, it takes on renewed meaning. In Arnold's films, blades of grass, flowers, fences, pylons, the material elements of quotidian experience, are elevated and transformed, enacting a process of poetic animation and re-animation. As we will see, her realist style encourages an involved mode of spectatorship and the process of heightened observation is also enacted by her protagonists diegetically – they are all outsiders whose views we share as they conspicuously interrogate their environments. For Arnold's human subjects, windows and doorways function as cinema screens, and by watching the watcher Arnold asks us to similarly make cinemas of our own worlds. As Amber Jacobs puts it, Arnold's films operate on 'a tactile, phenomenological level' to produce 'an embodied alignment between the projected subject and the viewing subject' (Jacobs 2016: 161). Similarly, for Jonathan Murray: 'audiences simultaneously look with and at the protagonists whose stories are being told' (Murray 2016: 208).

Just as with Joanna Hogg, Arnold's early career offered little indication of her later artistic pursuits. She came to prominence in the 1980s as a presenter on the ITV children's programme *No 73* (1982–8) and later wrote and presented *A Beetle Called Derek* (1990–1) for the same channel. She left the UK and moved to Los Angeles to study film-making at the American Film Institute and, after some further experience in TV, she made her first short film *Milk* in 1998. *Milk* concerns the response of Hetty (Lynda Steadman) to her miscarriage, and is a powerful examination of grief, motherhood and sexuality. Arnold's next short *Dog* (2001) would offer more clues to her later feature work. A young woman, Leah (Joanne Hill), who lives on a council estate (the film is shot on London's iconic Thamesmead estate), sees her boyfriend, John (Freddie Cunliffe) violently kill a dog after it interrupts the couple as they are about to have sex and eats John's supply of cannabis. Leah flees the scene and then seems to transform and begins to enact the spirit and behaviour of the dog in her fraught relations with her mother. Arnold's third short *Wasp* (2003) announced her on the international stage when she won an Oscar for best short film. *Wasp* is set in Dartford and follows a day in the life of Zoë (Natalie Press), a struggling mother of four who encounters Dave (Danny Dyer), an old flame who invites her for a drink. Not wanting to reveal that she is a mother and not able to afford childcare, Zoë takes her children to the pub and asks them to wait in the car park while she enjoys her date. Her youngest child, however, is almost stung by a wasp, causing a commotion that alerts Dave to Zoë's maternal status.

In 2006, *Red Road*, Arnold's first feature, made as part of Zoetrope's Advance Party initiative, was released. The film concerns Jackie (Kate Dickie), a CCTV operator mourning the death of her husband and daughter after a car accident. When she spots Clyde (Tony Curran) – the man who, while under the influence of drugs, caused the accident which killed her loved ones – on one of her cameras, she sets about exacting her revenge: she has sex with Clyde and then frames him for rape. At the film's conclusion, Jackie decides to withdraw the charges and appears to have found a degree of peace. Arnold's second film *Fish Tank* (2009) concerns troubled fifteen-year-old Mia (Kate Jarvis), following her attempts to be a dancer, her fraught relationship with her mother Joanne (Kierston Wareing) and her sexual relationship with Joanne's boyfriend, Conor (Michael Fassbender). The film won the BAFTA for best British film and repeated *Red Road*'s success at Cannes, again winning the Jury Prize. In 2011 Arnold took on Emily Brontë's *Wuthering Heights*, interpreting Heathcliff as a black former slave (with the older Heathcliff played by James Howson and the younger, Solomon Glave) and telling the story of his relationship with Catherine (the younger Catherine played by Shannon Beer and the older, Kaya Scodelario) from his perspective. Five years later, Arnold returned to a contemporary setting with *American Honey* (2016), a road journey narrative that follows an impoverished teenager, Star (Sasha Lane). Fleeing a sexually abusive father, Star joins a 'mag crew', a group of similarly disenfranchised youths travelling America selling magazine subscriptions, led by the tyrannical Krystal (Riley Keough) and Star's love interest, Jake (Shia LaBeouf). In addition to her film work, Arnold has also directed television dramas in America, most recently the second series of *Big Little Lies* (HBO 2017–).

Arnold's films are united by a number of recurring, thematic and aesthetic tendencies. As mentioned, the films all concern outsiders whose mode of looking upon the world we share, largely through point-of-view or over-the-shoulder shots. With this in mind, Arnold favours a handheld camera, and a 4:3 ratio that enables an immersive mode of portraiture, because, as she puts it, her films are 'usually about one person and their experiences of the world' (Robinson 2016). Like Hogg, Arnold evokes an embodied and textured sense of 'being there', but the proximal nature of her aesthetic creates a more involved effect to foster the illusion of 'being with'. The deep, static tableau, used by Hogg, is replaced by the relentless mobility of the participatory, mobile camera, and while Hogg privileges soundscapes that emphasise the weather, Arnold's films privilege an embodied evocation of breath and touch communicated by the intimate counters her films enact with their protagonists. This sense of a textured approach to form, one that fosters a mode of atmospheric embeddedness, is felt throughout Arnold's dual approach to landscape and the poetics of location. On one hand, the intensely subjective, experientially focused representation of a single character's interactions with a particular place enables it to be represented as lived in and experienced. On the other, the more contemplative dimension of Arnold's aesthetic constitutes a lingering emphasis on the details of the built and natural environments in which her characters are situated, and extends to a pointed and multidimensional treatment of non-human animals, not only as thematic counterpoints to human subjects, but as intrinsic elements of a multilayered evocation of space. At the heart of Arnold's cinema then is a kind of non-diegetic indeterminacy, one that we have also identified as being present in Hogg's and Hopkins's work. In part this is derived from all three film-makers' use of non-professional actors, whose status affirms the presence of narratives beyond the frame. More specifically, the environment is both central to meaning making within the fiction and operates as an element of place making which invites identification and participation, whereby the familiar and mundane elements of lived experience are deployed as resources to deepen the viewer's appreciation of character and situation.

With this multidimensional realist project in mind, it is once again useful to draw upon Doreen Massey's conceptualisation of space as dynamic:

> A reimagination of things as processes is necessary (and indeed now widely accepted) for the reconceptualisation of places in a way that might challenge exclusivist localisms based on claims of some eternal authenticity. Instead of things as pregiven discrete entities, there is now a move towards recognising the continuous becoming which is in the nature of their being. (Massey 2005: 20–1)

This notion of 'continuous becoming' and of the possibility of considering the cinematic landscape as in 'process' so that it operates diegetically but is also felt and identified non-diegetically by viewers, is critical to Arnold's realist project, and to those of the other film-makers explored in this book. Space is therefore neither backdrop to nor authenticator of fiction, but is represented, through a number of mechanisms, as mutable, malleable and ongoing.

While Arnold's work has its own specific concerns and points of formal and thematic emphasis, it is, then, clearly possible to consider it within a wider understanding of new realism. As I discussed at the beginning of this book, however, one of the ways in which the critical construction of realism and realisms within British film history has operated has been through the tacit construction of a monolithic notion of social realism against which auteurist analyses of particular film-makers or movements are positioned, in order to emphasise difference and contrast. Given the significant weight of critical attention that has been directed towards Arnold, it is no surprise that most commentators indulge in a similar discursive project. For example, in her discussion of *Red Road*, Sue Thornham suggests that the film contests 'the masculinity of social realism's focus on the gritty, provincial city' (Thornham 2016a: 141); on the same film, for Jonathan Murray 'the links between [*Red Road*] and Scottish/British traditions of social realist [. . .] are strictly limited in nature' (Murray 2015: 101). Michael Lawrence comments that the 'innovative formal complexity and intricacy of Arnold's films [. . .] complicates their affinity with a British tradition of social realism' (Lawrence 2016a: 158), while Lucy Bolton argues that '*Fish Tank* might look like social realism but is also phenomenological experimentation. This is a film about Mia, but it is not just a gritty exposition of her environment and the limits of her choices' (Bolton 2015: 76). Finally, Amber Jacobs comments that 'Arnold's films have a striking political reach, but not one that comes about through the conventional mode of social realist, didactic, message-based cinema' (Jacobs 2016: 163).

I will return to the question of the politics of Arnold's approach shortly, but for now it is worth reflecting on the implication in these positions; that there exists both a conjoined and consistent tradition, perhaps even a coherent genre, of social realism, one which Arnold should be viewed against, because she eschews didacticism in favour of a more phenomenological and formalised mode of poetics. My aim is not to argue against claims that Arnold is a bold and distinctive film-maker, but to acknowledge that these characteristics of apparent difference can be understood also in line with a new realism that extends beyond Arnold, one which is both experientially focused and aesthetically rigorous. For example, we have already seen how phenomenological realist film theorists, such as Kracauer and Bazin, and later thinkers such as Vivian Sobchack, and Laura U. Marks, building on these traditions, might be used to illuminate the sense in which British realist film-makers have concerned themselves, albeit in varying ways, with the perceptually grounded representation of experience. Indeed, Sobchack's discussion of cinema's treatment of the '*modes of embodied existence*' and '*the structures of direct experience . . .* as the basis for the structures of its language' (Sobchack 1992: 5), and Marks's identification of 'haptic *visuality*' and the cinema's encouragement of 'a bodily relationship between the viewer and image', through its 'offer' of 'haptic *images*' (Marks 2002: 3), absolutely chime with Arnold's sensorially driven aesthetic, and indeed, multiple critics draw on these theorists in their analysis of Arnold's oeuvre. Yet we also know that these insights are equally relevant when considering the work of Arnold's realist contemporaries, such as Hogg and Hopkins, for whom the representation of perception and lived, direct experience are also fundamental.

As I have already implied, Arnold's new realist credentials can also be identified in the highly considered nature of her realist *mise en scène*. Where we previously explored, for example, the lyrical, rhythmic effect of Hopkins's use of windows and Hogg's deployment of bedrooms and dining tables as spaces that are simultaneously familiar but also highly constructed in their capacity to convey symbolic meaning, we can, in Arnold's work, similarly identify a commitment to an everyday poetics that we might in turn think of as constituting image-led narration, whereby meaning is constructed in and through self-contained images and/or through recurring formal patterns. Arnold's cinematographer and long-time collaborator Robbie Ryan describes the process in a pleasingly direct fashion: 'Andrea [Arnold] would call it a poetic realism. You're trying to be lyrical with something that's real' (Jenkins 2015).

When reflecting on the creative process, and more specifically the genesis of her projects, Arnold has repeatedly stated that she begins with the image: 'Normally how I start writing is I have an image that bothers me and I have to go and explore it. It's a great way of starting because it actually helps me decide what to do. It becomes the thing that won't leave me alone' (Tolley 2009). I will explore the formal implications of this approach in more detail later, but for now it is worth reflecting on Arnold's self-conscious positioning of herself as a storyteller who is primarily motivated by visual stimulus rather than, for example, more developed structural themes. Even in *Wuthering Heights*, with an obviously established narrative, and having joined the project when it was already in advanced stages of development, Arnold still maintained this intuitive, visual approach, describing how she had initially imagined 'a huge animal climbing up the side of the moor at dusk, which you suddenly realise is a man carrying rabbits on his back' (Lee 2016). In *American Honey* the film's broad themes of economic marginalisation and its actualisation of the inhumanity of the free market, where the body itself is commoditised, are again imagined as being distilled within a particular image of the film's characters that directed Arnold's process:

> It was of them being on the outside of things and trying to get on the inside of things and get accepted by people in houses. There was this sort of vulnerability about them being on the doorstep or in a parking lot, sort of looking to get people to accept them, getting people to listen to them and to buy what they were selling. I have a very strong memory of seeing them selling and trying to attract people. They're sort of solitary figures on this huge tarmac or outside of a house where they were not really that welcome. That was a very poignant feeling I came away with, having spent time with them. I hope that's in the film. (Zuckerman 2016)

Here Arnold describes the relationship between a guiding image and the communication of a particular set of emotions associated with it. The film's complex themes are condensed within both a notional and an actual – there are numerous compositions in the film that chime with this description – visual iconography to give a 'feeling', rather than directing meaning. As Stella Hockenhull puts it, this constitutes a process whereby Arnold 'emphasises setting and privileges image over narrative' (Hockenhull 2017: 115). These images do not, however, imply distance or objectification. Instead, as Arnold is keen to point out, they offer ways into deeply embodied representations of characters and their environments:

> [. . .] the other day I saw a woman walking up to the station. It was very cold, it had been snowing, and she had not enough clothes on for the weather. She had a load of kids and she was pushing a pram up the hill, and she was kind of shouting at the kids, I don't know what they were doing. I could tell she was trying to hurry for a train. She had some

track-suit bottoms on and they'd kind of slipped down, and you could see this expansive flesh at the back. It seemed such an intimate thing to me. I was behind her, and I just started imagining her whole life and a house and what it was like. And that is the kind of thing that I will go and write down and think about. And it grows. I'm always saying that my films have all started with images, so I would consider that potentially a starting place for a whole story. (Smith 2010)

Here Arnold does not read the woman as a type or a representative figure, she is instead drawn to her individual story; a fleeting surface gaze enables a deep contemplation of human experience. It is also significant that Arnold is drawn to 'the expanse of flesh' and the 'intimate' status of this image. Ambivalently, rather than assisting the woman, she gazes at her from behind, and uses her as artistic inspiration. The identification of such close human and non-human details is an intrinsic element of her 'haptic' appreciation of the textures and surfaces that constitute the physical experience of everyday life – we might think of the repeated shots of Heathcliff's and Catherine's hair in *Wuthering Heights*, or the emphasis on Mia's wounded ankle in *Fish Tank*. What is clear then is that Arnold's privileging of the image in this way implies a deeply instinctive approach, which partly manifests itself in terms of a visual poetics that denies obvious socio-political application:

And if I'm writing, when I've got an image that I've decided I want to explore, I usually write around it and try and work out its context. I'll let my brain be quite free and see what happens. Then it will take more shape [...] I told you about that woman I saw. I wanted to go back and write about her straight away. That's how it works. I don't have an intellectual thought about oh, I'm going to make a film about this world or these people or this subject or theme. It's not like I have a plan, really. (Smith 2010)

Arnold thus connects this mode of affective, image-led narration to a wider acknowledgement that her films are not conceived instrumentally to be 'issue'-driven – Arnold's 'woman' is not a mechanism through which to mount an analysis, but rather a way into a lived experience and a conduit for a wider emotional project:

A film for me is a journey I have to go on. It starts with myself emotionally and moves outwards. I do make my films with a social eye. It's not a huge thing, and I don't want to ram it down people's throats, but it's there all the time in the way I feel and think. It's just how I see the world. (O'Hagan 2016)

This conflation of realist poetics with discourses of emotion and 'feeling' in place of didacticism has provoked critiques of Arnold's work. In two separate analyses of *Fish Tank*, Clive Nwonka has argued that Arnold's 'distinctive poetic realist address' (Nwonka 2017: 73) produces an 'objectification of the subject', rendering characters like Mia as 'insects under a magnifying glass' (Ibid.: 74). Nwonka connects Arnold's poeticism to a disavowal of politics: '*Fish Tank*'s poetic identification of space becomes fragmented: its character rendered attitudinal, culturally specific, and a location of power structures that are emotionally, rather than systemically, defined' (Ibid.:73). As I discussed at the start of this book, readings such as those put forward by Nwonka are part of a wider tradition of critiquing realist texts for apparently insufficient political analysis, and while it is fair to say that Arnold does not fully explore the 'agency of the state apparatus' (Ibid.: 74) in determining Mia's predicament, we should approach with caution the dialectical positioning of 'emotion' and 'system' as if they are mutually exclusive. The film concerns itself with Mia's emotional world and therefore adopts a style which necessarily foregrounds the subjective experience of life as a young woman living on a tough council estate; while this might efface structural analysis, it is – through the privileging of the perspective of a marginalised subject – nevertheless political. For Nwonka, however, this feature of Arnold's style, the tethering of the camera to Mia to convey a sense of how and when she feels, further curtails the film's social potential:

> Certainly in the first act Arnold's camera focuses on just one character, with Mia sharing the frame on very few occasions with her co-characters. Mia's visual detachment comes from a seeming desire to construct the story as an individual account rather than an account of class relations. Arnold consistently employs close-ups on Mia to draw visual attention to the protagonist's emotional state. (Nwonka 2014: 211)

Arnold's 'visual attention' to 'emotion' works against Nwonka's desire to see Mia's social context explored – again, then, the aesthetics of emotion are seen as disabling rather than facilitating the film's politics. Nwonka goes on:

> [...] the camera's almost surveillance-like hawking of Mia restricts *Fish Tank* from revealing any broader contextual meaning for the spectator. In this sense, the spectator is denied the crucial connection between the socio-economic realities of Mia's existence and the images on the screen. (Ibid.: 212)

However, the elements of Arnold's realism that Nwonka decries are those that other critics, such as Lucy Bolton, celebrate:

This is a film about Mia, but it is not just a gritty exposition of her environment and the limits of her choices; nor is it a straightforward vision of teenage girlhood in broken Britain. It is an evocation of her individual personality and experiences, through an immersive cinematic phenomenology of her space, time, and movement [. . .] This existentialist phenomenological approach enables us to understand how *Fish Tank* evokes the experience of what is *to be* a modern girl in modern Britain, rather than presenting a more conventional story of what happens to her within her social and cultural context. (Bolton 2015: 76)

The embodied immersion that Bolton draws from Arnold's depiction of Mia is framed in terms of the necessarily subjective representation of her *experience*, but it is this emphasis that Nwonka sees as depoliticising. Yet, as Amber Jacobs argues, the sensorially rich, close proximity of this depiction is precisely the source of Arnold's 'striking political reach':

Arnold's films occupy a new political terrain. Her candid, sensory mode of depicting the extremity of sexual/maternal embodiment transmits and implants into the viewer not a social (moral) message but, instead, a new mode of ethical and ontological relatedness. (Jacobs 2016: 163)

Jacobs describes how the 'close following of Mia, emits a sense of care, a being-with-ness' (2016: 173) which is at odds with Nwonka's suggestion that Mia is an object of scrutiny. Indeed, I want to suggest that what is evolving in Arnold's film-making in terms of realist practice is the opposite of what Nwonka describes, that the sense of 'being with' fosters hitherto unrealised dynamics of participation and even solidarity with the director's marginalised subjects. As Jennifer Barker puts it in her phenomenologically informed theoretical work, '[U]ltimately we feel and understand love and loss more profoundly by being immersed *in* and inspired by them than merely by thinking *about* them' (Barker 2009: 16). Arnold's realism is immersive and engaged, and invites us to feel with rather than to think upon its subjects.

This returns us to Arnold's framing of the guiding image as stimulating an instinctive relationship with narrative, one that is necessarily indeterminate because it privileges mutable, non-prescriptive imagery that transcends easy socio-political analysis. Let us take, for example, the ending of *Fish Tank*, where Mia leaves the estate with her traveller companion Billy (Harry Treadaway). For Nwonka, impressing a structural analysis on the film, the ending is akin to *Billy Elliot* (Stephen Daldry, 2000) whereby individual liberation overwhelms the collective experience and ignores the complexities of class analysis (Nwonka 2014: 213–14). In labelling the ending unambiguously 'escapist' (Ibid.: 214), Nwonka makes a number of assumptions. Precisely because of Arnold's highly subjective style, and her privileging of poetic image over prescribed narrative, we cannot know that Mia is liberating herself from her surroundings. As Lucy Bolton points out:

> Spending time with Mia in *Fish Tank* is to experience the uncertainties, ambiguities, and disappointments of a particular 15-year-old girl in modern Britain. We experience those ambiguities our not knowing the extent of her relationship with Billy, the intentions and deceptions of Conor, or what her future holds. (Bolton 2015: 83)

And for Emily Cuming the ending offers 'no sense that she is on the ascent, Mia's rejection of the spatial parameters of the estate is the only dance she has left to offer' (Cuming 2013: 338). For both critics the ending is consistent with the 'ambiguities' of the film's immersive depiction of Mia, and her reactions to and encounters with her environment. Just as in *Wuthering Heights* and *American Honey* we are left with a sense of closure in visual and sensory terms, one that is consistent with the established patterns and motifs that run throughout the films, but one that resists straightforward interpretation.

Ways into Arnold

Before looking in specific detail at Arnold's four feature films, I want to first spend some time exploring her other works, not least because they evidence the remarkable consistency of her cinematic concerns.

Arnold's most recent work in Britain is an advert for the Prince's Trust entitled *Youth Can Do It* (2017). While other realist film-makers, such as Shane Meadows, Mike Leigh and Ken Loach, are no strangers to the world of advertising, this is Arnold's first such venture and unlike the (by definition) commercially orientated work of her fellow British directors, Arnold's film feels remarkably consistent with her oeuvre.

The commercial is soundtracked by a poem, 'Bulletroof', performed, by sixteen-year-old poet Maya Sourie. The lyrics emphasise the resilience of youth: 'pain is nothing but fuel to reach my full potential'. The poem is backed by a youth choir that creates a rousing, chanting effect. Just as she does in her features, 'Arnold cast young people whose lives and circumstances reflected those in the script, filming the scenes in their own homes and dressing them in items from their own wardrobes' (Anonymous 2017), and the film is made up of short, fractured vignettes of the characters in a variety of scenarios which show them both experiencing adversity and illustrating defiance. The camera is handheld, and rests on particular details: close shots of a girl's face as she applies make-up; a temporary tattoo on a girl's arm; cobwebs as a young man opens a garage door; a buttercup in sharp focus before a cut to a young woman in a hijab performing sit-ups in a playing field. These ephemeral fragments of everyday experience give a textured distinctiveness to Arnold's portraiture, suggesting lives of depth and complexity beyond the fleeting glimpses offered here. These visual strategies are entirely consistent with the modes of everyday poetics that we have already begun to sketch out in relation to Arnold's work, and there are a number of other such motifs at work within the film. Images of a girl running through an estate, her breathing audible on the soundtrack, and two shots, one from behind and one from the side, as another teenager moves through a busy street, bring to mind Mia's restless mobility in *Fish Tank*, as does the film's final image, shot over the shoulder of a young man, where the room is dark in the foreground but light shines through a window at the back of the frame, making visible a block of flats outside. These images of young people encountering and making sense of the world are punctuated by shots which give a sense of the poetic potentials of their environments: in one short scene we see a flock of pigeons flying across a blue sky, in another ducks swimming across a pond. Despite its instrumental purpose, *Youth Can Do It* can be viewed as a distillation of Arnold's work to date, showcasing the consistency and pervasiveness of her artistic project.

Going back to the start of Arnold's film career, *Milk* presents a number of thematic and stylistic threads that would be developed in later films. As Amber Jacobs argues:

> Arnold's films are radical and inspiring in their bold and sensitive juxta-position of the maternal and sexual realms, and *Milk* is an early example of their powerful capacity to position the materiality of the experiential, maternal, bodily subject as a privileged site for the production and trans-mission of philosophical knowledge. (Jacobs 2016: 161)

Milk's image-led approach to its subject enables the radical convergence of these elements as they manifest themselves in the film's central character, the grieving mother, Hetty. Indeed, after Hetty's miscarriage, Arnold introduces the film's bold, central image, a close shot of a lactating nipple as Hetty lies in the bath, preceded by the words of her partner, Ralph (Stephen McGann), on the phone: 'she hasn't cried yet'. Later on, Hetty will cry, but only after she has had sex with another, much younger man, Martin (Lee Oakes), and has seen him feed off her breasts. Here, then, image-led narration comes to the fore, and is given heightened emphasis through the film's concise structure. Indeed, the white of the milk forms part of a consistent colour pattern in the film that distils its themes. When Hetty arrives at the hospital, she is driven in Ralph's red car, and when she sees blood on her hand our attention is drawn to Ralph's white T-shirt. Similarly, when Hetty wakes up having lost the baby, Arnold's composition sees the white-shirted Ralph sitting next to Hetty, who lies in her white hospital bed, with white bedding. Next, in the aforementioned bath scene, the milk and the white bath are contrasted with the red tiles on the wall, and in the following scene, Hetty is shown applying red lipstick. The patterned use of a specific colour palette is, as we will see, developed further in Arnold's first feature, *Red Road* – another film that deals with the complex intersections of sexuality, maternity and grief – and shows the way in which Arnold's rhythmic repetition and visual rhyme schemes structure meaning in her films.

In *Dog* (2001), Arnold's style more closely resembles her feature work. Most obviously, the use of the handheld camera marks a departure from *Milk*, and its close identification with its female protagonist, Leah, as she moves through her council flat location and through wasteland spaces around it is highly reminiscent both of *Wasp* and *Fish Tank*. Arnold alternates between this visceral, participatory framing and more painterly and observational compositions, again deploying motifs that will be more fully realised in her features. Indeed, in repeated compositions, the camera rests in low angle amongst foliage with sharply contrasting focus depths alternating foreground detail and clarity in the distant landscape, with wildlife and the flats themselves presented not in isolation but as part of a living, textured landscape. This sensitivity for ecologies of the estate and its surroundings facilitates the film's complex treatment of the relationships between humans and non-human animals in the film, when John kills the dog. This prompts Leah to run away, with a long shot showing her moving into the distance across the wastelands, but not before Arnold's camera rests on the dead dog's eye. This contemplative moment seems to trigger Leah's empowered move towards animality, and when she returns home her angry mother's violence is met by Leah barking like a dog, with the film concluding with a close shot, resting on her grieving face. The combination of animal death and adolescent suffering, and the embedding of these elements within and through the landscape, brings to mind Mia's relationships with the horse in *Fish Tank* and Heathcliff's encounters with dogs and rabbits in *Wuthering Heights*.

Just as she does in *Dog*, in *Wasp* Arnold emphasises the details and textures both of the internal and external environments that her characters inhabit and seeks to foreground their intimate, physical experience of those locations. For example, after Zoë meets Dave, the camera rests at a low angle taking in a pink flower, out of focus in the foreground, which in turn conceals what appears to be a grassed communal area, and in the distance a red-brick council estate. Again, the variations in depth work to both emphasise the layers of the landscape and its human and non-human constituents, and realise the potential for beauty in the setting. Next, Arnold's moving camera surveys a group of children from behind as they walk across the green, and then another textured landscape shot, this time with blades of grass gently moving in the wind in the foreground and two women on the balcony of a flat at the back of the frame. In the next shot we see clothes blowing on a line, and then another balcony shot, this time showing a dog, before Zoë's narrative is picked up again. Similar vignettes are used to foreground the life of the Mardyke Estate in *Fish Tank*, and work both to position Mia's story as one of many and to foster a sense of the estate as a kind of ecosystem of multiple entities. Indeed, the following shot, as we move into Zoë's flat, is a close up of a wasp on the window. Of course, the wasp will be narrativised more directly later in the film, but for now it is presented as another being contributing to the film's (and the estate's) rich, sensory terrain. For much of the scene Zoë is on the phone trying and failing to arrange childcare and feeding her children (bread and sugar) and searching for money. Shots of Zoë and the children alternate with decorations on the wall, such as drawings and stickers. The images work to deepen the film's visual and thematic reference points: one of the stickers states 'I want to be Barbie the bitch has everything' (pointing to intersecting spheres of class and gender), there is a photograph of David Beckham (a direct link to Dave), an image of a butterfly (evoking themes of redemption, transformation and liberation) and a hand-drawn picture of a flower and an insect (elements that have already been foregrounded through the *mise en scène*). Not only do these details condense symbolically significant elements of the film (and work in line with the image-led narration that we have already discussed), but they also suggest – in a non-instrumental manner – activities, preoccupations and experiences that exist beyond the frame, and therefore add further texture to the depictions of Zoë and her children. As I will go on to discuss, the privileging of these kinds of domestic and highly personal details features in all of Arnold's work and is particularly significant in place-setting scenes in Mia's bedroom in *Fish Tank* and at Star's home in *American Honey*. The scene ends when Zoë, having seemingly decided on her course of action (to take the children to the pub car park while she goes inside with Dave), opens the window and lets the wasp fly out, just as Mia's attempts to free the horse and Star's similar liberation of an insect function as a further move by Arnold to render the synergies between humans and other forms of life.

In the next sequence, Zoë and the children walk to the pub and Arnold's realism of proximity, a sense of 'being with' the characters, is again emphasised through the handheld, mobile camera, with close shots of feet, legs and other body parts conveying their movements through the landscape. Just as in the previous scenes, Arnold also emphasises a wider environmental context with a long shot from road level of a motorway, showing the family in the distance walking across a bridge, and then a close up of a ladybird clambering up a blade of grass, with cars blurred in the background. Again, then, natural imagery is used as an analogue for the film's human subjects.

There are other moments in *Wasp* that offer further avenues into Arnold's later work. While at the pub, as Zoë alternates between Dave inside and the kids outside, she comes across the neighbour with whom she had a violent argument at the film's opening. The woman sarcastically tells Zoë, 'you won't be laughing when you have your kids taken away', having previously threatened to call social services. At this point, we would be forgiven for expecting at the conclusion the exertion of discipline from some element of the state apparatus, as punishment for Zoë's transgressions, or as a way into understanding her environmentally determined victimhood, perhaps anticipating Nwonka's critique of *Fish Tank*. And yet, as in *Fish Tank*, there is no such assertion of structural forces. Instead, Arnold ends the film in both a poetic and generically atypical manner, re-asserting the foregrounded character of the environment with five static shots of the Dartford landscape at night but transforming the potential earnestness of the scene with the non-diegetic soundtrack of DJ Ötzi's 'Hey Baby (Uhh, Ahh)' – the song that the children had been singing in Dave's car after Zoë's secret has been revealed.

With the Oscar-winning success of *Wasp* firmly announcing Arnold's arrival on the cinematic stage, Arnold quickly made her way into feature films.

RED ROAD (2006)

Red Road emerged as the first part of the Advance Party initiative, a Scottish–Danish collaboration between Lars Von Trier, Gillian Berrie, Lone Scherfig and Anders Thomas Jensen, involving a set of pre-existing characters and a cast to be shared between three first-time directors across three films. Despite these restrictions, however, the film is in many ways consistent with the defining features of Arnold's film-making that I have discussed so far.

I want to focus particularly on Arnold's mode of image-led narration, whereby *mise en scène* and more sensorially rich elements of style work to construct and direct thematic meaning. In *Milk*, *Dog* and *Wasp* we have already noted the ways in which highly specific visual motifs are deployed as thematic vessels. This suggests a meticulousness on Arnold's part, which despite her instinctive, intimately character-focused shooting style, is directed towards the establishment of a precise mode of formal poetics. Indeed, as Michael Lawrence argues, '[t]he innovative formal complexity and intricacy of Arnold's films' is arrived at through a 'rigorous approach to framing, editing, sound design and colour' (Lawrence 2016b: 156). Such rigour is perhaps at odds with the assumption that realist style is subordinate to social theme, or that its aesthetic should be observational, inconspicuous and unobtrusive. As we have seen so far, however, the emerging traditions of new realism imply a rhythmic, often highly structured level of formalism, and Arnold's films are no exception.

Early on in *Red Road*, we learn that Jackie is engaged in an extra-marital affair with a co-worker, Avery (Paul Higgins). The relationship is shown to be loveless, functional and ultimately unfulfilling for Jackie – a transactional product of her grief and solitude. This narrative information is critical to a wider understanding of the film's complex exploration of the relationship between sexuality and grief, which reaches its peak through Jackie's highly charged encounter with Clyde and its aftermath, and is given lyrical articulation when the pair spend an afternoon together near the film's outset. Avery enters the control room where Jackie is working and points at a dog on one of the screens, complaining that it is defecating in the street. Jackie explains that the dog is unwell – at this point, we have already seen her concern at the dog's plight in earlier shots. We then cut to a close shot of another dog, sitting behind a caged partition in what appears to be a van, then a shot from behind the partition reveals the driver, Avery, and passenger, Jackie. The image of the caged dog connects the world Jackie observes to the one in which she lives and is one of many instances whereby the plight of the non-human animal is equated with that of the human. Indeed, this is a sequence that is entirely concerned with the multiple restrictions and barriers that exist for Jackie.

The shot through the partition, possibly from the dog's point of view, sees Jackie playing with a toy that hangs from Avery's window; after a jump cut but with the composition maintained, Avery informs Jackie 'my son gave it to me', and, in an early indication of the causes of Jackie's grief, we see her smile turn to an uncertain frown. Arnold then cuts to a succession of quick landscape shots, which might be seen to further hint at Jackie's sadness, as Stella Hockenhull argues:

> The camera is placed to the rear of the car, and hence Jackie is seen in close-up. Her inner turmoil, however, is perhaps better expressed in the surrounding *mise en scène*: at this juncture, Arnold cuts to the passing landscape. Dark trees fill the frame and, shown in silhouette, they are bare of leaves and create black outlines against the late afternoon's winter sky. The car speeds on, and the Scottish hills now overpower the image, but the spectator is unclear whether this is from Jackie's point of view or not because the next shot of a tiny window looking out is from an interior perspective. A further edit reveals the couple seated in silence at a table of a pub [...] (Hockenhull 2017: 115)

Just as in *Wasp* and *Dog* Arnold complements intimate framing with more expansive treatments of external space, lyrically contextualising her character portraits. As Hockenhull implies, the cut to the shot of the window feels abrupt; it is certainly not a conventional establishing shot and we only realise that we are seeing the window to the pub when the next shot is revealed. To add to Hockenhull's point, the view of the window is also significant because it is restricted by metal bars, which partially obscure the road, hills and a pylon in the distance. The bars here echo the cage-like composition in the van – already, then, a motif is emerging which conveys notions of imprisonment.

After the pub a wide shot of the van with the dog outside cuts to a closer shot outside the van, showing Jackie's face pushed up against the window, then, in the rear of the van we see a partially obscured image of two bodies moving together, before a close shot, again filmed through the partition, of Avery's bottom moving back and forth. Then in another shot through the partition, we catch Jackie's face in the wing mirror; she is clearly enduring rather than enjoying the encounter. We then see two more shots through the partition on Avery as he climaxes, another of Jackie in the window, and another nine shots, all obscured and shot through the cage as the couple put their clothes back on and exchange pleasantries. Sex here is neither liberating nor pleasurable, it is an act framed in terms of confinement and subjugation, at least for Jackie. As Avery drops her off, presumably to return to his wife and family ('See you in two weeks, then'), a long shot shows Jackie alone outside a bus station in silhouette as the sun sets, appearing, as Michael Stewart puts it, 'numb and lifeless' (Stewart 2012: 559). This composition of a specifically gendered isolation concludes a sequence in which a succession of highly composed images has inculcated particular tonal elements of Jackie's plight: her sexuality, her sadness, her relationship with Avery. Indeed, it is significant that when Jackie ends their relationship later in the film, Arnold's composition again recalls the visual patterns deployed in the earlier scene. Avery drives in his van alongside Jackie as she tells him to 'go look after your family' and she is repeatedly shown walking alongside a metal fence which consumes half of the frame; when Arnold cuts to Avery on repeated occasions, the shadow from the fence reflects on his vehicle, creating the illusion of bars covering the van and Avery.

Arnold's rigorous approach to *mise en scène* is also in evidence through her use of colour. As we saw in *Milk*, the deployment of specific colours to convey tonal and more specifically thematic effects is a significant element of image-led realism, and where red and white featured prominently in the earlier film, the titular 'red' is here highly prominent. In his analysis of the film, Jonathan Murray helpfully summarises the ubiquity of the colour in the film's early stages:

> Jackie sees a red tabard-wearing night cleaner make a low-paid, anti-social job bearable by singing and dancing [...]; Jackie's married lover decorates the dashboard of his van with a red soft toy given to him by his child; Jackie watches her sister-in-law and the latter's new husband emerge from their wedding ceremony clad in red and pink finery; a scene at the subsequent evening reception opens with a shot of a young girl dancing in a spangled red dress, while elsewhere in the room, Jackie converges with another lady in red, her elderly Aunt Kathy (Annie Bain).

[. . .] Jackie reads a handwritten red shop window that advertises hamster babies for sale. The raw redness of Clyde's hair seems initially to be the main source of Jackie's shock as she follows his nocturnal rutting on CCTV; during her frantic attempts to track Clyde's subsequent movements, a surveillance camera image shows a fox racing across a deserted street; red bed linen then frames a sleepless Jackie before she gets up later that night to compulsively scour a hoard of old press cuttings that cover the death of her loved ones and Clyde's subsequent trial. Following a pattern by now well-established, despite the fact that *Red Road* remains less than one-fifth of the way through its running time, viewers see that Jackie stores these bitter relics inside a tattered red carrier bag. (Murray 2015: 99)

He goes on to suggest that a specific thematic purpose is at play, since '[e]ight of the ten deployments of the colour red that precede the introduction of the Red Road flats are clearly linked to ideas of sexuality and procreation' (Ibid.: 101). Thus, Murray identifies a kind of image-led rhythm, increasing in intensity until the film's carnal themes converge at the Red Road flats. Having identified that red is of significant thematic significance, taking into account the meticulous construction of *mise en scène*, it is possible to follow the use of the colour throughout the film as a form of leitmotif, which might even transcend the primary meaning Murray identifies. *Red Road* is comprised of some 1,084 shots, and in 279 of these a red object or lighting effect is in some way an element of the *mise en scène*. This represents 25.7 per cent of the film, underlining the prominence of this particular element of its visual lexicon. Considering the pervasiveness of the colour, and given our earlier discussion of the film's and Arnold's broader privileging of the image over more direct means of narration, it is possible to read *Red Road* in a more loosely atmospheric fashion; as a sequence of poetic and lyrically foregrounded images anchored by and through Jackie's journey through grief.

Considering *Red Road* through its use of specific colours in this way reveals further non-verbal, more loosely tonal means of articulating Jackie's experiences in the film. A focus on the ubiquity of the colour red, and its use in the objects, people and buildings that Jackie comes into contact with and coldly observes – thus reading the film through its use of colour – brings to mind the counter use of blue. For example, as Jackie steps up her surveillance of Clyde she steals CCTV tapes from work, viewing images of Red Road at home. As she watches a tape she sees an image of the flat with its red door prominent, and we then see a further six shots of varying lengths showing Clyde and his friend Stevie (Martin Compston), who wears a red jacket, attempting to drag a tree into the flat (we later learn that this is to facilitate Clyde's woodcarving hobby). As Jackie watches, an answering machine message from the solicitor is heard explaining the details of Clyde's early release. Jackie turns off the video and the dominant colour turns from red to blue, with a sea life documentary replacing the images of the flats. We then observe Jackie as she gets the bus to work. In the control room the colour blue is prominent: the walls are painted blue, the uniform is blue, and the screens collectively give off a blue shade. As Jackie's attention turns to Red Road, she observes a group of young boys walking down the street, and one of the boys is wearing red. She then picks up the trail of Clyde and the red-jacketed Stevie. They get into a blue van which is revealed to be associated with 24-hour locksmiths. Jackie makes a note of the telephone number on the side and observes Clyde and Stevie parking the van and pulling a red sofa from a red skip. Jackie then rings the number and reveals that Clyde is an ex-convict. It is significant that Jackie seeks to disempower Clyde here by seeking to remove his blue van, a colour that is increasingly associated with Jackie in contrast to Clyde's red. Jackie is diverted and misses a stabbing incident on one of the other screens. One of the perpetrators wears a red coat, and a man dressed in blue gives attention the victim, with the red blood of her hands just visible.

With this colour pattern now established, Jackie decides to go to the flats and we follow her as she arrives to observe Clyde in person. As the bus stops, it passes a red car; Jackie then walks past a red letter box, Arnold cuts to a shot of a red cycle pole, and then lingers over a red-and-white football. Jackie then loiters outside the flats, with the red colours of the building prominent behind over two shots, hiding when Clyde and the red-coated Stevie arrive. Jackie then follows Clyde into a laundrette, and then a café, along the way passing a red fence (where she picks up a sharp piece of glass, presumably to kill Clyde), and a red car. In the café Clyde is seated in front of another man wearing red and the walls are red. A red ketchup bottle is prominent throughout her observations of Clyde, and Jackie departs after watching Clyde lick baked bean residue from his plate.

From a sequence where red has been highly prominent we then return to the blue space of the control room. On the blue screens, Jackie observes Clyde and a group of friends buying large quantities of alcohol, and in the next shot, having obviously seen an opportunity to re-connect with her target, Jackie is shown in a low-angled shot against the red expanse of the flats. Arnold then moves to a close shot of Jackie drinking from a blue bottle of VK Blue with a red Escort car in the background. She then tries to gain access to the flats, using the red door and the red intercom and then going outside into the red phone box, pulling out a blue purse with a close shot showing red stamps, and she then rests the purse against a blue sign. Jackie then spots Stevie, as ever in his red jacket, and gains access to the red flats with him and his partner, April (Natalie Press). Jackie watches as the red numbers dial up and the lift moves upwards. As she enters, the walls are blue, but the red lights of Clyde's party soon overwhelm them, and we observe Stevie pulling a dog from his red coat. Jackie talks to April in the kitchen, as Jackie clutches her blue drink with a collection of blue bags (from the off-licence) on the side. April feeds the dog off the floor, and a shot from Jackie's point of view sees the dog consume its food against the blue tiling. Arnold alternates between shoots of the floor and further compositions of Jackie alone with her blue objects. As we move into the living room the red light of the dance floor starkly contrasts with the colour code of the kitchen scene. We see eight quick shots of Clyde and a group of predominantly male friends singing the Oasis song 'Morning Glory' before a slower song sees Jackie and Clyde lock on to each other. Then, a sequence of thirty-three shots shows the rapidly escalating physical intimacy between the pair, as they are bathed in red light while dancing. Jackie, suddenly horrified, runs out of the room and into the lift – the sequence ends with her being violently sick in the lift, producing a red shade of vomit and suggesting a bodily response to the colour, and all that it has come to represent.

These scenes are driven by Jackie's instinctive, emotional desires: for sexual contact, for revenge, for an end to her grief. Such forces exist beyond the realms of language and therefore manifest themselves non-verbally. Here image-led narration is directed towards the representation of innate and embodied feeling, and Arnold's realism of proximity, of 'being with' her protagonists, is given further intimacy through an approach to *mise en scène* whereby objects and landscapes are subtly transformed both to reflect and determine deeply embedded elements of character.

By the end of *Red Road*, Jackie seems to have found peace. After she and Clyde discuss the circumstances of her daughter's and husband's death, and Jackie uses her CCTV knowledge to share with Clyde the information that his own estranged daughter has been looking for him, she informs her in-laws that is she is ready to spread the ashes she has been protecting up to this point. The film ends as it started with a grainy CCTV image, but this time Jackie is one of the (many) subjects of the image. Indeed, throughout the film, the CCTV images that she consumes can be seen to offer reflections on her own emotional crisis – the recurring images of the dying dog, for example, or the forlorn, dancing cleaner. The film's ending makes symbiotic Jackie's relationship with these 'other' stories and the multitude of narrative possibilities that they represent. Just as in *Wasp*, and as we will see in her later films, Arnold's intense character portraits do not deny the presence of multiple co-existing narratives. Indeed, as if to confirm the synergy between these glimpses of other lives and the singular life that we have been focused on, at the film's conclusion Jackie meets the dog owner on the street and admires his new canine companion. Jackie's journey is therefore from observer to participant as she interacts with and becomes an agent within the world from which she was once alienated, which for Sue Thornham affirms the film's radical politics, as Jackie 'enters the city's life as subject of her own story' (Thornham 2016a: 145). Similarly, Paul Dave sees the film's ending, and Jackie's denial 'of the culture of vengeance' that permeates the 'political mainstream', as a marker of the way in which 'Red Road seeks grounds of commonality' (Dave 2011: 52). Indeed, in making Jackie a component rather than a subject of the 'master shot' the film reaffirms Arnold's self-conscious examination of experience of watching, both within and beyond the diegesis, enabled here by what Thornham calls the film's 'doubled viewing structure' (Thornham 2016a: 139). Earlier in the film, when Jackie confesses to Angus that she failed to get any close ups of the stabbing incident, Arnold immediately cuts to a close up of Jackie's hand, as if to make conspicuous the malleable relationships between the modes of watching (and watching as filming) at work in her cinema.

As Jonathan Murray argues, this impulse is at work in Arnold's next film, *Fish Tank*:

> Mia exhibits many skills that might make her a considerable director instead: this young woman is an active viewer, rather than (or as well as) an apparent victim, of the world in which she lives. Windows (both literal and figurative) endlessly attract Mia throughout the narrative's course, and resonant images therefore abound of her looking for things abstract and psychological by looking at things actual and physical. Mia's repeated aerial views of the estate from the deserted high-rise flat to which she retreats in order to practice her dance routines, her voyeuristic fascination with the erotic and emotional intensity of Joanne and Connor's abortive relationship and the ardent sincerity of her scanning of television and online videos of R&B culture and choreography are all of significance here. [. . .] We might even go so far as to see Mia as an authorial surrogate in several key regards, rather than as an authorial subject pure and simple. (Murray 2016: 210)

With this in mind, *Fish Tank* might be seen to begin where *Red Road* ends. Jackie is no longer the alienated observer, but is now one of many, and so it falls on Mia to inherit the role of watcher in a film which is similarly committed to transforming the mundane through the poetic gaze of its protagonist.

FISH TANK (2009)

The film's opening distils these thematic concerns and formal tendencies, along with many more, and is therefore worth considering in detail. *Fish Tank* begins with Mia head down in medium shot, before she moves up to look. She is panting and the sound of her breath is prominent alongside the ambient noise of the constant traffic outside. Arnold cuts to a shot behind Mia, who is in the dark in the aforementioned flat, and the wide landscape (housing estates, some trees, and pylons in the distance) is visible through the window and prominent in the light. We have already seen this kind of composition in *Youth Can Do It*, and in *Wasp* in the scene where Zoë frees the titular insect, and the effect is similar: the internal and external spheres of the protagonist's experience are held in balance. Arnold cuts to a closer shot, as Mia makes a phone call, leaving a message: 'you know what I'm like, I was pissed off, ring me back, you bitch'. Throughout the shot Arnold varies the depth of field with the handheld camera moving gently, seemingly in rhythm with Mia's breath. While the call is being made, the view of outside is prominent and our attention is drawn to the landscape, whereas Mia, closer to the camera, is out of focus. When she puts the phone down and gathers her things into a bag, she then comes back into focus – although she is still in the dark, parts of her body are sharply visible, and again, her breathing is prominent. When she leaves, the focus is immediately altered, almost in response to Mia's departure, and the camera rests briefly on the again clear and comprehensive sight of the landscape beyond the window.

For Stella Hockenhull, Arnold's use of the external landscape in these opening moments points to a wider project within her work to reveal the beauty of otherwise maligned spaces:

> Here, Arnold creates a romantic aesthetic at the outset, with Mia shown in silhouette set against the view from the flats. Far from introducing the area as the rundown housing estate that it is, Arnold cinematographically manipulates the *mise en scène* to create a scene of beauty, the camera bypassing the building in the foreground to prosaically observe the rural distance. (Hockenhull 2017: 116)

Hockenhull's identification of Arnold's 'manipulation' of the image is worth reflecting on here. In effect, what Hockenhull is describing are the ways in which Arnold emphasises, de-emphasises and re-emphasises particular elements of the *mise en scène*, often within the same shot, to either draw to or divert viewer attention from highly specific details and/or to emphasise the subjective relationship between the protagonist and her environment. We have already noted this device at work in *Dog* and *Wasp* as a means of enabling texture and resisting staticity within landscape shots, and here, owing to the close proximity of the camera to Mia's body, alongside the film's repeated foregrounding of landscape, the device is even more prominent. This quality of lingering on the image and manipulating its components has the effect of creating a lyrical accent on the quotidian materials that the film is repeatedly drawn to. As a device of everyday poetics, Arnold's shifting focalisations work to add weight to specific elements while also deepening the involved process of spectatorship that is initiated by her films. Here we might think of Jennifer Barker's account of an embodied symbiosis between audience and text:

> The viewer caresses by moving the eyes along an image softly and fondly, without a particular destination, but the film might perform the same caressing touch through a smoothly tracking camera movement, slow-motion, soft focus cinematography, or an editing style dominated by lap dissolves, for example. The film and viewer each respond in their own uniquely embodied ways to one another's style of touch. (Barker 2009: 32)

Barker's identification of specific cinematic techniques which might be seen to stimulate and call upon the experiences of observing or touching objects and bodies in reality, might easily include Arnold's alterations of depth of focus, given its ability to conjure the sensation of looking in close detail, and the selective processes of emphasis and de-emphasis that are involved in sight. Here, then, Arnold converges a realism of experience, one that is physically grounded and embodied, with an aestheticised poetic impulse, which seeks to re-imagine and make lyrical images of everyday life.

In her reading of the scene, Kate Ince is also drawn its phenomenological richness:

> When she stands up and moves over to the window to phone a friend with whom she has argued, only her head and shoulders are filmed, from behind and out of focus, meaning that the only image of her face viewable in this opening scene is riveted to her breathing, exercising body. This opening scene of *Fish Tank* could serve as a model to both women directors and theorist-critics of how to approach the screening of embodied female subjectivity – head-on, with attention to activity, effort and movement, and without fetishistic fragmentation of the female body. It illustrates feminist phenomenological theory in practice [...] (Ince 2017: 51)

Thus, the textured approach to composition, as well as being sensitive to the intimate representation of physical experience, in turn denies the objectification of Mia. Following Ince, we might argue that Mia's breathing is crucial here, given its near rhythmic, continual presence in a scene that is, visually at least, fragmented. As we will see, breath is a critical element of the film's soundscape, tied, as it is, to Mia's body, one which will go on to dance, walk and run throughout the film, and one which will guide our sensory experience of the narrative. Davina Quinlivan has argued for the importance of considering 'breath' when analysing embodied modes of spectatorship and representation:

> Importantly, breathing suggests a relationship with the image that involves the *mind* of the viewer as well as the body. [. . .] my attentiveness to the breathing questions not only what the film is showing us as a 'breathing encounter', but also what we, as breathing human beings, are mimetically, ontologically sharing with the film. (Quinlivan 2012: 21)

In foregrounding breath as an intrinsic element of the film's sensory, poetic vocabulary, Arnold might be seen to call upon this profoundly ubiquitous act both as a familiar auditory and bodily process and as an ambient sound which locks in our affect-centred relationship with the protagonist, just as the perceptual realism of wind and birdsong and architecturally centred sound design function in Hogg's films. This is not to say, though, that the emphasis on breath is purely an instrument of verisimilitude. Just as colour functions in *Red Road* to emphasise the instinctive carnal urges of its protagonists, so too this critical, accented element of sound operates symbolically in *Fish Tank*. Mia's movements of course justify the repeated foregrounding of her breathing, and, given that such sequences often occur when she is alone, attention is not diverted by dialogue. However, when Arnold slows down the image during moments of intimacy between Conor and Mia, the soundtrack emphasises the pair's shared breathing, as Tanya Horeck explains:

> There are several key moments in the film before they have sex, where there is close bodily contact between Mia and Connor [*sic*]. These scenes are choreographed in such a way that the speed of the camera changes ever so slightly and everything slows down; the sounds of breathing are amplified, and the tactility of the moment is emphasized (when, for example, Connor carries her sleeping figure to bed). (Horeck 2011: 175)

Horeck is right to suggest that the accented movements of breathing anticipate Conor's and Mia's eventual sexual encounter, which is itself presented with, naturally, close attention to the couple's heightened, emphatic panting. What emerges here is a poetics of breathing, which connects us to the violence and vitality of Mia's experiences on an intimate level. This aural pattern can be seen to reach a climax in the sequence when Conor and Mia have sex. The morning after, Mia, waking up to her mother's tears, learns from her sister Tyler (Rebecca Griffiths) that Conor has gone. She attempts to pursue him, and the camera is again highly mobile, moving with her as she first chases his car out of the estate while still wearing her pyjamas, and then goes back into the flat, getting a phone number from her mother's bag. Here the aural continuity from the sexual encounter the night before is maintained through Mia's restless, desire-driven panting, as she sets out, impetuously, to pursue Conor. In the following scenes, Arnold shows Mia's seemingly relentless walk to

Conor's home in Tilbury. Here, the motif that Lucy Bolton identifies whereby 'the camera picks up on her energy through its urgently unsteady hand-held motion and the accompanying sound of her exercised breathing' (2015: 75) alongside her footsteps, escalates, as Arnold shows shots of Mia walking through multiple landscapes, moving in and through traffic. She arrives at the home and is promptly shuffled out by a clearly panicked Conor, who drives her to the station. Mia, however, soon returns to the house and, this time, finding that Conor is not at home, breaks in. Because of the physical exertions of the break-in, the emphasis on Mia's breath returns, as short jump cuts and the now customary, intimate handheld camera communicate her encounter with this foreign space. When she turns on the video player, realising that Conor has a daughter, Keira (Sydney Mary Nash), her breathing increases and a close reaction shot shows her beating chest, after which multiple quick cuts reveal elements of Keira's existence (toys, for example), as the sound of Mia's frenzied breaths remain alongside the sound of the child singing on the video. Suddenly, Mia urinates on the floor, in an act that for Kate Ince expresses 'horror and disgust in the most spontaneously physical way imaginable' (Ince 2017: 134). Indeed, the emphasis on breath and instinctive movement and behaviour up to this point means that Mia's action seems logical in the terms of the film's intimate, bodily poetics.

From this point onwards, instinct will drive Mia's behaviours. Accordingly, Mia's kidnapping of Keira is driven by the combination of the close, handheld, moving camera, the sound of the wind and the water crashing against the shore, and both Mia's and Keira's breath as they move through the landscape. Arnold chooses this moment to deploy another of her slow-motion shots as Keira runs, drawing further attention to Mia's heavy breathing as she watches her and recalling the way in which Keira's father and Mia interacted in a similar edgeland space earlier in the film, furthering the sense that breathing acts as a poetic thread akin to the colour coding of *Red Road*. Indeed, once Mia returns Keira to her home, the combination of the relentless motion of movement and her frenzied breath is again prominent. Conor pursues her down a country lane, and then chases Mia across a field. Three separate moving shots show Mia running, her breath increasing in intensity, before Conor catches up with her and hits her across the face. Mia's breathing reaches a peak at this point, and then slows down as Conor's shocking act of violence sinks in, and as he goes back into the night. Here the sensory aural rhythm (arrived at through the movement of Mia's body and both her and Conor's breathing) is made conspicuous because of the absence of dialogue. The physical nature of the act between Conor and Mia here recalls their earlier sexual contact – particularly the sense of a building rhythm and highly physical, bodily release – and reaffirms the sense in which breath functions both lyrically, operating to convey desire, and as an instrument of the film's deeply perceptual realism.

Our exploration of the poetics of breathing in *Fish Tank* also necessitates further examination of the general nature of movement in the film. Indeed, the two are connected as part of *Fish Tank*'s highly intimate portrayal of Mia and might be viewed more broadly in terms of its radical feminist politics, as Kate Ince suggests in her analysis of Mia's actions following Conor's departure from the flat: 'a young woman's desire is filmed in all its raw spontaneity, in the fierce, determined walking and actions with which Mia counters anyone who acts upon her (any other subject who would objectify her)' (Ince 2017: 135).

Again, then, we might connect the film's visceral, participatory mode of address to a broader thematic end. Similarly, as Lucy Bolton argues, the film's intimate privileging of the kinetic poetry of Mia's movement is central to its phenomenological feminism:

> It is in the rhythm and relations of *Fish Tank* that Mia's embodied charac-
> ter is developed and the cinema style in which time is created, protracted,
> and interfered with, can be understood as a feminist phenomenological
> statement of *this* girl's experience. (Bolton 2015: 78)

Bolton is absolutely right to suggest that a 'rhythm' is established through the focus on Mia's moving body, as we have already identified in relation to her breath. The film contains 88 (out of 886) separate shots of Mia walking, either shot from behind, frontally, or by the side. In percentage terms this means that 9.59 per cent of the film constitutes shots of Mia walking. A number of these shots are continuous and unbroken, in line with the illusion of temporal verisimilitude, which is accounted for in the film's average shot length of 7.8 seconds, almost two seconds longer than the combined average of Arnold's other features (6 seconds).

The pervasiveness of this device recalls the highly conspicuous walking Steadicam shots in Alan Clarke's television and film work in the 1980s. David Rolinson's reading of Clarke's use of this particular device offers some insights for our analysis here. For Rolinson, Steadicam 'both positions the viewer as participant and places the character's story within wider society' (Rolinson 2005: 108). This observation chimes with both Ince's and Bolton's observations around the political force of Mia's movement and its representation. In his analysis of Clarke's seminal treatment of Jim Cartwright's *Road* (1987), Rolinson goes further:

> Clarke captures the wasted energy of unemployment by portraying
> working-class characters walking nowhere through deserted communities
> – reflecting the paradoxically static 'road' of Cartwright's title – and, in
> the subjective rhetoric of Steadicam attachment, queries the myth of indi-
> vidual participation propagated by Thatcherite rhetoric. These effects are

3.1   The 'rhythm' of Mia's movement.

rooted in the mediation of the experiential, recalling Raymond Williams's (1979) concept of 'structures of feeling', as Steadicam places us within the characters' lived experience, as they walk 'their' streets, demonstrating a fragmented but, in Williams's term, 'knowable community'. (Rolinson 2005: 115)

Taking Clarke's use of Steadicam as broadly analogous to Arnold's use of the handheld moving camera suggests the potential for a more nuanced and embodied representation of realism, which denies the aesthetics (and politics) of detachment to convey both intimate feeling and a sense of societal context. Rolinson argues that the Steadicam enables an environmental focus which is also tethered to an individual's experience of that environment, suggesting in the process the possibility of a critical realism, which, in a further challenge to Nwonka's criticism, works both at the level of empathy *and* analysis. Thus, our engagement with Mia's story is also an engagement with her landscape, and our sense of place in the film is directly connected to Mia's encounters with her environment. For example, we have already discussed the ways in which Arnold manipulates focus to emphasise and de-emphasise elements of *mise en scène* and this is particularly true of the scenes in which Mia walks, with Mia's body and environment vying against each other for primacy. Thus, with Mia as our guide, Arnold repeatedly foregrounds the landscape and, with the exception of the external punctuation shots of the estate, these views are shaped by our engagement with Mia's mobility. To return to the aforementioned Tilbury sequence, Kate Ince discusses how

> [Mia] sets out on foot to Tilbury, a distance of at least six or seven miles. Arnold films here at four or five different moments in this walk, despite the drab similarity of the surroundings at each of them, emphasizing the distance involved, which is confirmed when Conor – after the briefest of conversations that is as evasive as it is reassuring – redeposits her at Tilbury station to get the train home. (Ince 2017: 134)

Ince is right to suggest that the conspicuous emphasis on the process of Mia's journey foregrounds her desire-driven determination, what Ince terms her 'spontaneous and raw ... movements ... entirely unreflected upon' (Ibid.: 134), but what should also be noted is that through the repetition and frequency of their foregrounding, Arnold invites us to engage with the landscapes beyond the level of their drabness. Indeed, in perhaps the most arresting shot of the sequence Mia walks past a wide expanse showing housing estates and pylons in the distance, with a busy road in the foreground, the sun edging through the dark clouds. It is the same landscape that we encounter at the outset but now Mia moves through and beyond it. Her journey to 'the new estate' where Conor lives is of course a journey from one highly class-bound landscape to another. This is reflected in the soundscape: the pervasive presence of the cars dulls as Mia moves towards the estate, and birdsong is audible. Mia slows, and Arnold opts for a wider establishing shot of the estate, pausing temporarily from the relentless forward motion of the journey up to this point, as if to reflect the uncharacteristic tentativeness of Mia's encounter with her new surroundings. For Tim Edensor, the landscape(s) that Mia encounters on this journey fit with a broader sense in which the film's action can be seen to unfold within an innately ubiquitous framework, calling upon our own everyday geographies:

> *Fish Tank* [. . .] evokes a generic English contemporary landscape replete with a host of mundane settings that diverge from any notion of a romantic urban and rural Englishness. [. . .] The scenography features an abundance of ambient quotidian spaces that are usually unreflexively apprehended but are simultaneously deeply familiar: there are elevated sections of motorway that look out onto low-key, semi-industrial townscapes, with the banal kinds of fencing and roadside fixtures that extend out of many large towns and cities across the UK. There are poorly maintained post-war housing estates, with their scruffy communal play areas and run-down stairways and balconies, and the low-key shopping precincts typical of many urban English areas, but also the neat, bland

sections of low-grade suburbia that have superseded the pre-war estates that surround the outskirts of English towns [. . .]. English viewers are likely to be familiar with some or all of these settings, and though they certainly convey a sense of grittiness, this is not merely symbolic but is embedded in the ways in which such environments are felt and sensed, and chimes with prior experiences of actual space. (Edensor 2015: 68)

The repeated foregrounding of these spaces does therefore function, in similar ways to the everyday spaces and soundscapes of Hopkins's and Hogg's work respectively, to place us within the diegesis by evoking parallel experiences of space between audience and text. This might be seen as another element of the film's and Arnold's perceptual realism, and the embodied nature of its realist address, and it certainly coheres with the use of similar landscapes in *Wasp*, *Dog* and *Red Road*. Yet, as mentioned, we should also keep in mind that we are experiencing these 'deeply familiar' landscapes *with* Mia and thus they are offered up both as intuitively authentic and as open to subjective and lyrical transformation through her very specific interpretation of them, as Lucy Bolton argues:

The multi-layered temporality of the film, focused on Mia, works to create a viewing experience of acute intensity and tension. These layers are, simply, the world as experienced by the striding Mia, and how those elements relate to other people and lives in the film. Present and partaking to various degrees are elements of nature, music, and non-human lives (a nocturnal hamster trying to sleep, an observational dog, a dying fish, a lonely horse). All these different types of physicality and different rhythms of life are present in the film's temporal landscape, thereby enabling the specific elements of Mia's experience to emerge. (Bolton 2015: 78)

These are the symbolic tropes and narratives that emerge from within the spaces that Edensor describes and they are the units of Arnold's image-led narration which work to elevate and poeticise the mundane – we might think of the travellers' site in which the horse resides and its abundance of prison-like imagery and pervasive atmosphere of entrapment. Much like the narratives behind the CCTV screens in *Red Road*, these motifs both enable reflection on Mia's experiences and acknowledge the presence of other stories besides hers.

WUTHERING HEIGHTS (2011)

Arnold's interpretation of Emily Brontë's *Wuthering Heights* is entirely consistent with the pervasive nature of her realist practice as discussed so far across this chapter, despite the canonical nature of the source material and its period status. Indeed, the film's opening is highly reminiscent of *Fish Tank*'s, both in its distillation of the film's primary formal and thematic concerns and in its use of specific motifs that recur throughout Arnold's oeuvre.

The first shot is an etching on a wooden wall-panel of a house, shot with a handheld camera while heavy breathing is audible on the soundtrack alongside the creaking of the room against the wind from outside. A side-on shot reveals an out-of-focus older Heathcliff with the bed beyond him in focus; he takes deep breaths as he stares at the wall and Arnold brings him back into focus as the bed becomes blurred – again, then, variations in depth of field work to emphasise and de-emphasise multiple elements of *mise en scène* within the same frame. Heathcliff then turns away from the wall to look out of the window. This particular window will be shown on 24 occasions in the film (31 out of the film's 1,143 shots are of windows) and is shown to literally frame Heathcliff's view of the world around him. The motif of the marginalised watcher is therefore again evoked here, and we think immediately of similar window shots or framed observation compositions in *Wasp*, *Red Road* and *Fish Tank* – and, as we will see, in *American Honey* – where characters' emotional and political detachment from their surrounding is given distinctive visual articulation. As Sophie Mayer argues, 'Catherine . . . and Heathcliff . . . are, differently, marginal as a girl under patriarchy and a black child under colonialism' (Mayer 2015: 38), and particularly in the case of Heathcliff, this marginalisation will be visually inculcated – as it is for Jackie and Mia – through a physical evocation of being on the outside of things, of watching through windows, doorways and the cracks in walls. As Jonathan Murray argues, 'Arnold's *Wuthering Heights* thus unfolds as a chain of pregnant, largely wordless vignettes in which an imperfectly maturing human being watches, wonders and wants in relation to his wider world' (Murray 2016: 201) – thus the repetition of the window as a device can be seen both as an instrument of subjective realism, and as an enabling element of Arnold's image-led narration in which the subject of the 'wordless vignette' invites lyrical interpretation.

The rest of the scene is made up of further quick, close shots of an unsteady, clearly distressed Heathcliff, kicking at the walls, and eventually crying (we later realise that he is mourning Catherine) and the physical, highly affective nature of his grief recalls the instinctive bodily responses of Mia to the revelation of Conor's fatherhood. Arnold cuts to further etchings, the letters 'CE' and a drawing of a lapwing, later revealed to be Catherine and Heathcliff's favourite bird, and 'Catherine' and 'Heathcliff' scratched into the wall. These markings are significant as mementos of Catherine and Heathcliff's early life together, but also as fragmented glimpses of lives lived beyond the immediacy of the diegesis, in the same way that the aforementioned wall decorations function in *Wasp*. We might think, too, of the close shots of photographs of

Mia and her former friend Keeley (Sarah Bayes) in *Fish Tank*, or the drawings
and stickers showing cats in the room where Mia reluctantly watches television
with Tyler in the same film – these are images which function as symbolic aug-
mentation, while also offering fleeting contextual glimpses to enable breadth in
otherwise highly subjective narratives.

The penultimate shot of the scene returns us to the window in closer composition this time, with the wind causing a twig to hit against the panes of
glass on four occasions in quick succession. We then move to a close shot of
Heathcliff who violently bangs his head against the floor with the same rhythm,
four times. This mirroring of the outside and the inside, and the conflation
of Heathcliff's physical articulation of emotion with the textured movement
of the landscape itself succinctly illustrates the film's broader engagement with
the environment. Indeed, to return to Murray's observation, the film's sense of
'wordlessness' places greater emphasis on the sensory application of the image,
in line with *Fish Tank*, and this is primarily developed through the repeated
foregrounding of the landscape with intensely visceral detail, either through
close framing of Catherine's and Heathcliff's encounters with external space,
whereby touch and breath are emphasised just as they are in *Fish Tank*, or
through punctuation shots either foregrounding the grimly spectacular isolation of the Yorkshire Moors, or, more commonly, through close focus on
highly specific elements: feathers, insects, plants, blades of grass, for example.

In line with this understanding of the symbiotic nature of the landscape,
Sophie Mayer identifies the scenes of horse-riding as particularly significant:

> In these early scenes, Catherine teaches Heathcliff to ride, and they share
> sensory experiences through the body and movement of the horse. Close-
> ups of the horse's muscles even convey a cinesthetic sense of *being* the
> horse, and of the horse's being as movement, energy, scent and place [. . .]
>
> Through Robbie Ryan's tight framing and handheld camera, the horse
> subsumes Cathy and Heathcliff so that the three become one flesh, and
> moreover, one being with the moor, rather than the human/animal/
> landscape. (Mayer 2015: 21)

The foregrounding of the horse in relation to the marginalised child is also
apparent in Mia's encounter with the chained horse in *Fish Tank*, as, more
broadly, is Mayer's sense of Arnold's evocation of '*being*' with as a further
illustration of the participatory nature of her realist address.

Such a sense of sensorial intimacy and immediacy has the effect of disrupt-
ing expectations associated with literary adaptation. Indeed, multiple critics
have noted the way in which Arnold's visceral realist style works to radically
re-interpret the novel's themes. For Jenny Bavidge, this is most primarily felt at
the level of the soundtrack:

[. . .] repeatedly through the film's mode of narration, the points of narrative tension found in the novel are dissolved. Instead our attention is turned outwards, to the speaking landscape. Some critics protested about the 'grunting' of the characters, or the fact that dialogue is frequently indistinct, muttered or excised, but Arnold's insistence on an 'empty' soundtrack [. . .] returns us to the very landscape, soil, rocks, animals and so on that the characters invoke as the correlations of their feelings. [. . .] the layering of these sounds creates a soundscape which does more than authentically represent the environment: it expresses instead something of the process and mesh of the experience of place. (Bavidge 2016: 129)

Bavidge's discussion of 'layering', 'process' and 'mesh' develops Mayer's observations around the film's textured tactility, further suggesting the film's complex and highly considered interrogation of landscape. On a similar note, Luis Rocha Antunes describes how Arnold's 'camera penetrates the intimacy of the characters and films their perceptual experiences as if through first-hand experience' (Antunes 2015: 5), a process which in turn 'creates the conditions for spectatorial engagement with the story through the senses', and constructs 'a world, which appears real and within reach' (Ibid.: 7). This mode of embodied, sensorially felt spectatorship and representation is of course even more striking when the subject matter is so obviously grounded in the distant past. Arnold thus fosters a distinctive sense of 'presentness' within a historical setting, unlocking a non-linear palimpsest of ecological, cultural, and political narratives in the process.

Indeed, in drawing attention to the highly textured and perpetually evolving relationship between the landscape and its inhabitants on a physical level, Arnold once again calls upon the viewer's perceptual experience of familiar environments. While there are no housing estates and A-roads here, the denial of more conventional distanced and painterly treatments of the landscape in *Wuthering Heights* in favour of close, detailed compositions affirms the ubiquitous rural iconographies of contemporary landscapes, with the literal foregrounding of the present (filmed landscape) within a diegetic framework of pastness further promoting a critical engagement with our own lived environments, as Michael Lawrence argues:

A great many times the film presents shots of various trees with branches filling the entire frame and the sky visible behind; these shots are placed at the beginning of a narrative episode and indicate a shift forward in time, typically signifying a new day since the images of the trees tend to follow the darkness of preceding night-time scenes. While the types of trees function metonymically to present a particular place – the English countryside – and provide material evidence of the shoot in the Pennines,

3.2 The ongoing life of the film's landscape.

several timescales are presented simultaneously. The size of these trees suggests that they are several centuries old – as old, if not older, than the novel on which the film is based – while their usually leafless state indicates a specific time of the year, the season during which the shot was taken, early in the twenty-first century, and the season during which the narrative episode takes place, in the late eighteenth century. (Lawrence 2016b: 187)

The trees therefore point to diegetic temporalities that exist before, during and long after Catherine and Heathcliff, and they assert their non-diegetic status within the ecological present tense – underlining the sense of landscape as lived, experienced and felt rather than as backdrop. We might also think of the other forms of life that are foregrounded through Arnold's textured approach to landscape as functioning in a similarly counter-diegetic fashion, to affirm setting as perpetually present and containing multiple lives within it. For Lawrence, Arnold's conspicuous treatment of the landscape in this way enables 'a post-humanist distribution of attention' (Ibid.: 178), further suggesting that the 'privileging of non-human elements in Arnold's film . . . produces an equitability of attention which defies humanist solipsism' (Ibid.: 184). This is of course in line with the representation of the environment and the non-human animal in Arnold's other films, and we might also see these observations in terms of new realism – they are further invitations to reflect critically on the viewer's lived experience and not just that which is offered up within the parameters of the diegetic world.

In the chapter on Duane Hopkins we identified similarly perceptually layered representations of rural space – indeed, we might also consider Hogg's use of sound in the same way – and I drew on Doreen Massey's work to suggest that a critical aspect of new realism and its everyday poetics is the representation of the environment as never static and always in motion, containing within it multiple stories. Sue Thornham extends this critical position in her discussion of *Wuthering Heights*:

> In *For Space*, Doreen Massey has suggested that rather than thinking of space (or landscape) as emptiness, stasis, the exterior to a heroic subject's interiority, we should imagine it as presence, as 'co-existing multiplicity . . . a simultaneity of stories-so-far' (Massey 2005: 54). Perhaps, then, another way of viewing Arnold's teeming, borderless landscape, with its abundance of lives and deaths glimpsed vividly for a moment, is to see it as a space of multiple narratives, in which our sense of time as well as of space is disrupted. The film's two presents are frequently intercut, to create a sense not of flashback or flash-forward so much as of multiple temporalities. [. . .] What we know, or feel, is this space, with its multiple intersecting, temporally uncertain narratives of life and death. (Thornham 2016b: 225)

Thornham's use of Massey to identify the way in which Arnold challenges the assumption of a single story and acknowledges the existence of multiple parallel narratives goes beyond the discussion of flashbacks in the film *Wuthering Heights* and has been similarly reflected upon throughout this chapter across Arnold's oeuvre – we can think again of the multiple screens in *Red Road*, the foregrounding of the estate in *Wasp*, and the similar glimpses of coexisting lives in *Fish Tank*. This reading is of course even more significant in light of *Wuthering Heights*'s representation of multiple temporalities, identifying, as Thornham does, its spatially orientated disruption of monolithic notions of history and literary tradition. For Massey, where space is fixed and static it might be seen to colonise the representation and experience of reality, and, in line with Thornham's arguments, reduce it to one story:

> Space conquers time by being set up as the *representation of* history/life/the real world. On this reading space is an order imposed upon the inherent life of the real. (Spatial) order obliterates (temporal) dislocation. Spatial immobility quietens temporal becoming. It is, though, the most dismal of pyrrhic victories. For in the very moment of its conquering triumph 'space' is reduced to stasis. The very life, and certainly the politics, are taken out of it. (Massey 2005: 30)

Again, then, Arnold's perceptually rich, temporally disruptive representation of space *and* history can be seen to work against this sense of fixity and to in turn present a newly disruptive, critical encounter with history as something experienced, felt and therefore alive in political terms – and this is, of course, emphasised again through the film's broad ecological emphases and its interpretation of Heathcliff as black. As Massey continues:

> Conceiving of space as a static slice through time, as representation, as a closed system and so forth are all ways of taming it. [. . .]
>
> If time is to be open to a future of the new then space cannot be equated with the closures and horizontalities of representation. More generally, if time is to be open then space must be open too. Conceptualising space as open, multiple and relational, unfinished and always becoming, is a prerequisite for history to be open and thus a prerequisite, too, for the possibility of politics. (Ibid.: 59)

In *Wuthering Heights* the collapsing of the distinction between the historical (the temporally fixed) and the contemporary landscape, which is 'always becoming', both radicalises the representation of the past depicted within the diegesis and calls our attention to the presentness of the past in everyday life.

To return to the question of form in *Wuthering Heights*, one of the ways in which the landscape (and Catherine's and Heathcliff's encounters with it) is so wilfully disrupted is through fragmented close shots, both of physical details and of tactile encounters between living beings and the landscape. Accordingly, these shots while not traditionally 'short' are of course often wordless, and their repetitive placement fosters a spatial and temporal rhythm that is accompanied by the aforementioned aural emphasis on breath and on elements such as wind and rain. The film's median shot length is 4.8 seconds, and there are just 17 shots in the whole film (out of 1,143) that go beyond 20 seconds, and just 4 that exceed 30. These longer takes are deployed in the second half of the film, following the older Heathcliff's return, and all are thematically linked. In the first, Heathcliff is shot from behind as he returns to *Wuthering Heights* for the first time since his departure years before; he moves to the door, notices a young Hareton (Michael Hughes), and then encounters a vomiting Hindley (Lee Shaw). In the next, having located Catherine, he is moving through the corridors of Thrushcross Grange, where Catherine now lives with her husband Edgar (James Northcote), where again he is shot closely and from behind just as he is throughout the film, in a manner which evokes the 'being with' mode of participatory realism that we have already discussed and which more specifically evokes Heathcliff's back as a site of suffering, as it is shown at the outset to literally bear the scars of his former life as a slave. In the third such sequence, the longest at sixty-three seconds, Heathcliff is again in Catherine's home, having been let in by Nelly (Simone Jackson). While he waits for Catherine, the shot holds Heathcliff in the foreground side-on and out of focus while Isabella (Nichola Burley), in focus in the middle of the frame, looks at Heathcliff and asks questions of his past with a mixture of lust and fascination. When Catherine arrives in shot, moving down the stairs, she comes into focus, and Isabella moves out, with Heathcliff moving up to meet her and almost consuming the frame entirely – again the handheld camera follows his back. In the fourth and final such shot, Heathcliff is back at Wuthering Heights where he now resides, again held side on, and out of focus as Hindley, in focus and at the back of the frame, pleads for more money. All the shots and the scenes of which they are a part emphasise both Heathcliff's physical presence and his reversed fortunes, and all are associated with his desire for Catherine. Viewing them as part of a broader sequence in this way, and drawing attention to their regimented structure, provides further evidence of the rigour and rhythms of Arnold's style. Here, the dominant stylistic grammar – defined by its meticulous and repeated foregrounding of a perpetually indeterminate landscape – is temporarily balanced by a differing formal structure, one which subtly draws attention to Heathcliff's body as both an object both of desire and exploitation.

AMERICAN HONEY (2016)

American Honey finds Arnold on familiar ground. It is centred around the lonely observations of a marginalised protagonist; it balances a subjective treatment of its human subjects with a close interest in the landscape and its multiple layers, favouring handheld moving shots alongside symbolically loaded punctuation shots and lingering treatments of animals and insects; it blurs distinctions between human and non-human animals, often as a mechanism to enable the exploration of carnal instincts; it is centred around an intimate character portrait which nevertheless does not compromise the possibility for an exploration of the socio-economic conditions and their deterministic relationship with identity; it deploys unknown and non-professional actors alongside established performers; and it is anchored by poetic rhythms born from repetitions of quotidian routines, offered up for lyrical transformation through music and other forms of emphasis.

Despite its American setting, then, the film continues to develop Arnold's recurring formal and thematic concerns. For example, early on in the film we are introduced to Star's home life, as if to establish the conditions for her escape with the mag crew. As ever, the *mise en scène* is carefully structured to convey thematically significant elements while evoking a visceral sense of the lived experience of the characters. There is a close shot of soggy cornflakes, an uncooked chicken that had been prised from a dumpster in a previous scene is being speared by Star's brother, Star's sister is applying make-up, there are shots of the sparse contents of the fridge, and of the dogs, and Star's father comes in drunk, shouting abuse at his son. The camera rests on a photograph on the fridge, showing Star's sister with a smiling woman (later shown to be the girl's reluctant mother). Star prepares food for her dad and siblings, but he beckons her into the living room, where she is abused. Close shots that alternate between him licking her neck and squeezing her buttocks, and Star's crying eyes are intercut with multiple photographs on the wall of the younger siblings, while a Confederate flag is conspicuous in the background. As Jack Cortvriend points out, the flag anticipates a later scene where Star's boss Krystal 'emotionally abuses' her while wearing the bikini in Confederate colours, enabling Arnold to hint at the 'systemic abuse Star faces in contemporary American society', and indeed Star's racial identity (the actress Sasha Lane is mixed race) is never explicitly referred to (Cortvriend 2017: 210). Cortvriend is right, too, to suggest that this scene invites 'us to imagine the lived-in experience of her everyday life which, through steeping us in the material-reality of Star's everyday life via a preponderance of ordinary things' (Ibid.: 212), and this detailed evocation of quotidian materiality recalls many of the scenes we have already discussed, particularly in *Wasp* and the shots of Mia's living space in *Fish Tank*.

After Star has been abused we join her outside on the swing alongside her siblings as they play, as if to remind us of her youth. Arnold then provides us with further close shots of the lived environment. We see close shots of a butterfly against a window; a small spider crawls across the wall against a hand-drawn etching; we see a close shot of a pair of red shoes; photographs of a tortoise and some dolphins; two photographs of wolves; a wider shot showing the wolves alongside images of a sunset, elephants and a tiger next to more shapes hand-drawn directly on to the wall; there is an image of a bird; a dog leaping on a beach; and tadpoles in the bottom of a plastic bottle, before Star gathers the children to escape the home. As Cortvriend argues, 'these images come to be symbols which are returned to throughout the film' (Ibid.: 211), and this is therefore another distillation of the ways in which Arnold's non-verbal mode of image-led narration can be seen to condense key themes within elements of *mise en scène* which are both lyrical and grounded in material reality. For example, the tortoise foreshadows the turtle that Star returns to the water in an act of re-birth at the film's ending, the wolves refer to Jake, who howls throughout the film to signify his presence to Star and who, during a moment of post-coital reflection tells her that his father taught him to make the wolf noise if he was ever lost. This recalls the association between Clyde and foxes in *Red Road*, first hinted at when Jackie sees Clyde on CCTV having sex (when she loses sight of him she instead sees a fox) and as Jonathan Murray argues 'the . . . symbol of the fox associates Clyde with animal nature, rather than artificially disciplined culture' (Murray 2015: 104). Jake can also be viewed in this way, evoking a wider symbolic system in Arnold's work – also visible in *Fish Tank* – which equates sexual desire with animality. The drawings on the wall also seem to evoke concerns beyond the immediacy of the narrative, alluding instead to familiar instances elsewhere in Arnold's work – the drawings on the wall, for example, recall both *Wasp* and *Wuthering Heights* and suggest a poignant affirmation of the combined spatiality and temporality that we discussed in relation to the latter film, with a literal writing on the domestic landscape here capturing both a specific moment in time and a sense of 'becoming' in a similar way to the glimpsed images of the family photographs. Finally, the 'red shoes' are an obvious self-conscious allusion to *The Wizard of Oz* (Victor Fleming, 1939), and soon after we see them the mag crew will arrive in Kansas City.

Cortvriend argues that the highly selective nature of the *mise en scène* construction here, 'brimming with textual signifiers', contrasts with the road scenes which reflect what he terms 'spaces which Arnold could not control' (Cortvriend 2017: 209). However, this is not to say that these scenes are not rigorous in their construction. Indeed, *American Honey*, the longest of Arnold's features at 156 minutes, is given shape and order through the repeated journeys on the bus. The film is made up of eleven of these trips and they work as an anchoring mechanism, imbuing our experience of Star's narrative with a sense of structure. Accordingly, the scenes are constructed around a repeated aesthetic: the shot is handheld from within the bus itself, and while we are most commonly drawn to Star's point of view or over the shoulder shots, there is also a dispersal of focus across the other members of the crew. This can be seen as a further example of the 'being with' mode of participatory address that we have called upon throughout, and Arnold herself describes how '[i]t was fairly intense. I used to get out of the bus at the end of the day going, ugh. It was a tiny space at the back. It was the DP Robbie [Ryan] and [Rashad Omar] who does sound recording' (Zuckerman 2016). Here Arnold (along with her skeleton crew) is explicitly foregrounded as a participant – literally a fellow traveller. Indeed, in other interviews she describes the shooting of the film in terms that blur the boundaries between the fictional world and the actual process of constructing the film:

> It was a real road trip movie in that sense [...] We were all together from the beginning, with no one flying in and out. Crazily, we went up to the Dakotas, where I had never been on my road trips, and started in Muskogee [Oklahoma], one of the poorest towns in America. It seemed as good a place as any to start from. (O'Hagan 2016)

Again, we come back to broader questions of the experiential and embodied qualities of Arnold's realism, and might in turn think of the relationship

3.3   Watching with Star.

between Joanna Hogg's similarly immersive aesthetic and the highly involved nature of her production strategies.

This ritualised emphasis on participation creates the conditions for a further instance of Arnold's interest in watching, both as an element of her narratives, and more broadly as a routine of everyday life. The view from the window is here hugely significant, recurring as it does some fifty-eight times in the film (accounting for more than five per cent of the film's shots). In most cases it is Star's view that we share as the multiple and changing landscapes unfold throughout the film. In one sense, the shots serve a narrative function, introducing the viewer and the characters to new spaces and providing an indication of the nature of those spaces (urban, rural, wealthy, poor, for example) as the crew members comment on their new surroundings. The repetition and ubiquity of the shots however also evoke the sense in which Arnold's other films, intensely focused as they are on individuals, recognise the presence of alternate or parallel narratives and resist narrow individuation in the process – yet again, we think of the screens in *Red Road*, of the estates in *Wasp* and *Fish Tank*, and of the conspicuous foregrounding of the ever 'becoming' landscape in *Wuthering Heights*. Once more, Doreen Massey offers insights that can substantiate our thinking about the textured nature of space and narrative in the new realist text. In discussing the sensation of viewing the outside from a train window, she writes:

There is a famous passage, I think from Raymond Williams . . . He too is on a train and he catches a picture, a woman in her pinny bending over to clear the back drain with a stick. For the passenger on the train she will forever be doing this. She is held in that instant, almost immobilised. Perhaps she's doing it ('I really *must* clear out that drain before I go away') just as she locks up the house to leave to visit her sister, half the world way, and whom she hasn't seen for years. From the train she is going nowhere; she is trapped in the timeless instant.
[. . .]
Thinking space as the sphere of a multiplicity of trajectories, imagining a train journey (for example) as a speeding across on-going stories, means bringing the woman in the pinny to life, acknowledging her as another on-going life. (Massey 2005: 116)

I am arguing then that Arnold's approach to space and time in *American Honey*, and in her other films, similarly acknowledges the recognition of ongoing stories and, in turn, through the participatory address, calls upon our own physical and conceptual positions within these multiple 'trajectories' and lives. The repeated evocation of the window shot as a way of figuring both Star's and our own comprehension of the multilayered landscapes that we occupy and pass through does not entrench a sense of passivity – the static consumption of passively observed timeless, immobilised instants – rather, *American Honey* compels us to imagine and acknowledge multiple parallel narratives alongside Star's.

For example, towards the end of the film, the crew arrives in Rapid City, Krystal's home town. Star approaches a house and knocks on a door. Two children answer and a peeling sticker of the American flag is visible. Star is invited in. The TV is on loudly and she notices another child playing with a cat while another sings to her. Star is told that the mum is sleeping. Her eyes are drawn to photographs on the wall and stickers on the fridge, and Star requests a drink, which allows her to catch a glimpse of another sparsely filled fridge. As she does so the children's mother emerges from her room, unsteady on her feet and oblivious to the stranger in her house, and slumps on the sofa. Star notices drug paraphernalia next to her. The atmosphere in the home clearly recalls Star's own, foregrounded at the outset – from the innocence of the children, the place of animals, the neglectful parent, the sense of poverty, the preponderance of photographs and stickers, the subtle reference to discordance between national ideology and economic reality. Accordingly, Star quickly falls into her role as benevolent sister, and in the next scene is shown in a supermarket – just as she was at the start of the film – buying eggs, milk, bread and fruit for the family. As she leaves fireworks can be heard, and with Star shot from behind as she moves through the car park, a focus shift reveals two figures in the distance unfolding a large American flag, suggesting perhaps that it is Independence Day – tellingly, Star, and certainly the poverty-stricken family are oblivious. In an earlier scene, Star has revealed that her own mother died from an addiction to Methamphetamine and as if to make the parallels explicit, Krystal tells the crew on their arrival: 'It's just poor people like y'all'.

Arnold's journey through America is thus both a deeply intimate examination of Star as she experiences the country, and of multiple intersecting narratives that reveal, albeit elliptically, the fabric of the place that she inhabits – balancing the politics of identity and of structure. In this sense then, Arnold's poetic treatment of the worlds that her characters inhabit, something that I have anatomised throughout this chapter, enables an intricate and nuanced environmental analysis. As Jonathan Murray argues, 'Arnold's interest in exterior topography stems from her apparent conviction that people are profoundly shaped by the places they inhabit. Depicting places constitutes an effective way of delving deep into the hidden complexities of people' (Murray 2016: 197). This examination of location as a determining factor of identity brings us back to a sense of Arnold's place in the context of new realism. We have seen how Hogg and Hopkins in distinctive but intersecting ways lyrically foreground the environments their characters occupy, not as mere decoration but as a fundamental element of their poetics, an impulse which seems to underpin Arnold's approach too:

> Because to some degree, with the stories I've been telling as well, where you're born and where you grew up has a huge impact on how your life is. Your circumstances and the things you're born into are everything, especially when you're young. I think maybe that's why I get wrapped up with the environment and location when I'm filming. It matters and it says something about people – who they are and how they live. All my films have had that element. When I think about the next thing I'll do, I know I'll do it again because it's almost like a character, the location. (Smith 2010)

To return to the debates I explored at the beginning of this chapter, for all its accented and aestheticsed treatment of environment, new realism is concerned with the relationships between location and identity and it is precisely through its poetic examination of this dynamic that the films enable an intimate and embodied address. This is fundamentally attentive to experience, both in terms of representation – foregrounding the textured and tactile encounters between its characters and the landscapes they occupy – and spectatorship – calling upon familiar sites and senses to viscerally engage the audience and to in turn effect re-imaginations of our own sense of place and of being in the world. For Arnold and her contemporaries, we have seen how this is arrived at through highly structured and meticulous approaches to *mise en scène*, what we can term image-led narration; an intimate participatory mode of filming that evokes a sense of 'being with' a protagonist; and a construction of detail and foregrounding of visual perspectives which call attention to and transform conventionally overlooked aspects of everyday life. While these modes of poetics are immersive, they do not wholly subsume the viewer in a fiction, but rather evoke and transform the 'stuff of life' – the visual and sensory spheres that we share with the characters – effecting renewed critical engagement with the experience of reality. In discussing phenomenology as a research practice, Vivian Sobchack draws conclusions that can similarly be applied to Arnold's phenomenological realist practice:

> And, because it turns us toward the origins of our experience of phenomena and acknowledges both the objective enworldedness of phenomena and the subjective embodied experiencing of them, such radical reflection opens up not only fresh possibilities for reflective knowledge, but also fresh possibilities for living knowledge and experiencing phenomena, for seeing the world ourselves in a critically aware way. (Sobchack 1992: 28)

Arnold's films evoke and maintain a material sense of 'enworldedness' while also fostering a relatedness to the intimate perceptual and corporeal experiences of that world. It is this poetic appeal to the materials and experiences of our everyday lives that underpins the work of all the film-makers that are explored in this book, and it is one that we will continue to examine in the next chapter.

4. SHANE MEADOWS

Like many of his new realist contemporaries, Meadows's career trajectory is somewhat unconventional, and began, at least tangentially, within the broader visual arts. He was studying photography in Burton-on-Trent when he met Paddy Considine, who would go on to work with Meadows on *A Room for Romeo Brass* (1999) and *Dead Man's Shoes* (2004), as well as a range of shorts. Meadows describes how breaking into the 'exclusive, condescending medium' of film 'came about by accident, by me being thrown off a photography course' (Wilson 2012), and his output in the 1990s was defined by a prolific, DIY, community-focused ethic. He came to wider attention with the short documentary *King of the Gypsies* (1995), a profile of the bare-knuckled boxer legend Bartley Gorman, a man whose accent and mannerisms would inspire Considine's depiction of Morell in *A Room for Romeo Brass* four years later, and then, in 1996, with the BFI production board-backed *Where's the Money, Ronnie?* and *Small Time*, two films that captured Meadows's ability to meld the aesthetics and sensibilities of Hollywood genre film-making with an intimate feeling for everyday life in non-metropolitan England.

Meadows's first feature was 1997's *TwentyFourSeven*. Notable for its use of black-and-white cinematography and the casting of Bob Hoskins alongside a cast of unknowns, the film follows the efforts of Hoskins's Darcy, a melancholic but idealistic figure, to galvanise a community of young, hopeless unemployed men by setting up a boxing gym; ultimately, however, Darcy's inner demons manifest themselves in a violent outburst which brings an end to the enterprise. The film's depiction of a charismatic father figure falling victim to a bout of uncontrolled, destructive violence anticipates similar moments in Meadows's later films. Not least *A Room for Romeo Brass*, a semi-autobiographical work based on Meadows's and co-writer's Paul Fraser's childhood relationship, which follows Gavin, a boy with an unspecified spinal problem (Ben Marshall) and his best friend and next door neighbour Romeo Brass (Andrew Shim). Gavin and Romeo meet Morell, an older loner who strikes up a divisive relationship with Romeo, who is keen for a masculine role model owing to the strained relationship with his errant father, Joe (Frank Harper). When Morell's advances towards Romeo's sister Ladine (Vicky McClure) are rebuffed, he reacts violently, beating Ladine's new boyfriend in the street and attacking Gavin's father, before Joe apprehends him.

The film suffered due to poor distribution and was little seen, but Meadows's next film, the Film Four/UK Film Council-backed *Once Upon a Time in the Midlands* (2002), placed him into a different commercial sphere, with an estimated budget of £1,950,000 and a cast of highly prominent British actors (Rhys Ifans, Kathy Burke, Ricky Tomlinson, Shirley Henderson and Robert Carlyle). The film nevertheless treads familiar thematic ground, being structured around the battle between competing father figures, Carlyle's Jimmy and Ifans's Dek, and infusing American genre codes with a typically English setting. It was, however, commercially unsuccessful and Meadows has sought to distance himself from the film. As he puts it:

> It wasn't quite a flop, but what I learned is that whether a film costs 50 pence of £50 million there has got to be a challenge and it must mean something personal. If you want to go into long-term development with somebody you perhaps don't get on with, you ended up with this kind of communal film-making in the end I was so shattered with developing the script I just went along with it. It's not a terrible film, but I'm far more complicated than that. (Lawrenson 2004: 35)

This was clearly a formative experience for Meadows, as he realised the need for control that now only seemed possible in smaller productions. Accordingly, *Dead Man's Shoes* was made for less than half the budget of his previous film. The film established a partnership between Meadows and Warp Films, and was another collaboration with Considine, who co-wrote the film and plays its central character, Richard. Richard is a soldier who returns to his working-class rural community to seek to avenge his disabled brother, Anthony (Toby Kebbell), who has been bullied by a local gang. The film is a generic hybrid, melding a characteristic sensitivity for everyday dialogue and location with traces of the gothic, western and thriller traditions, and was a commercial success, paving the way for Meadows's next film, the career-defining *This Is England* (2006).

Set in 1983, the film is focused on Shaun Fields, an obvious avatar for Meadows. A thirteen-year-old boy played by Thomas Turgoose, Shaun is dealing with the recent loss of his father, a soldier killed during the Falklands conflict, when he is befriended by benevolent skinhead Woody (Joe Gilgun) and his friends, amongst them Andrew Shim's Milky. Shaun quickly embraces the style and camaraderie of his new subcultural family, but the group splits when Combo (Stephen Graham) is released from prison, having developed fervent English nationalist views. Seizing upon Shaun's desire for a new dad, Combo draws in the youngster and Shaun is temporarily seduced by the racist narrative Combo presents, one which helps him to make sense of his real father's death. The film ends in brutal fashion, with Combo beating the mixed-race Milky in front of Shaun, and the youngster symbolically throwing his English flag in the sea.

Following this significant critical and commercial success, Meadows's next project was noticeably modest. *Somers Town* (2008) was commissioned by Mother, the creative agency, on behalf of their client, Eurostar. Accordingly, the film, Meadows's first and so far only project in the South of England, is set in the Somers Town area of North London, next to St Pancras station, UK terminus of Eurostar. The film concerns Tomo (Thomas Turgoose), a teenager from Nottingham who has run away from his care home to start a new life in London. After being mugged and beaten up, he meets and sparks up a friendship with Marek (Piotr Jagiello) who has moved to London with his father, Mariusz, (Ireneusz Czop), who is working on the re-development of St Pancras. Tomo and Marek both fall for the same French waitress, Maria (Elisa Lasowski); when she leaves unexpectedly, the pair drown their sorrows, before Marek has an emotionally honest conversation with his father about their absent mother, and Tomo finds an unlikely father figure in 'wheeler-dealer' Graham (Perry Benson). The film ends with a shift from black-and-white to colour as, in a utopian twist, Tomo and Marek travel on the Eurostar and are reunited with Maria in Paris.

Following this, Meadows made an even lower budget film, a 'rock-umentary', *Le Donk and Scor-zay-zee* (2009), about a roadie, Le Donk (Paddy Considine), with delusions of grandeur. Meadows then moved to television, with Channel 4 broadcasting his three mini-series sequels to the *This Is England* film, *This Is England '86* (with the first two episodes directed by Tom Harper), *This Is England '88* and *This Is England '90* (referred to as '86, '88, and '90 hereafter), in 2010, 2011 and 2015 respectively. Between the second and third series Meadows returned to the big screen, with *The Stone Roses: Made of Stone* (2013), a film documenting the reunion of the eponymous Manchester band.

The *This England* serials have allowed for a dispersal of the narrative focus established in the film, with a shift towards Lol (Vicky McClure) particularly. The first series deals with her affair with Milky, and the return of her violent and sexually abusive father, Mick (Johnny Harris), who rapes Trev (Danielle Watson) and is killed by Lol in self-defence when he forces himself upon her. Combo takes the blame for the murder, but, by the second series, Lol is constantly haunted by the memory of her father, and a combination of this trauma and post-natal depression contributes to a suicide attempt. In the meantime, Shaun's relationship with Smell (Rosamund Hanson) ends after he cheats on her, and Woody is ensconced in a new relationship, before reuniting with Lol by the end of the series. In '90 the focus shifts to Lol's sister, Kelly (Chanel Cresswell), whose descent into heroin abuse is exacerbated by the revelation that her father was a rapist and that he was murdered by her sister. The series also sees Milky take revenge on the newly rehabilitated Combo, but ends on a positive note, with the wedding of Woody and Lol and with Shaun having found satisfaction and a creative outlet through a photography course at the local college.

Meadows's willingness to work across the mediums of film and television evokes the traditions of British realist practice, and it is no surprise that he frequently cites Alan Clarke as a major influence on his work, stating of his films and TV plays that, 'I don't think they inspired me. It's more that they're a part of me' (Fuller 2007). This is significant because it further connects Meadows's work to that of his contemporaries, particularly Hopkins and Arnold, both of whom, as we have seen, reference Clarke, and his visceral, stylised realism, over more prominent and widely known figures such as Leigh and Loach.

Indeed, as this chapter will show, despite a highly distinctive and recurring set of thematic and aesthetic concerns across his oeuvre, Meadows's work can be productively located alongside that of his contemporaries to examine wider developments in the language and politics of realist practice in Britain today. It might seem initially far-fetched to compare the films of Joanna Hogg, with their static frames, sensory landscapes and emotionally constipated middle-class protagonists, to the work of Meadows – avowedly working-class in focus, revelling in a bawdy humour and often highly stylised in the use of music and slow motion. Yet, both film-makers are instinctively realist in their casting techniques (willingness to use non-professionals), writing methods (openness to improvisation, drawing on personal experience), and performance methods (encouraging actors to live together and immerse themselves in the filming locations), while both deploy *mise en scène* for poetic effect rather than mere authentication – this is what we have called image-led narration, where quotidian locations are imbued with lyrical meaning. Thus the reading strategies that we have deployed so far to establish a poetics of contemporary British realism are equally applicable here.

Accordingly, this chapter will seek to anatomise the processes by which

Meadows deploys and employs markers of everyday verisimilitude for narrational and affective purposes, to further explore and call attention to new realism as a practice. With that in mind, it is worth briefly considering the extent to which scholars have described Meadows's realist project in ways which align with our consideration of film-makers discussed elsewhere in this book. For example, Beth Johnson argues that while Meadows acknowledges the 'often-harsh realities of working-class life', he is 'not confined to merely documenting and reproducing', but that he is also committed to 'a delicate and poetic transformation of the mundane and the familiar' (Johnson 2018: 140); while in their introduction to a dossier of articles devoted to Meadows's work in *The Journal of British Cinema and Television*, Martin Fradley, Sarah Godfrey and Melanie Williams describe his tendency to create moments which 'transcend quotidian reality' (2013a: 824). As we will see, instances of stylisation are common in Meadows's work, and function in the way implied to elevate, draw attention to and re-imagine everyday phenomena for lyrical purposes. One such moment in Meadows's first feature, *TwentyFourSeven*, occurs when the film's protagonist Darcy takes his Auntie ballroom dancing, with the scene shot in slow motion, a decision which Meadows justifies in poetic realist terms:

> If it had just stayed at normal speed, it wouldn't have meant much. But with the slow motion, it says, 'hold on a minute'. This dance takes you back to the 50s, it gives you a link to where Darcy comes from. What may be a crappy village hall would at one time have been beautiful, and the only way I could show that was through my camera. (Macnab 1998: 16)

It is significant that Meadows sees the shift to slow motion, a technique used throughout his oeuvre, as an opportunity to encourage reflection on the part of the audience and to in effect signal the temporary suspension of the delivery of narrative information. Moreover, Meadows sees this poetic interruption as necessary for opening up the hitherto linear representation of this location into something that is more temporally complex and palimpsest-like in form. Thus, just as in the work of the film-makers that we have discussed so far, the relationship between environment and identity is formal as well as political.

Indeed, even more common amongst scholarly engagements with Meadows's work are observations about the importance of the representation of place and the use of space in his films. Accordingly, much of the work in this chapter will similarly concern itself with the critical exploration of that particular dimension of the films, not least because, as we have seen, the representation and poetic transformation of familiar environments and place-specific sensory encounters is a pervasive feature of new realism.

Academic accounts of Meadows's work are quick to point out setting as crucial to his meaning making. For Fradley, Godfrey and Williams, 'Meadows' awareness of social place is matched by an equivalent attachment to geographical space, more specifically the East Midlands region of England in which he grew up and which has provided the setting for the majority of his films to date' (2013: 825), while Sarah Street notes how Meadows's films 'reference place and identity as major themes, but this time from a non-metropolitan, local perspective. This is invariably Nottingham or, if not directly referenced, its environs in the Midlands' (Street 2009: 145). Vicky Lebeau's reading is broader, highlighting Meadows's interest in the 'disinvested spaces of the Midlands' housing estates' (2013: 885). These summaries all point to a key feature of Meadows's work (and, again, of other new realists): an autobiographical proximity to subject and, by extension, location. Moreover, Meadows seeks to represent generalised regional space which might in turn be understood as consisting of sites which counter the dominant presence of London and the South East in cultural representation, and in economic and political terms. Going further, Jason Scott describes how:

> Meadows' films use *mise en scène* and dialogue further to fix their representations in the East Midlands, combining regional speech with local place to construct 'accented space' [... and] make recurrent use of local space, by which I mean the referential specificity that derives from the particularity of location shooting, through the combination of shooting style and choice of locations (often 'as found'), and the inclusion of passers-by or local extras. (Scott 2013: 836)

However, as we will see as this chapter unfolds, Meadows's connection to the specificities of East Midlands place is increasingly slippery. Elsewhere in Scott's article, he acknowledges Meadows's 'selective' use of location which in turn creates an 'imaginary geography' (Ibid.: 136), and this observation is given heightened currency when applied to Meadows's most recent work, where the locations of Nottingham and Grimsby, used in the *This Is England* film, are jettisoned in favour of Sheffield in the TV series. This bold invitation to suspend our investment in what Scott calls the 'essential realism' of the director's use of location (at least up to this point in his career trajectory) underlines the impressionistic, collage-like approach to 'real' space that defines Meadows's oeuvre, one which is given added complexity due to its deployment in constructing representations of the past.

Thus, despite the impression of fixity in Meadows's use of location, his work rarely references specific places, with the obvious exception of *Somers Town*, and frequently multiple actual locations converge to create an amalgamated, imagined landscape. Even in *Somers Town*, the film's use of black-and-white cinematography seems to have been partly motivated by a desire to transform the urban landscape by nullifying its specificities, as Meadows argues:

> I actually started taking photographs of the various locations, because there was a massive range of buildings from a massive range of times we ended up with a huge variation in colour. [. . .] I had some of the photographs converted into black and white and suddenly it started to look like the same place rather than this mish-mash. (Wilkinson 2008)

Meadows is therefore keen, it seems, to render the environment as mundanely ubiquitous, to minimise the extraordinary nature of the capital and instead to emphasis its ordinariness, those qualities which bind it to rather than distinguish it from other landscapes within Britain: 'At first it just seems another amorphous inner-city neighborhood [sic], but you quickly realise it's just like every other community. You see the same people going to the same shop at the same time every morning' (Anonymous 2009). This is not to say that location in Meadows's work is secondary, far from it: rather, its mutability is necessary for his particular brand of universal poetic realism. As Sarah Petrovic argues, Meadows's films are by virtue of their titles alone always 'spatial':

> In *The Practice of Everyday Life*, Michel De Certeau suggests that 'Every story is a travel story – a spatial practice' (De Certeau 1984: 115), and this is certainly true for Meadows' films, nearly all of which have spatial titles. In addition to *Somers Town* and *This Is England*, Meadows' works include *Once Upon a Time in the Midlands* and *A Room for Romeo Brass*. Even the title *Dead Man's Shoes* suggests a personal perspective and space. (Petrovic 2013: 127)

This suggests an immediate foregrounding of environment as an organising strategy in both narrational – providing a space for the action to unfold – and less instrumental, poetic terms, suggesting that the location is open to multiple interpretations, as in *Somers Town*. Shorn of the necessity to depict landscape prescriptively and exactly, Meadows is liberated to transform real spaces for symbolic ends. Let us take, for example, the use of Matlock in *Dead Man's Shoes*. A location never referred to explicitly, the town is presented in a highly impressionistic fashion, an assemblage of familiar but equally generic council houses, rural landscapes and market town streets, and de-populated in sinister fashion, suiting the film's gothic inflection – it is a space which is both universal and avowedly fictional and constructed. As suggested, the manipulation of realist space in this way opens up the location to broader interpretative possibilities. For Clair Schwarz, 'the film's sparsely populated *mise en scène* resembles the post-social desolation and economic impoverishment of the Western "ghost town"' (Schwarz 2013: 105), and for Fradley, Godfrey and Williams, this locational sparseness is similarly redolent of socio-economic figuration:

> Despite the sparse plot, *Dead Man's Shoes* is dominated by a palpable sense of stasis and social decay. Understated montages of agricultural debris and rotting council houses underscore its hermetically sealed depiction of life on the social and economic peripheries [. . .] (Fradley, Godfrey, Williams 2013b: 8)

Here the writers pick out the metonymic signifiers of marginality that abound in the film, units of meaning that operate symbolically and universally precisely because they are conspicuously emphasised through their placement in this ambiguous landscape and are not connected to pre-existing place-specific narratives. This again seems to open up the space as palimpsest, one which for the writers operates at the autobiographical level, as the reference to Meadows's own home town of Uttoxeter indicates. While the layered iconographies of the film's uncertain landscapes function to emphasise its social scope, the conspicuous looseness of the space enables other readings to emerge, ones which, as Beth Johnson and Joe Andrew show, generate multiple points of emphasis:

> Thus the empty male site could be imagined as the whole of a town like Matlock, bereft of male trades, employment and purpose, which not only casts out and destroys the very men and the homosocial bonds that it seeks to protect, but renders the 'other' – its women – invisible, silenced and excluded. (Johnson and Andrew 2013: 872)

Crucially, this is not Matlock, but 'a town like Matlock', and thus this is authentic landscape as simile, which in Johnson's and Andrew's reading, enables the revelation of important intersections between post-industrial decay and gender relations.

It is striking, too, that in Meadows's first feature, *TwentyFourSeven*, implicitly located in Nottingham but temporally ambiguous and visually stylised and defamiliarised through the use of black-and-white, scholars have sought to reveal the poetic effects of figurative landscapes. As Jill Steans suggests: 'the social and political legacy of Thatcherism is evident from the film's opening scene. Tim walks his dog along a disused railway line, his body swamped by the surrounding landscape of urban decay' (Steans 2013: 69), and thus the themes of decline and destitution are written into the *mise en scène* from the outset and rendered through their (aged) photographic presentation. Paul

Elliott connects the film to *Dead Man's Shoes* on the basis of their shared themes of recurrent and barely suppressed trauma, both at the collective and individual level:

> If Richard and Anthony had their Edenic countryside, then Darcy has his abandoned railway carriage; each psychogeographical space is a literal rendering of the otherness that trauma engenders. As the narrative develops we again realise that we are being presented with two more temporal series: a recent traumatic past that is characterised by violence and a distant past that is enshrined in memory. (Elliott 2013: 90)

Eliott's evocation of psychogeography connects Meadows's use of space to his complex characterisations of bereft and marginalised protagonists, and I would suggest that these figurative effects are only generated because of the ambiguously selective assemblages of multiple landscapes that take place within Meadows's films, enabling a wilful denial of the locational and temporally specific in favour of a universal ambiguity.

This poetic disruption of geographical specificity is not solely delivered through Meadows's treatment of space. Although Scott is correct to point to Meadows's use of Nottingham's Television Workshop as a recruiting ground for his actors – Vicky McClure (*A Room for Romeo Brass*, *This Is England*, *This Is England '86*, *'88*, and *'90*) and Andrew Shim (*A Room for Romeo Brass*, *Once Upon A Time in the Midlands*, *This Is England*, *This Is England '86*, *'88*, and *'90*), chief amongst them – Scott's claim that this casting emphasises a 'localised' and 'regional' sense of identity needs further development (Scott 2013: 836). While Meadows draws upon performers from the East Midlands, he also casts actors from Yorkshire, and the North West, particularly. Again, then, Meadows's use of the 'local' and the 'regional' is necessarily loose. The coexistence of multiple geographically specific accents within seemingly cohesive groups and communities of characters is supported by the symbolic rather than specifically authentic use of landscape that we have already identified. Thus, the imagined geographies of *This Is England* enable the relationship between a Liverpudlian (Combo), a Lancastrian (Woody) and an East Midlander (Lol) to appear authentic in the 'any town, anywhere' poetics of Meadows's filmic world. The sense of 'regionality' is thus again purposefully mutable, generating a collage of reference points 'local' to any of us who live outside of London.

Landscape and performance are thus inextricably linked in Meadows's films; authenticity at the level of affect is privileged at the expense of geographical accuracy to construct imagined spaces that are nevertheless formed from quotidian referents. Meadows is motivated by what feels real rather than the verisimilar construction of authenticity through setting and performance:

I didn't really need actors; I needed human beings. It wasn't like I was some kind of magician, I just believed that everyone could act, because on a daily basis most of us do already. It's not about training at RADA; it's about giving people confidence and making them feel comfortable in their own skin on camera. (Wilson 2013: 913)

As we have noted in relation to the other film-makers discussed in this book, lived experience is here positioned as a rich resource in the construction of emotionally authentic characters. Just as landscape functions as spatial and temporal palimpsest in Meadows's films, so too performance operates through figurative layers of individual memory and dramatic representation. Vicky McClure has described how Meadows would tell her, 'Don't worry about where the camera is, all you need to do is just act', and that 'he will only give you the stories you need to hear, but it's more about the freedom that he gives you' (Wilson 2013: 918), thus the 'freedom' exists within parameters which stimulate the performers' own emotional histories, the connections they have formed with each other and those which exist beyond the realms of the text, as McClure goes on to explain in her discussion of *This Is England '88*:

For the scenes when Woody and Lol had been apart for a long time, he literally wouldn't let us see each other, on set or after filming. Joe stayed with the rest of the gang in digs and I got put up in a separate hotel. That's a definite style Shane has in terms of getting you to that emotional level. But it just helps you to become that character even more. (Wilson 2013: 919)

Thus, the authenticity that pervades Meadows's texts is constructed through an intimate process of performance whereby actors, recruited for their experience and their emotional literacy rather than their training, offer their labour on an almost embodied level, as McClure again explains:

The isolation of living on my own for a few weeks fed into the work. If we had been going out having the craic every night, it would have been different. Not as organic or emotionally real. So it is all in the aid of the art.
[...]
We have that weird feeling of enjoying the pain. You know it is not real, but because you are living it and breathing it you really hurt. And it is so important to do justice to women out there who are really suffering. (Lobb 2011)

This quotation is also revealing in that it points to the socio-political effects of representing suffering on screen, and in the case of Vicky McClure the performance becomes an act of solidarity which connects the dramatic representation of Lol to the 'real' lives of women who are victims of abuse, depression and socio-economic marginalisation, such is the extent of her immersive creation of the character. Beth Johnson has usefully theorised McClure's performance in terms of 'emotional suffrage' and as evincing a wider 'feminist . . . concern regarding emotionally honest representations of working-class women's stories and lives' (Johnson 2017: 17). What Johnson frames as McClure's 'emotional labour' (Ibid.: 20) in mining her own experiences and in seeking to represent and do 'justice' to those of other women, is also then conceived as an act of authorship, and considered alongside the way Meadows's improvisational methods both draw upon and are shaped by the contributions of his actors. This also serves to illustrate a crucial point about Meadows's working practices. As Martin Fradley and Emma Sutton argue: 'the casual normalization of a term such as "the Meadowsian" is fraught with problems, not least due to Meadows' enthusiasm for collaboration in his creative practice' (Fradley and Sutton 2014: 6) and Meadows's deep and involved collaborative relationships with performers such as McClure, Andrew Shim, Thomas Turgoose, Stephen Graham and Paddy Considine are matched by the depth of his partnerships with co-writer and childhood friend Paul Fraser, Warp Films's Mark Herbert, the late singer-songwriter Gavin Clark and the contemporary composer Ludovico Einaudi, and more recently Jack Thorne and Tom Harper.

Yet, despite the dispersal of Meadows's authorial practice and the symbiotic, gang-like mentality of his creative communities, consistent themes abound in his work. As mentioned, the non-specific Midlands or Northern space as metonym for post-industrial marginalisation and decay, the connected notion of community, both familial and more broadly social; the centrality of fatherhood and the trap of toxic masculinity to working and underclass experience, and a related and problematic focus on what Louise FitzGerald and Sarah Godfrey term 'male violence towards women' (FitzGerald and Godfrey 2013: 159); and a pervasive sense of mourning, arrived at through narratives set in the past or whereby characters search painfully for a lost or never existent time before the impossibility of the present moment, are particular prominent concerns across his oeuvre. Perhaps most significantly, the inspiration for Meadows's films can be repeatedly found in his own experiences, in another connection to his new realist contemporaries.

The consistency of Meadows's thematic concerns might also be due to his prolific output as an amateur film-maker, in what seems a highly productive period before the *Where's the Money, Ronnie?* and *Small Time* brought him wider attention. Indeed, Jack Newsinger's analysis of the structural and institutional ecologies of Meadows's creative outputs highlights the importance of a regional film culture that was enabling for young, working-class talent, with Meadows borrowing equipment from Intermedia, a now closed, but once publically supported 'Nottingham institution that gave Meadows and many other local film-makers their first production experience', as Newsinger puts it, implies the 'support structures' (Newsinger 2013: 31) which helped Meadows to emerge are rapidly evaporating in what is now a global rather than regional film sector which is both increasingly market-driven and socially exclusive. The development of Meadows's career then should also be seen in this context – his emergence at least partly aided by a cultural climate which more clearly recognised and sought to remove barriers to creative participation.

A ROOM FOR ROMEO BRASS (1999)

As mentioned at the outset, the commercial failure of *A Room for Romeo Brass* means that it is one of Meadows's lesser-known films. As Fradley, Godfrey and Williams explain, 'Despite critical acclaim . . . *A Room for Romeo Brass* suffered from catastrophically poor marketing and distribution, barely recouping £100,000 of its £3.2 million budget on its theatrical release in February 2000' (Fradley, Godfrey and Williams 2013b: 7). However, it remains a key film in Meadows's oeuvre because of the way in which it distils so many of the formal and thematic features that would come to define his film-making across the next two decades, and new realism more broadly.

Much of the most perceptive scholarly analysis of *A Room for Romeo Brass* has focused on its problematic representation of gender, and it is worth contextualising what is to come in light of these readings of the film. For example, Louise Fitzgerald and Sarah Godfrey have sought to highlight the ways in which the representation of Romeo's mother Carol (Ladene Hall) reflects a 'generalised and over-determined understanding of black lone motherhood' (Fitzgerald and Godfrey 2013: 165), pointing out how 'Carol's inability as lone mother to foster a protective and supportive relationship with her male child is central to the narrative' (Ibid.: 167). The character, Fitzgerald and Godfrey argue, stands in contrast to her next-door neighbour and Gavin's mother, Sandra (Julia Ford): 'Carol's ambiguity towards her son is juxtaposed with the emotional support given to Romeo's friend Gavin by his white married mother, who is maternalised according to a very different set of discursive norms' (Ibid.: 167). Fitzgerald and Godfrey also argue that Carol is only 'able to access an acceptable configuration of motherhood once the nuclear family is re-established through her reconciliation with Romeo's father, who had been expelled from the family home as a result of his violence' (Ibid.: 167), which in turn invites inquiry into Meadows's related thematic preoccupation with fatherhood. As Fradley and Kingston argue, Romeo's uneasy relationships with his father and mother create the conditions for his friendship with Morell (Paddy Considine), a 'man-child' who 'emerges as a quasi-paternal figure' (Fradley and Kingston 2013: 177). The film's climax is a troubling 'dad-off' between the hammer-wielding Morell and the imperfect but loyal Bill (James Higgins), who sits stoically, protecting Romeo, Gavin, Sandra and Carol, but endangering his own life. Bill is, however, rescued by Joe (Frank Harper), who violently and decisively dispatches Morell with ease, and calms the situation – the film ends shortly afterwards, with Romeo and Gavin performing a magic show for their happy families. Although Fradley and Kingston argue that the playful and surreal nature of the ending, with its 'camp theatricality', critiques the 'bleakly masculinist' (Ibid.: 179) scene that has preceded it, Fitzgerald and Godfrey are right to point out that 'the father's violence is enacted under the guise of paternal protection' and 'with his physical attack on Morell, his role within the family is restored and the patriarchal family structure is regenerated' (Fitzgerald and Godfrey 2013: 168), thus connecting the harmonious conclusion to the problematically restorative nature of the violence. Indeed, the sense of Joe's beating of Morrell as in some way satisfying is doubly reinforced by the screen presence of Frank Harper. Although he also appeared in *TwentyFourSeven* (and would work with Meadows again in *This Is England*), Harper would have been most familiar to viewers for his role in the highly successful British crime thriller, *Lock, Stock and Two Smoking Barrels* (1998), and has since gone on to feature in a range of similar but much less successful British gangster films. Undoubtedly the means by which stylised violence is instrumentalised as a generic feature in these films is conspicuously embodied in and through performers such as Harper, and this is doubly reinforced here by his cockney accent, incongruous amongst the cast of East Midlanders and thus repeatedly announcing his intertextual presence.

In privileging a particular kind of masculinity and restoring a particular kind of familial structure, the film arguably reduces its otherwise complex and nuanced exploration of the socially marginalised Morell to that of a villainous obstacle to the restoration of order. As Fradley and Kingston argue: 'With no apparent state support despite his obvious mental ill health and oscillating between vulnerable sociability and self-aggrandising individualism, Morell is ultimately both a victim of and atomised cipher for the logics of contemporary neoliberal culture' (Fradley and Kingston 2013: 178), yet by so conclusively dispatching Morell (via Joe) and reducing his presence in narrative terms, the complexities of his actions – the environmental conditions that explain his violence – are overwhelmed.

Romeo Brass, then, might be seen to reveal some of the problematic elements of Meadows's characterisation, particularly in relation to the representation of gender, while illustrating the dangers of narrative closure – features that recur throughout his oeuvre. Yet the film also serves to provide an early illustration of many of the formal features that pervade Meadows's work, and particularly those that connect his practice to that of the broader tendencies of new realism. For example, the film is anchored by six montages set to music, and these extended sequences suppress dialogue through the frequency and repetition of often self-contained, painterly images, repeatedly accented by the use of slow motion, and are therefore conspicuously marked as distinctive from the rest of the narrative action. In addition to these sequences, Meadows uses music elsewhere to punctuate scene transitions. While Ian Brown, The Specials, The Stone Roses, Gavin Clark and Beth Orton feature, Meadows also uses American artists such as Beck, Donovan and Fairport Convention in ways that subtly disturb the otherwise conspicuously national character of the landscapes that the film surveys. It is this subtle process of defamiliarisation – of a temporary elevation and transformation of quotidian material – that characterises Meadows's poetic realism here and across his oeuvre.

For example, the opening composition begins with a striking tracking shot, as Gavin and Romeo walk across a rural expanse, both their full bodies in side-on profile against rolling farmers' fields and trees in the background. The shot rests as they reach a tree and is held for a total of one minute and twenty seconds, the gentle sounds of wind and birdsong accompanying Gavin and Romeo's conversation, which in turn establishes their personalities, Gavin as whimsical ('I'd like to build a house out here') and Romeo, no-nonsense ('you talk a load of bollocks'). The scene precedes the first montage, set to The Specials' 'A Message to You, Rudy' which accompanies both the titles and Romeo's purchase of fish and chips (bought from a chip shop owner played by Meadows himself) and subsequent consumption of his mum's and sister's meals. The arresting, heavily stylised composition in combination with the earthy dialogue serves to distil the means by which Meadows throughout the film combines a textured and authentic sense of quotidian performance with a distanced, almost romanticised imagery. Indeed, I have previously discussed the way in which these types of shots replicate the iconographic compositions of the New Wave (Forrest 2009), but overcome the ethical barriers of such imagery (Higson 1984; Hill 1986) through Meadows's own autobiographical inscription of the landscapes, and Gavin's and Romeo's undercutting of earnest romanticism and the sudden shift to the two-tone soundtrack similarly work to disrupt the associations of aestheticised distance.

In the second montage of the film, Romeo accompanies Gavin and his mother to Gavin's hydrotherapy session. Again, the scene is played to music, with Ian Brown's track 'Corpses In Their Mouths' providing the soundtrack. The scene is comprised of four gentle tracking shots, with the final in slow motion, each showing Gavin and Romeo peacefully enjoying the water. This is another moment where Meadows asks us to 'hold on a minute' (Macnab 1999: 16), with the music and slow motion and the consequently dream-like presentation of the pool serving to distinguish this episode from those that precede and follow it. Indeed, the scene comes after Romeo is told off following the chip shop saga, Gavin's father embarrassingly chases a pair of children looking for

4.1 'I'd like to build a house out here.'

their ball out of his garden, and Gavin's mother discovers her husband's stash of pornography in a giggling Gavin's room. The scene afterwards is markedly different in tone: it involves Gavin and Romeo getting into a fight with a pair of much older teenagers at the local park, is shot with a handheld camera and viscerally evokes a sense of 'being there and being with', particularly when Andrew Shim stumbles over his lines and his assailant reacts with improvisation ('You stuttering fuck!'). The scene is notable as the moment where Morell is introduced, as he intervenes in the fight and takes the injured Romeo and Gavin home. Thus, the hydrotherapy sequence, with its heightened, poeticised quality, works as a bridge between and as a counterpoint to scenes occupying a differing formal register. This might be seen to function as pattern or visual rhyme structure in similar ways to the formalised lyrical strategies that we have seen deployed by the other film-makers discussed in this book. For example, another montage later in the film begins after Morell and Romeo have visited Gavin, who is recovering from his operation at home. This particular scene confirms that Morell has temporarily at least replaced Gavin in Romeo's affection, and that Gavin fears the intimidating older man. The montage begins with a highly stylised, fast motion aerial shot of the city as it moves to night and is sound tracked by Beck's 'Dead Melodies'. Gavin lies in bed and reads creative writing to his home tutor, his poetic prose sitting alongside the music to add another layer of melancholic lyricism to the sequence:

> He eats children and pulls down houses
> And to add to that, he makes the town look bad
> Happy's a word nobody knows
> It wouldn't have been shown in films or shows
> cos in this land, happy's a word that nobody knows.

Shots of Gavin and Mr Laws (Bob Hoskins) are interspersed with visits from an animated and over-talkative school friend, whose presence for Gavin only serves to underline Romeo's absence. Thus, while the montages serve to condense narrative information – in this case the distance between the two friends and Gavin's recovery – they also can be seen again to offer a means of poetic contextualisation. Indeed, the scenes that follow this montage and precede the next one are also significant in terms of the film's poetic structure: Morell's unwanted sexual advances towards Ladine (Vicky McClure); Ladine's reconciliation with her father, anticipating the film's conclusion; an uncomfortable one-minute-and-fifty-second-long take from the top of Morell's stairs as he attacks Romeo, essentially under the auspices of training him to be a 'warrior' but confirming his move from oddball to sinister and violent threat. The accumulation of these scenes, signalling as they do a significant narrative shift, therefore precipitates another montage, this time set to Gavin Clark's forlorn love song 'If This Is Love'. The sequence here is more obviously focused around Romeo's sense of loss, with images of him forlornly walking down the street alone and, in another shot, staring up at Gavin's window; these are complemented by a shot of Morell alone in his flat, one which gently pans out to reveal a gas canister presumably used by his late father, both reminding the viewer of the potential causes of his behaviour and symbolically pointing to the film's wider themes. Indeed, the montage also gives a space to Joe's sadness, with the film having previously deployed him in often fraught dialogue with other characters; he is now shown standing outside his van, smoking pensively in the cold. The repeated lyric, 'If this is love, then it's crucifying me' works to conjoin this sense of homo-social longing, finding commonality across the characters in the montage. This sense of lyrical synthesis is then quickly, in line with the film's structure, contrasted with the scene that follows the montage's conclusion. After Romeo and his mother share a tender exchange, with her cheering him up with offers of beans and sausage on toast, he is shown leaving the house and is quickly apprehended by an unhinged Morell. Morell and Romeo then watch from Morell's car Ladine in her place of work talking to her new boyfriend. Morell then proceeds to drive up to the man, gets out of his car and starts viciously beating him. Here the scene is shot handheld and although the camera moves away from the beating as it worsens, the shot is held for an uncomfortably long one minute and twenty seconds, the dull blows of the weapon against the man's increasingly inanimate body audible alongside Morell's unhinged rant; the violent scenes that follow, involving Morell's attack on Bill and Joe's treatment of Morell, are shot in a similarly immersive fashion, evoking Alan Clarke's use of the Steadicam, and therefore are further contrasted with the musical montages that have preceded the scene.

This balancing of registers, between on one hand a sense of 'being there and being with', and on another the use of montage, synthesising narrative and thematic threads and effecting a temporary distance from the cut and thrust of dialogue-led action, is part of a wider process in Meadows's work whereby the representation of everyday images is in the continual process of subtle transformation – images that are at once familiar and strange. This is also visible in the film's use of space and place. *A Room for Romeo Brass* constructs, in line with Meadows's other works, a generic and convergent sense of locational realism. Indeed, the film's economy of space locks in a kind of patterned familiarity, with the repeated use of Romeo's and Gavin's red-brick suburban homes, often introduced through aerial establishing shots which emphasise their uniformity, particularly prominent alongside the shopping precinct, housing the jeans shop in which Ladine works, and the park, where Romeo and Gavin first meet Morell. These particular locations are all found in the village of Calverton, some seven miles from Nottingham, but they are typical of the 'every/any spaces' found in Meadows's work, with no explicit reference to their actual filmed location. The repetitious use of the space is not only a tool of narrative structure, but also serves Meadows's subtle defamiliarisation of these conspicuously mundane environments.

Let us take, for example, the shopping precinct. This is a significant space in the film, since it is where Morell, Gavin and Romeo watch Ladine at work, where Morell lusts after her, and it is ultimately the site of his violent outburst. The exact location is in Calverton's St Alfred's Square, but it is typical of the kind of mid-century suburban shopping precinct found in British towns and cities; indeed, it is very similar to the one used in *This Is England*. Yet here it houses a cowboy-themed denim shop (Ladine's place of work), with saloon style doors and a mural depicting cacti and cowboys. When Gavin tricks Morell, convincing him that Ladine has a particular preference for men who wear shell suits and encouraging him to buy an outfit made up of second-hand sportswear from the charity shop in the same precinct, Meadows follows Morell in Steadicam as he confidently strides down the street; he is laughed at by a group of lads because of his eccentric new style, but dismisses them and confidently enters the shop through the saloon doors, passing a man wearing a Stetson on his way in. As Morell arrives he immediately falls to the floor in slapstick style. The stylised treatment of Morell's journey through this site of quotidian suburbia – evoking Meadows's heroes Alan Clarke and Martin Scorsese with the walking shot – is offset by the atonal slice of filtered Americana, the shell suits, the swinging doors and the comedy fall. Indeed, we are reminded again of the ersatz nature of this Western setting when, in a later scene in the shop, Romeo pleads with Ladine on Morell's behalf while Steps' hit '5, 6, 7, 8' is playing in the background and Ladine's co-worker, dressed in PVC trousers, performs the line-dance moves from the music video in the background, as Meadows continues to make strange this simultaneously familiar and tangible environment. Indeed, the lyrics from the Western-themed song might be seen to enable a further playfully self-conscious disruption: 'My rodeo Romeo, a cowboy god from head to toe. Wanna make you mine, better get in line'.

Thus, the layering of Midlands suburbia with strains of camp Americana works to make strange Meadows's otherwise normative landscape. Certainly, the non-specific nature of the precinct is critical to the poetic effect of its subtle disruption, but Meadows similarly disrupts the representation of the one specific location in the film, when Morell, Romeo and Gavin visit the seaside village of Chapel St Leonards near Skegness in Lincolnshire. It is here where Morell secretly threatens Gavin, but the sequence is largely built around a montage set to the guitar-led track 'Civvy Street Fiasco' by Unisex. Multiple long shots of Morell, Gavin and Romeo on the beach, shots of the waves and, most strangely, a wide-angled shot of Morell performing a kind of pseudo-breakdance to an audience of enthusiastic pensioners in a seafront ballroom, work to loosen any sense of the seaside location as a specific place and rather open it up as a collage of dream-like locations, albeit anchored by a generic and familiar national iconography.

THIS IS ENGLAND (2006)

This subtle transformation of the familiar through a symbolic construction of space and location was to be more fully realised in Meadows's most successful film to date, *This Is England*. As I mentioned at the outset, the film's sense of place is in typical fashion non-specific, with the multitude of varied accents reinforcing a sense of locational ambiguity. Here again, then, real spaces are synthesised to construct multilayered landscapes, which retain authenticity but are simultaneously positioned to convey meaning on figurative levels, something that is crucial to *This Is England*'s particular exploration of the subjective geographies of nationhood. As Caitlin Shaw argues, these factors generate a sense of 'placelessness', which activates the film's figurative inter-rogation of the national, describing the 'town' in the film as a 'synecdochic stand-in for all English towns and cities outside of London in the 1980s' (Shaw 2015: 209), which creates an '[a]nywhere, England' quality (Ibid.: 210). Again, non-specificity is positioned as enabling a more universal address to emerge, which might in turn convey themes in broader, more figurative terms. Similarly, Mark Sinker comments on the 'dreamy inexactness of these strangely underpeopled Northern cityscapes', and a pervasive feeling that the film operates in 'unreal time' (Sinker 2007: 25). Here, then, ambiguous space is linked with the film's evocation of 1980s England to further suggest a loose and broad palimpsest that is both temporal and geographical. The extent of the film's denial of specific place and period can be felt in Hannah Dyer's otherwise excellent article on the film's exploration of private and public mourning. Dyer, a Canadian scholar evidently unfamiliar with English geography, offers the following synopsis: 'Shaun is a lonely child who lives in working class Exeter in the early 1980s, a city bruised by economic recession and deeply impacted by resultant miner's [*sic*] strikes and protests' (Dyer 2017: 315). Dyer's description, comprising as it does of a synthesis of superficially generic features of 1980s working-class history and inaccurate geographies, actually serves to illustrate Meadows's success in constructing a patchwork of multiple temporalities and spatial signifiers – despite the film's evocation of period through its engagement with the Falklands conflict and use of archive footage –which function, as the title suggests, to emphasise a broad national story rather than a specifically local one.

A lyrical and convergent approach to location thus constructs a collage of nation, but *this* England is an England of post-industrial decay which conspicuously bears the scars of economic neglect and profound regional inequality – here the national story looks to make emphatic rather than conceal the momentous politics of the period and their corrosive effect on working-class communities. Meadows's wilfully indeterminate approach to space and place therefore amplifies and draws explicit attention to these themes. For example, in the scenes that build up to the film's violent climax we are with Combo and Lol inside Combo's car and outside Lol's place of work, a factory. It is here where Lol tells a heartbroken Combo that the night they shared together before his imprisonment was 'the worst of her life'. Before this exchange, Meadows deploys five shots of housing estates from multiple perspectives, with the first an aerial composition which shows both residential and office spaces in the distance in a manner typical of an urban environment, and the fourth showing a flock of pigeons flying against a city skyline. While these images unfold, we hear an interview with Margaret Thatcher discussing the Falklands conflict, presented alongside the diegetic sound of birdsong, before a cut to Combo in his car waiting for Lol. After the exchange, we cut to Shaun's home (Thomas Turgoose), in a comedic scene where he is introducing his girlfriend, Smell (Rosamund Hanson), to his mother. Meadows then cuts to an interior shot of Combo's sparsely furnished flat, where Gadget (Andrew Ellis), Meggy (Perry Benson) and Banjo (George Newton) are watching an episode of *Blockbusters* (1983–93, ITV), before a low-angled shot shows Smell and Shaun walking through the housing estate and making their way towards the flat, and another shows them entering the doorway, with Shaun shouting 'Combo!'. However, Combo is yet to arrive, as the next shot shows: a low-angled, wide long shot reveals him in a wasteland space, sitting on the bonnet of his parked car next to a crumbling wall, all that remains of a demolished building. The space around him is also made up of more ruined buildings, and Milky (Andrew Shim) and his girlfriend, Pob (Sophie Ellerby), stop to talk with him (Combo wants to buy weed from

4.2   England as collage.

Milky to numb the pain of Lol's rejection). Meadows cuts to a closer shot which makes the wall even more prominent. The sound design is critical here, with the ambient sound of seagulls, heavy wind and boat horns made prominent. Thus, the film's internal geography has in the last four scenes presented us respectively with an urban industrial landscape, a suburban house, an urban council estate, and now a coastal space, one that is also heavily indicative of post-industrial ruination. While these spaces are ostensibly divergent in actual terms, they are entirely coherent in terms of the film's wider figurative logic: this is England as symbolic palette, a series of authentic but non-specific landscapes which balance private and public malaise.

Meadows thus constructs an iconography which is simultaneously familiar and variable, open to symbolic transformation because it is not beholden to place or period-specific narratives, poetically charged but also reliant on a sense of referential universality. In his description of the shopping precinct used by Woody's gang, as mentioned, one very similar to that which is depicted in *A Room for Romeo Brass* – Tim Edensor emphasises the way in which such locations work at the level of affect; that they feel real:

> The scene is a familiar setting from a low key, post-war, distinctively British modernism, located in a very unglamorous shopping precinct. [...]
>   This setting instantly conjures up a host of familiar sensations. We can feel the hard concrete materialities that dominate the plaza, imagine

seeing the stubs of cigarettes and chewing gum stuck in the tub and in the cracks between the slabs, taste the greasy rashers of bacon and sausage that are served up in the café alongside the plastic condiment containers on the surface of the formica tables (that we subsequently see), and empathetically sense the steamy atmosphere and murmur of chatter inside. (Edensor 2015: 75)

This is a generic production of quotidian Englishness which invites subjective interpretation and (re)habitation at the sensory, empathetic level. While these spaces *feel* authentic to us, or at least to a national audience with a shared set of reference points, they also work symbolically to emphasise elements which are specific to the film's themes and are responsive to the diegetic world constructed from within this familiar landscape. As Sarah Petrovic argues, 'the film uses its presentation of physical space to represent the internal experience of Shaun, and perhaps by extension English society' (Petrovic 2013: 131), thus the *mise en scène* again invites symbolic interpretation. Indeed, earlier in her psychogeographical reading of the film's spaces, Petrovic suggests: 'The film's setting seemingly portrays the East Midlands with a coast, which is an iconic geographical marker for this island nation' (Ibid.: 130), which similarly points to Meadows's collage-like construction of nationhood as operating on a figurative level.

For example, in line with Petrovic's discussion of the layering of location as both national imaginary and subjective canvas for Shaun, it is worth exploring the first significant montage in the film. This takes place following the scenes which show that Shaun is bullied at school, and that he is struggling to cope with the death of his father. The sequence is played to the Gravenhurst track 'Nicole', a contemporary piece that might be seen to further disrupt the scene's sense of temporal rigidity. The first image is a close shot of a dandelion seed head wavering gently in the wind, with birdsong audible on the soundtrack; there is then a low-angled shot of what appears to be a block of low-rise flats, with a pebble-dash wall next to a tree which again blows gently in the wind. The sun dips behind the clouds and the shadow fades against the wall. These lingering images work to foreground a sensory atmosphere, in line with Edensor's analysis, and serve to lyrically preempt the images of Shaun that follow. Indeed, we see nine shots of Shaun, on his bike, washing cars and outside a toyshop coveting a catapult, before a medium shot from within long blades of grass shows him walking alone, emerging with his new toy. Now seagulls are audible on the soundtrack, as another close shot evokes the sensory experience of the landscape, while Shaun picks up a stone from amongst a pile of weeds, and we then see three shots of Shaun shooting his catapult at a target made from polystyrene. The next shot is closer again, as Shaun is shown biting at a fried egg sweet, before an aerial shot reveals that he is sitting in dilapidated small boat. There is then a four-shot sequence of Shaun playing in an empty dockland warehouse, followed by a seven-shot sequence, alternating handheld and longer, aerial shots, on the beach, which culminates with Shaun throwing stones into the water. The music fades and is replaced by a news report on the Falkands war, and three punctuating images outside the pebble-dash walls again, with a fourth internal shot confirming the source of the radio to be Shaun's bedroom. Just as in the sequence involving Milky and Combo that I described earlier, this montage converges multiple actual geographical locations in Nottingham, Grimsby and Cleethorpes (just three miles down the coast). In so doing, it creates a collage that evokes both a sense of the felt and lived experience of generic but universally familiar space – the textured, close shots of natural imagery, the pebble-dash walls, the suburban streets – and which works figuratively. For example, the representation of the sea, the shell of the boat and the warehouse reflect both Shaun's personal grief at losing his father in war on a distant island and a wider national elegy that is here written into the land (and seascape). That these images are accented through the montage invites such interpretation, while also meeting the more immediate narrative demands of conveying Shaun's solitude. Clearly these spaces, specifically their sense of liminality, are central to Meadows's symbolic lexicon in the film. Indeed he has remarked, '[o]riginally we had the idea to set it all at the edge of England, by the coast, with the sea lapping against it' (James 2007: 41), suggesting a locational instinct which is first and foremost governed by a poetic impulse to construct rather than merely reflect an existing geography. It is significant that these coastal spaces are returned to for the film's final scenes, as Shaun walks past the boat and throws the English flag, given to him by Combo, into the sea. While this again evokes Shaun's private grief, mourning his father and the now shattered illusion of paternal comfort offered by Combo, the nationally symbolic nature of the location opens up further figurative interpretation, as William Brown suggests:

> The film ends with a shot of the St George's Cross sinking into the sea: what *This Is England* seems to be saying is that society breaks down when one is forced to live according to an arbitrary notion of 'nationality' defined by flags and other symbols of national identity. (Brown 2009: 412)

Similarly, Jill Steans notes: 'At the boundary of the national body, a desolate seashore, [Shaun] hurls the St George's Cross (with its associated nationalist connotations) into the sea' (Steans 2013: 77). In both readings, the nation is evoked figuratively, since obviously the flag is as direct a national symbol as possible, but the generalised sensibility that is here evoked, what Meadows called 'the edge of England' (James 2007: 41), once more reveals the lyrical capacities of these ubiquitous iconographies. Steans's reading locates and personifies the creaking national imaginary in the seascape, and by extension in Shaun himself, a feeling which is reinforced by Meadows's nod to Truffaut's film *The 400 Blows* (1959), as the now hardened teenager looks directly at the camera.

The fact that these critical moments take place at the 'edge of England' actualises an otherwise abstract notion of nationhood, making tangible the hitherto imagined geographies that the film deploys. As Michael Sley argues in his analysis of Englishness and everyday life, '[n]ational boundaries also make both individual national spaces and the globe as a whole, knowable and, in setting limits, manageable' (Sley 2011: 24), and the film's emphasis on coastal spaces in this way asserts the national in physical terms. This is significant given what we have already identified as the film's lyrical construction of national iconographies and offers a further way into understanding its complex engagement with the politics of nationalism.

Steans's evocation of the nation as a 'body' is therefore a useful starting point for understanding how *This Is England* asserts its complex political project in symbolic terms. The film's themes are organised through the central tension between two father figures vying for Shaun's allegiance, both of them representing competing visions of nationhood. Indeed, the contrasts are made explicit through Meadows's characteristic use of montage, with two parallel sequences showing Shaun with Woody's gang and later with Combo's, as Paul Dave argues:

> Meadows quickly establishes the exhilaration of belonging to a group which is open to the stranger. In central scenes detailing the outfitting and initiation of Shaun, a strong affect of solidarity is generated through music, the use of space and cinematography to the extent that when the skinhead Combo (Stephen Graham) appears, the soundtrack tunes out his racist provocations (Combo's monologue fades, solemn, classical music dominating in the mix) and we are left with a sense of the unspoken opposition of Woody's faction to Combo's encroaching racist nationalism. (Dave 2011: 33)

The divisions are made explicit when Shaun is forced literally to choose a side, in a critical encounter in Combo's flat. Combo delivers an impassioned speech to the group in an attempt to convey his newfound political position:

> That's what this nation has been built on. Proud men. Proud fucking warriors. Two thousand years, this little tiny fucking island has been raped and pillaged by people who have come here and wanted a piece of it. Two

fucking world wars, men have laid down their lives for this. For this, and for what? So we can stick our flag in the ground and say, 'This is England.' 'And this is England. And this is England.' And for what? For what now? Eh, what for? So we can open the fucking floodgates and let them all come in? And say, 'Yeah, come on, come in.' 'Did you have a safe journey? Was it hard?' 'Here's a corner, why don't you build a shop?''Why don't you build a shop and then build a church?' 'Follow your own fucking religions. Do what you want.' When there's single parents out there who can't get a fucking flat and they're being given to these . . . And I'm gonna say it, people. We're giving the flats to these fucking Pakis. Right? Who've got 50 and 60 in a fucking flat on their own. Right? We're giving that to them. There's three and a half million unemployed out there. Three and a half million of us who can't find fucking work. Cos they're takin' em all. Cos it's fucking cheap labour. Cheap and easy labour. Fucking cheap and easy, which makes us cheap and easy. Three and a half fucking million! It's not a joke! It's not a fucking joke! And that Thatcher sits there in her fucking ivory tower and sends us on a fucking phoney war!

Combo's use of repetition is particularly significant, as he points first to the room (this is England as a physical community), to the heart (this is England as an abstract feeling), and then to the head (this is England as a political ideology). The re-assertion of a territorial politics of fixed and essential identity is therefore also enacted at a corporeal level, and further illustrates the extent of the film's figuratively layered geographies. Indeed, at the conclusion of his speech, Combo spits on the ground, as if to literally assert a border and make explicit the notion of the hitherto complex nation as embodied, tangible and knowable: 'Now yous all either cross that line and go your merry little way, or you stay where yous are and yous come with me. The choice is yours, boys.' The evocation of the Falklands evokes literal and metaphorical signifiers, pointing both to an actual geopolitical narrative and an abstract notion of imperial belonging, which initially incites Shaun's rage but ultimately intoxicates him, connecting his personal grief to Combo's all too compelling national narrative. Later, this will be made explicit when Combo and Shaun confirm their new bond as they sit in Combo's car:

Combo: You loved him, didn't you?
Shaun: Yeah.
Combo: And then you lost him.
Shaun: Yeah.
Combo: I know what it's like to have people walk out on you. To have people just fucking leave you. Honest, lad, I know how you feel. You ever want anyone to talk to . . . someone to cry with, or just to fucking have

a hug or punch the fuck out of em, I'm telling you, I'll be there for you. I won't turn me back on you. I promise you that.

Combo then spits on his hand and offers it to Shaun, telling him, 'That's a man's handshake, that. I promise you. I won't let you down', in another bodily assertion of masculinity, paternalism and nationalism. This scene is particularly significant for its suggestion of the link between both Combo's and Shaun's shared personal grief and their use of the nationalist narrative to assert certitude in their otherwise emotionally adrift worlds, coming as it does directly after the speech in the flat. Combo's offer to Shaun is one that draws on and animates the national imaginary as a controlling fiction to re-direct their shared grief, as Hannah Dyer argues:

> In fantasy, Combo creates the enemy he needs to unleash anger upon (an anger that's [sic] origin is surely to do with an inability to mourn his own losses). Part of Combo's healing may be that the nation must become a whole object, good and bad, a geography and psychic formation that he is ambivalent towards. His reverence to the nation and propensity for splitting has precluded and damaged his ability to mourn. His confused longing and obdurate attachment to a fantasy of mastery seek to repair a difficult past, and perhaps, his own childhood traumas. In Combo, we are given a demonstration of what could become of Shaun should his childhood grief not be cared for. Reciting his injuries, and re-playing the structure of events that has made him enraged, Combo tries to teach Shaun that through political loyalties he will fortify himself against vulnerability. Together, they retreat to the nation as a holding place for their rage and defend against the difficult work of mourning and reparation. (Dyer 2017: 320)

Dyer rightly asserts that Combo's, and by extension Shaun's, psychosocial project is predicated on a direction of grief and unrequited longing to an ideology of nationhood enacted spatially, which enables the illusion of agency and mastery. Thus, the nation is once more rendered in symbolic form, and accordingly Combo and Shaun begin their project of racially motivated intimidation in territorial fashion. For example, during the aforementioned montage scene, the gang come upon a group of Asian boys playing football, against the same wall that Shaun played with Woody and his friends in an earlier parallel scene. Combo speaks to one of the boys: 'That's our ball now. And we're playing here. So, I suggest you take fucking Tweedledum and Tweedledee [pointing to his two friends] and fuck off home! If I see you on my streets again . . . I'll slash you.' Combo delivers the last line while holding a knife to the boy's face, which anticipates the gang's next attack at Shaun's local newsagent. Shaun was told off by Mr Sandhu (Kriss

Dosanjh) earlier in the film for reading a comic in the shop, but the present act is no such innocent transgression, as Shaun demands cigarettes and alcohol from the outraged Mr Sandhu, whom Shaun calls 'a Paki bastard' and then soon afterwards follows up with 'you filthy Paki bastard'. The gang then enter and proceed to raid Mr Sandhu's shelves. One of them, Meggy, attempts to defecate on the floor and while Combo's reaction is one of amused shock, the moment powerfully conveys again the corporeal and territorially focused manifestation of racial violence. Combo then holds a machete to Sandhu:

> Don't you dare backchat me, cos I will slay you now where you stand, you fucking Paki cunt! Right? You listen to fucking me! That fucking kid's dad died for this fucking country! What have you fucking done for it? Fuck all, but take fucking jobs off decent people! Now, listen, son, listen good. We'll be back here whenever we want, cos this is fucking ours now. This is ours, fucking Sandhu. Don't forget that. Any fucking time.

This is, in effect, an actualised version of Combo's speech in the flat, representing a violent assertion and reclamation of the national through a territorially asserted narrative of racial hierarchy. The film's violent climax, and Shaun's symbolic repudiation of nationalism at the 'edge of England', effectively counter these discourses, but the manner in which Meadows presents the fermentation and manifestations of Combo's violent nationalism is part of his heavily symbolic and collage-like approach to space (seen here through the assertion of territorial discourse and the recurring evocation of the spatial myth of England) and opens up the film's political themes to further theoretical reflection. In essence, the narrative that Combo presents is one bathed in false nostalgia, which evokes Svetlana Boym's seminal and increasingly pertinent analysis in *The Future of Nostalgia*:

> The danger of nostalgia is that it tends to confuse the actual home and the imaginary one. In extreme cases it can create a phantom homeland, for the sake of which one is ready to die or kill. Unreflected nostalgia breeds monsters. (Boym 2001: xv)

Combo's politics, spatially articulated and enacted as they are, are thus constructed around an 'imaginary' idea of 'home', which festers and takes on dangerous form through what Boym later terms 'restorative nostalgia', which is contrasted with the more malign 'reflective nostalgia':

> Restorative nostalgia puts emphasis on *nostos* and proposes to rebuild the lost home and patch up the memory gaps. Reflective nostalgia dwells in *algia*, in longing and loss, the imperfect process of remembrance. The

first category of nostalgics do not think of themselves as nostalgic; they believe their project is about truth. This kind of nostalgia characterizes national and nationalist revivals all over the world, which engage in the antimodern myth-making of history by means of a return to national symbols and myths, and occasionally, through swapping conspiracy theories. Restorative nostalgia manifests itself in total reconstructions of monuments of the past, while reflective nostalgia lingers on ruins, the patina of time and history, in the dreams of another place and another time. (Boym 2001: 41)

The malleable and blended approach to national space that Meadows adopts in *This Is England*, evoking and re-deploying familiar but generic signifiers of nationhood, thus makes visible the ease with which feelings of national and personal loss can converge to construct a powerful and destructive ideology. This is what Boym later describes as the nationalist impulse to build 'on the sense of loss of community and cohesion', to offer 'a comforting collective script for individual longing' (Ibid.: 42). These are sentiments felt through Combo's and Shaun's haunting personal experiences of mourning, feelings which are transformed by an apparently rousing idea of England. Thus, the film presents us with two forms of nostalgia. On one hand there is Meadows's own 'reflective' brand, itself a selective and highly personal impulse which nevertheless draws attentions to and lingers on the literal and figurative 'ruins' of the recent past as they exist in the present tense:

> As a kid growing up in Uttoxeter, Staffs, it was a time of great music, brilliant fashion and a vibrant youth culture that makes today's kids look dull and unimaginative by comparison [. . .] In 1983, people still cared about society as a whole but now they'll keep their mouth shut as long as they've got the house, the job and the car they want. If you were a kid in 1983, you wouldn't have a PlayStation to sit indoors alone with. You got your entertainment from mixing with a variety of different people. (Meadows 2007)

On the other hand, we see Combo's restorative version, which is altogether more sinister, in line with Boym's description:

> Restorative nostalgia evokes national past and future; reflective nostalgia is a more about individual and cultural memory. The two might overlap in their frames of reference, but they do not coincide in their narratives and plots of identity. In other words, they can use the same triggers of memory and symbols, the same Proustian madeleine pastry, but tell different stories about it. (Boym 2001: 49)

The 'frames of reference' that Boym describes can be understood as the quotidian iconographies that Meadows evokes and offers up for symbolic transformation. In diegetic terms we might also see the battle being between these two forms of nostalgia as enacted through the struggle between Woody and Combo and the markedly different national stories that their subcultures seek to tell, again made explicit through the contrasting montage sequences with Shaun as the overlapping presence. As I have argued throughout, the locational collage that Meadows constructs is drawn from multiple regional and national iconographies converged, and this renders the past tense of the film with contemporary urgency, bringing attention to the visibility of history within the landscapes of the present and asserting the continued resonance of the film's underlying politics of class and nationhood. This realist palimpsest is thus complex and ambiguous, and is further disrupted through the layers of Meadows's own 'looking back', to contrast with the horrifying simplicity of Combo's articulation of nationhood, which again evokes Boym's reading of nostalgic forms:

> National memory reduces this space of play with memorial signs to a single plot. Restorative nostalgia knows two main narrative plots – the restoration of origins and the conspiracy theory, characteristic of the most extreme cases of contemporary nationalism fed on right-wing popular culture. The conspiratorial worldview is based on a single transhistorical plot, a Manichaean battle of good and evil and the inevitable scapegoating of the mythical enemy. Ambivalence, the complexity of history and the specificity of modern circumstances is thus erased, and modern history is seen as a fulfillment of ancient prophecy. 'Home', imagine extremist conspiracy theory adherents, is forever under siege, requiring defense against the plotting enemy. (Boym 2001: 43)

In depicting in spatial terms these competing visions of history and nationhood, *This Is England* powerfully realises the political potential of Meadows's non-specific and wilfully amalgamated presentation of real locations, and his stylised emphasis upon and transformation of quotidian English landscapes. The politics of *This Is England* is centred on a critique of the certainty that its title implies – England is shown not to be a place but an idea, one that is imagined, perpetually mutable and always contested, and thus Meadows's approach to realist space must be similarly uncertain. The decision to return to the characters and to breathe new life into the film through the television adaptations, however, raises questions on the sustainability of these strategies – and those of new realism more broadly – across media.

This Is England on TV

As David Rolinson and Faye Woods explain, the series was part of a wider revitalisation of Channel 4's drama output, following the cancellation of '*Big Brother* in 2010', which saw the channel drawing 'on the "quality" status legitimised by its filmic roots and British "auteur" [. . .]' to present an 'an "event serial" offering period drama with a twist'... and 'positioned within a discourse of quality drama' (Rolinson and Woods 2013: 187). Thus the 'quality' status accorded to the film, validated through its critical acclaim and award successes, creates the conditions for its transmedia expansion into television, in the process re-stating the heritage of Channel 4 as a producer of high-end drama which converges the realms of film and television. Initially, at least, the series therefore invites interpretation as a text which emerges directly from *This Is England*, a view explicitly propagated by Meadows himself:

> Not only did I want to take the story of the gang broader and deeper, I also saw in the experiences of the young in 1986 many resonances to now – recession, lack of jobs, sense of the world at a turning point. Whereas the film told part of the story, the TV serial will tell the rest. (Holmwood 2009)

Thus, for Meadows, the series presented an opportunity to move the narrative focus away from Shaun and to revive the political project enacted by the film, understood here as an attempt to reflect the parallels between the contemporary socio-economic situation and that which faced marginalised communities in the 1980s. Paul Dave seems to endorse Meadows's position, suggesting that the move to the serial format better enables the facilitation of the themes developed in the film:

> Formally, it seems appropriate that *This Is England* was followed not by a film sequel but two television series (*This Is England '86* [Channel 4, 2010] and *This Is England '88* [Channel 4, 2011]. The resultant dispersal of narrative agency across a collective cast and the opportunities for slower development of and response to events, alongside, of course, the unprepared for trauma of unforeseen violence and entrapment, help to capture central aspects of the social conditions of working-class existence, opening out the common culture visible in the film and detailing its relocation within the wider social forces pressing in on it. (Dave 2013: 758)

However, although the 'dispersal of narrative agency' does, as we have already discussed, enable a much-needed focus on a female character in the shape of

Lol, I want to argue here that these processes of 'dispersal' might be seen to dilute rather than actually broaden attention and 'agency'. If, as I have argued, the film's complex interrogation of nationhood is enabled by its collage-like and conspicuously symbolic treatment of location alongside its nuanced portrayal of the origins of Combo's and Shaun's racist nationalisms, the serials' necessary widening of focus and the narrative demands of its format naturally limits the potential for these themes to be developed further.

The opening moments of '86, however, do acknowledge explicitly the film. Hitherto unseen moments show Combo and Shaun together after the attack on Milky, with the older man telling Shaun, 'I let you down, didn't I?' We then see the young Shaun holding out his hand in the rain, and a match-cut to his hand reveals the older Shaun in school uniform, presumably now sixteen since we learn that he is undertaking his final CSE examination as the flashback ends. The serials' filmic preface might therefore be seen as an attempt in narrative terms to move on from the traumatic events of *This Is England*, and although Combo will return, and in '90 the consequences of his violence against Milky will be realised, the themes that evolve through the film are largely contained within this televisual tying up of loose ends. Accordingly, the rest of the episode is directed toward a re-induction of Shaun into the wider ensemble and the beginning of a process to foreground the individual characters of the group, no longer functioning as mechanisms to illuminate elements of Shaun's character development (as they were in the film). Thus there is an immediate focus on Woody and Lol's relationship, with Milky's role as a third party initiated by the end of the first episode, while Harvey (Michael Socha), a school bully in the film, is now seemingly a part of the gang and characters such as Gadget, Banjo and Meggy, previously members of Combo's gang, are re-initiated into the wider group in more obviously comedic roles – the generic shift from the film to the serials is thus felt immediately.

These invitations to suspend disbelief are significant in light of the film's relationship to the serial. The site of the group's reconnection to Shaun is a hospital, which they go to when Meggy has a heart attack at Woody and Lol's aborted wedding. When they are invited to Meggy's room they tell the doctor that they 'are all family', and the scenes in the hospital contain other galvanising moments such as a montage where the younger members of the gang race around the hospital corridors on wheelchairs to the Housemartins' track 'Happy Hour', released in 1986. In the next episode we will be re-introduced to Mr Sandhu, who performs a comedic Marlon Brando as Don Corleone impression when offering Shaun a job in his VHS job and, although he is later revealed to be in a relationship with Shaun's mum, Cynthia (Jo Hartley), a revelation that initially drives a rift between son and mother, Sandhu operates comfortably as ancillary role in the other episodes and is a permanent, albeit superficial, fixture in the following serials, operating as Shaun's step-dad and his mother's domestic companion. Effectively, then, we are asked to forget that as a thirteen-year-old, Shaun called Sandhu 'a fucking Paki bastard', that Meggy, now re-imagined as a comedy figure, attempted to defecate on the floor of his shop, and that Combo held a machete to his face and hurled violent threats at him amidst the sinister bluster of his white supremacist invective. In this way, the film's nuanced examination of the psychosocial constitution of violent nationalisms and its powerful interrogation of 'restorative nostalgia' is here re-cast and reduced to a narrative backdrop at best, and a contextual afterthought at worst. Indeed, the encounter that seemed to trigger Combo's violent outburst in *This Is England* (film, 2006), his conversation with and rejection by Lol, is in '88 revealed to have been based on a lie, and that despite what Lol said in the film, their night together was meaningful after all. In Caitlin Shaw's words, '[t]his self-adaptive moment reframes Combo's previous behaviour, smoothing over inconsistencies between his filmic and televisual representation' (Shaw 2015: 215). More broadly for Shaw, the serials' 'self-adaptive' relationship with their source text sees it 'reprise memorable elements from the film . . . to de-politicise them' (Ibid.: 216). Shaw goes on to identify the ways in which the serials – and this is clearly a consequence of the narrative dispersal – are more focused than the film on 'domestic issues: sexual abuse, the deaths of parents and sexual relationships' (Ibid.: 218), and that they are also driven by a series of crises: 'in '86 Woody is unable to commit to marrying Lol, Lol's sexually abusive father returns, raping her friend Trev (Danielle Watson) and attempting to rape her, and Lol murders her father. In '88 Lol is revealed to have given birth to Milky's child and attempts suicide' (Ibid.: 217) – we might add that in '90 the traumatic focus shifts to Kelly as the corrosive legacy of the sexual abuse continues. As Shaw continues, 'the excessive degree of trauma experienced by the serials' characters requires suspension of disbelief, as do over-the-top characters . . .' (Ibid.: 218). Shaw here cites Trudy (Hannah Walters), another implausible re-development of a character from the film, as Shaun's shoe-shop assistant becomes a comedic sexual predator who chases Gadget and is the mother to Meggy's illegitimate son. As Shaw argues, then, 'the saga's transmedial shift to television draws it generically closer to melodramatic genres like soap opera' (Ibid.: 218) and thus the dispersal of narrative and the process of adaptation work to effect a shift away from the looser formulation of the film.

The episodes of the serials tend to follow a defined structure: alternating moments of comedy; the foregrounding of the group in a musical montage which communicates communal harmony, such as the wheelchair race or the football match in episode two; a reference to and further development of the traumatic narratives, usually involving Lol, but transferred to Kelly in the third series; mournful montages often in slow motion and most commonly using a Ludovico Einaudi composition, in which characters from the episode are brought back together in light of its darker themes – in turn the episodes are bookended by relevant archive footage which works to historically locate, albeit superficially, the fictional narratives. While these strategies seem consistent with the first film, and with Meadows's oeuvre in general, when deployed consistently across the serials they undoubtedly come to represent a formula, one which is effective in maintaining the narrative dispersal across the ensemble while emphasising the narratively important moments of dramatic development, but which by its very nature contains and orders meaning, resisting the complexity and ambiguity of the film.

This generic transformation might in part be explained by Meadows's recruitment of new collaborators. His co-writer on all three serials is Jack Thorne, who had previously written for *Skins* and *Shameless*, and the director of the first two episodes is Tom Harper, who had previously worked with Thorne and, indeed, Turgoose, on the film *The Scouting Book for Boys* (2009) and had directed *Misfits* (2009–13) for Channel 4. Meadows therefore worked with figures who had experience in television and undoubtedly the features of the serials, both textually and in terms of their extra-textual branding, can be more productively read alongside those of their televisual counterpoints rather than the film made by Meadows or his new realist contemporaries. As Rolinson and Woods argue:

> However, the serials emerged in a period of 1980s revivalism, embraced by *Skins*' tendency towards constructing its cast's identities from reassemblages of past youth cultures, their promotion illustrating Drake's point that 'the styles of the past' can help texts to 'be branded and marketed to audiences' (Drake 2003: 183), here both the nostalgic Generation X-ers and the Millennials targeted by British youth television. The trailer's aesthetic brings connotations of the distinctive early trailers for *Skins*, in which bright lights pick out youthful bodies in darkened rooms of destructive hedonistic partying, while Woody's introductions also echo the Frank Gallagher voice-overs which open each *Shameless* episode. Thus it positions '86 as youthful, fun and decisively 'Channel Four'. (Rolinson and Woods 2013: 188)

This Is England, then, might be understood alongside texts such as *Shameless*, *Skins* and *Misfits* as exemplars of what Woods, in an article on the latter series, labels 'skewed social realism . . . threaded through with a strong comic voice and fondness for the fantastical' (Woods 2015: 230). Woods identifies some of the ways in which *Misfits* blends its embrace of 'the fantastical' with an engagement with 'social-realist visual codes' (Ibid.: 232), most readily identified in its use of brutalist architecture, more specifically the Thamesmead Estate in South East London. The estate, however, is never named and the characters' accents are varied so as to diffuse the possibility of regional specificity, thus creating a similar collage effect to that which is found in Meadows's work. For Woods, the flats are 'social-realist markers, connoting the gang's underclass status and potential – yet unrealised – threat' (Ibid.: 236). This generalised and generic landscape 'enhances the sense of ordinariness that grounds its elements of telefantasy or flights of surreal fancy, asserting these programmes' authenticity through their verisimilitude to the lived experience of viewers' (Ibid.: 239). While the *This Is England* serials are less consciously fantastical than the sci-fi inflected *Misfits*, we might argue that the comedic and melodramatic features already discussed are similarly grounded by a visual discourse which projects quotidian familiarity and constructs an illusion of lived experience. Woods, though, is also quick to point out the possible dangers in attempting to construct the poetic and universal from the real and specific:

> However, the telefantasy of *Misfits* disrupts the socio-cultural expectations imprinted in its concrete; the cinematography and production design construct the sprawling Thamesmead estate as a familiar yet unfamiliar world, a stylised social-realist space. (Ibid.: 240)

Woods rightly identifies the tension when real spaces, particularly spaces rich in complex socio-political and cultural histories, are mined for a generalised purpose, to in effect authenticate a fictional narrative. The use of Sheffield as a setting in *This Is England* presents similar questions. As mentioned earlier, the sense of *This Is England* as a transmedia narrative operating amongst and within a range of imaginary geographies is illustrated through the move from Nottingham to Sheffield across film to serial. This is not to say, however, that locations from the film are jettisoned entirely. For example, when Shaun falls out with his mother in '86 he returns to the seaside site of his solitary walks in the film, once more suggestive of an imagined landscape that enables its inhabitants to move freely from dense urban areas to seaside vistas. Similarly, in '90, Lol asserts that she wishes to have her wedding reception at the 'Miners Welfare Club': 'it means a lot to me', as she tells her unimpressed middle-class future in-laws, 'it's where my granddad used to drink', but the location of the club used in the episode is Conisborough, some fifteen miles from Sheffield, so again an imagined assemblage of regionalised, working-class space is constructed into an authentic narrative backdrop, one which converges multiple thematic and period-specific signifiers into a generic national space.

As I have suggested elsewhere in this chapter, the text's refusal to be grounded by a specific geographical and temporal framework is clearly a key ingredient of its universal resonance but, just as Woods points out in relation to Thamesmead, this strategy is rendered problematic when it comes into conflict with the very narratives that are woven into the real, pre-existing landscapes that the fictional texts occupy. This represents a fundamental issue of representation in realist practice more broadly, and the layering of real location and fictional narrative is particularly apparent in the serials.

Just as in *Misfits*, the *This Is England* serials exploit to great effect the presence of arresting modernist architecture, specifically Sheffield's Park Hill flats, seen as the one of the finest examples of post-war British Brutalism, and the huge Gleadless Valley estate. Gleadless Valley particularly is used extensively in the first series – it is the estate on which Woody and Lol live and houses the church which is used in the final episode to stage their (second) aborted wedding; moreover, the dramatic vistas the estate generates are used to punctuate the narrative throughout the serial, often after commercial breaks, and are put to particular effect in designating the changing of seasons in *This Is England '90*. In one sense, the prominence and continual re-assertion of these spaces as non-specific but paradoxically authentic markers of a particular kind of urban, and suburban, life function to support Meadows's stated political project, that is the ruefully nostalgic lines of continuity between the depicted past and the contemporary socio-political situation, and a nostalgic longing for a lost sense of community. This particular political impulse is aptly summarised by Owen Hatherley:

> What might be at work here is the common contemporary phenomenon of nostalgia for the future, a longing for the fragments of the half-hearted post-war attempt at building a new society, an attempt that lay in ruins by the time I was born. These remnants of social democracy can, at best, have the effect of critiquing the paucity of ambition and grotesque inequalities of the present. [...] The intriguing thing is that there are two real survivals in present-day Britain of the brief rush of Bevanite Socialism that followed the war: one, the National Health Service, is considered so sacrosanct that even while dismantling it, Tories or New Labour have had to pay it fulsome tributes. The other is the council blocks that still stand all over Britain's cities, monolithically making their point about its essential failure. (Hatherley 2009: 9)

Thus, in foregrounding these buildings as symbolic entities, as ruins of a lost future, Meadows realises their hauntological presence in our everyday lives – making visible the residual traces of the municipality in an increasingly privatised contemporary landscape. However, it is clear that in the serials the spaces do not only function in this way, but that they also evoke the specificity of their histories and their existence in the present tense of their filmed articulation.

Sheffield's proximity to the Peak District means that, more than any other city in Britain, it juxtaposes green space with residential housing, and its hilly topography means that arresting views, which draw into focus living space alongside more untamed landscapes, are common. The serials realise the visual potential of these landscapes through the aforementioned punctuation shots, which, in common with Meadows's work for the big screen, work to assert a sense of locational verisimilitude while also enabling a persistent lyricism. The best of Sheffield's housing developments themselves call upon the contrasting nature of landscapes, as Hatherley argues in his survey of the city's estates: 'Practically any view here provides you with a photogenic picture of either the cityscape or the Peak District, so you're always conscious of being in the presence of both a big city and an abundant countryside' (Hatherley 2011: 106).

Sheffield's best modern architecture thus exploits what is 'special' about Sheffield, and the serials similarly draw upon these 'photogenic' landscapes by repeatedly foregrounding an architecture that accentuates them, most notably the Gleadless Valley Estate. As Hatherley continues:

> Places like the Gleadless Valley, planned under Womersley at the same time as Park Hill; a bizarre and beautiful landscape, Bruno Taut's Berlin via Neutra's Los Angeles refracted through the English Picturesque. After 1945 many British architects and thinkers appropriated the idea of the Picturesque for Modernist purposes, under the influence of Nikolaus Pevsner's ideas about the 'Englishness of English Art'. Schemes like the Lansbury neighbourhood or the Alton East estate in London are the best known of this attempt to create a specifically English integration of architecture and landscape, but Gleadless shows the aesthetic at its most stunning, set in a dramatic natural landscape and with an equally dramatic abundance of parkland which is lush and planted rather than bleak and scrubby. (Hatherley 2011: 107)

Again, then, it is important to note that the architecture and the broader landscape with which it symbiotically operates are framed in terms of its extraordinary qualities. This is not merely a generic signifier of social housing; it is a visually arresting and significant example of a specific moment in the history of post-war Britain. Indeed, the serials seem to revel in the vistas produced by the estate's relationship with the rolling hills that surround it, and the contrasts between its sharp-edged modernism and the spectacular green space – we might think here of the shots of Lol pushing her daughter in a pram up the hill in at the start of '88 with the vast estate in the background, and soon after the same view being used to frame the weary Milky as he returns from working away, carrying an oversized teddy bear for the same child.

The Park Hill estate, which is located closer to the city centre, is similarly aestheticised, and plays a key role in '90 as the location of Gadget and Harvey's flat. Park Hill again carries with it a very specific heritage as an iconic example of post-war British architecture and, having been listed by English Heritage, is currently undergoing a significant re-development process, the first phase of which saw many of the flats repurposed as upmarket dwellings. While some social housing remains, the flats house local design businesses, a café-bar, an art gallery, and plans are afoot to convert a large section of the estate into private student accommodation. At the time of writing, then, this location has an ongoing narrative life, one that speaks to contemporary economic, political and social concerns. In episode three of '86 the group play football outside the flats – on the other side of the new development – and the flats later provide the backdrop for a comedy fight between the gang and Shaun's sportswear-clad, scooter-riding bullies, made all the more surreal by the involvement of The Stone Roses's Ian Brown playing a police officer. Thus, these architecturally arresting spaces are made conspicuous within the serials, which in turn invites the complex and layered socio-political histories to be interpreted – while they operate here as lyrical decoration of a collage of the past (the Park Hill sequence is layered with archive footage from England's 1986 football World Cup campaign), their depiction becomes entangled with their continued existence in the non-diegetic present.

As mentioned, the use of Park Hill flats in *This Is England '90* is particularly prominent. Towards the conclusion of the series, Shaun's photography course is empowering him – we see him listening attentively in a lecture about Henri Cartier-Bresson and the notion of 'the decisive moment', and the lecturer sends the students out to find their own moment. Shaun uses the assignment as an opportunity to cultivate his relationship with a female course mate, Juliette (Poppy Corby-Tuech), and they decide to work together. Shaun suggests as a location 'the flats, you know just behind the train station, the big high-rise ones' where his new friend has not been before, but Shaun assures her, 'it's nice up there. It looks really good on the camera and stuff'. There is much of significance here already. Shaun's role as a budding photographer and the parallels with Meadows's own journey into film-making (we might also think of Marek in *Somers Town* as another photographer avatar for Meadows); the lecture, which raises questions about the ethics of realism and reportage; and the attraction to the flats for what they look like, rather than what they represent (their residents, indeed, Shaun's friends). Moreover, Shaun's description of the flats is consistent with their actual location in Sheffield (the estate is behind the train station), and this rendering of the flats as a specific place rather than a generic location intersects with Meadows's imaginary geography. Shaun and his friend seem to thrive in their artistic engagement with the space, as he puts it: 'Look at the light around here. You can see straight through, it's so strange', until they are interrupted by a clearly distressed Gadget, who has just had an argument with Harvey after he found Kelly injecting heroin. Shaun breaks away from his assignment to help Gadget find the missing Kelly, and in this moment Meadows seems to self-consciously reveal the tension between

4.3   'It looks really good on the camera and stuff.'

the space as imagery and as an environment which contains within it complex, multiple narrative lives – a tension which underpins the treatment of location in the series more broadly.

There is perhaps a danger that in seeking to raise questions about the transformation of real locations into a collage of imagined geographies, I am informed too heavily by my own subjectivities: I live in Sheffield, almost exactly between Park Hill and Gleadless Valley, and my engagement with the estates' representation on screen in *This Is England* is indeed layered with my own personal narrative. Yet, I want to suggest that despite the texts' assertions of realist authenticity, which emerges from the performance of its characters, Meadows's mining of his own personal biography and the surface level quotidian referent, there is a tension inherent in their impressionistic use of actual locations – locations which contain specific, historicised and ongoing narratives. This tension exists precisely because of the subjectivities involved in interpreting a realist text; a text that invites us to reflect on and call upon our own lived experiences as resources for interpreting and inhabiting the narrative. To illustrate this point, I want to call upon Paul Mason's discussion of *This Is England '90* in *The Guardian*:

> In *TIE 90*, young people sit around on sofas in the daytime talking bullshit. They sit, they smoke, they watch TV, they indulge in prolonged and pointless conversations.

Nobody looks at their mobile phone because – as thousands of parents will have had to explain – there weren't any. Nobody goes on the internet because it didn't exist. Nobody flicks through movies and games on TV because, back then, the box beneath a TV was for playing tapes.

[...] That's not the only difference between now and 25 years ago. In 1990, intelligent twentysomethings sit around in the daytime because they are unemployed. Britain was in recession. Estates such Sheffield's Gleadless Valley, where the series is filmed, were as stark and poor as Meadows makes it look. There is no self-loathing, yet, among the spliffed-out youngsters. The estate is trashy but not yet dysfunctional. The precarious low-paid job has barely been invented – so people without work are still referred to as 'jobless' not 'welfare recipients'.

[...] A glance at the deprivation figures for the real Gleadless Valley (2013) reveals the legacy of this turnaround. According to Sheffield council: 'The entire population live in areas classed amongst the 10% most deprived areas in England.' Just under a third of children in the ward live in poverty. More than half the women booked in for childbirth are overweight or obese.

Lol and Woody, the couple at the centre of the series, would now be aged 45. Lol's a dinner lady in 1990 and Woody's on the dole. What they would be doing now depends on whether they have escaped Gleadless Valley estate. That was the issue for working-class kids in the first years of globalisation. Could you escape the trap that was opening up, and how would you do it?

So as we laugh at the hapless youngsters of *TIE 90*, and snicker at the analogue drabness of their world, let's remember. This is what it was like just before we got divided into the saved and damned: when you could still riot without a balaclava, walk into a jobcentre with your head held high, and when a whole family could – if it had to – live on the earnings of a dinner lady. (Mason 2015)

There is much to unpick here, and the first point to make is that like myself, Mason perhaps brings his own experiences of these locations to his analysis. Mason was a student in Sheffield in the 1980s and so his reading of the location in specific terms originates from his prior knowledge of it, given that there is no explicit mention of the city in the series. Secondly, Mason suggests that the series was filmed on Gleadless Valley, and then goes on to make a number of points which emerge from a specific engagement with that specific estate, drawing on its deprivation figures and using the data as an anchor for his speculative discussion of the fate Woody and Lol. Yet by '90, the couple have 'escaped' Gleadless Valley and live in a semi-detached house in the Lowedges suburb of Sheffield. Indeed no characters live in Gleadless Valley in '90; Gadget and Harvey, the unnamed TV watchers Mason is referring to, as we know, live in Park Hill. Thus, Mason's comprehension is here fundamentally mistaken. Yet the point of this is not merely to identify inaccuracies, but to reveal the ease with which Meadows's imagined geographies of 'anywhere, England' are not always evocative of a loosely ambiguous sense of place and time but can be redeployed as the basis for a highly place-specific analysis; for Mason, this is not only England, it is Sheffield. Here the realism of the text comes from Mason's engagement with its authentic and precise location. Mason's reading of the serial of course reveals his own politics: he has written extensively about the dangers and utopian possibilities of automation and the digital future, he is a fierce critic of 'neo-liberalism', and a vocal supporter of Jeremy Corbyn's leadership of the Labour Party, but the malleable landscapes and characters of '90 animate and give shape to Mason's politics, rather than the other way around. The points he uses to evidence his interpretation are not drawn from the text – there is no mention of Gadget's and Harvey's employment status, and there are no jobcentres, and no riots. Mason's analysis reveals the tensions inherent in the serials' attempt to balance multiple realisms. While the film seemed to deny the specificity of place to project a symbolic national body, the sheer repetitions of a *specific* kind of landscape in the serials – one which, to many, is iconic - has the effect of diluting the earlier film's assertive and politically coherent imagery.

With this in mind, I want to spend what remains of this chapter considering in more detail the ways in which the demands of the serial format affect the transfer of Meadows's particular brand of realism from film to television. At the start of this analysis of the serials, I suggested that the episodes maintain a repeated structural and aesthetic formula, one that enables the dispersal of narrative attention across multiple characters while superficially retaining traces of the source text. For example, '90 begins with Gadget, Shaun and Milky surreptitiously acquiring school dinners from Lol, Trev, Smell and Chrissy, with Gadget explaining the importance of school dinners to Milky in a moment of self-consciousness: 'it's about the nostalgia . . . it means having meals that we used to have when we were happy, when we were kids', with Milky eventually reassuring him, 'Don't worry, Gadge, them good times will come again'. This triggers a montage of archive footage (the Happy Mondays, The Stone Roses, Italia '90, the Iraq War), which works to situate the historical context of the film, yoked together by images of Margaret Thatcher leaving office soundtracked by The La's 'There She Goes'. The rest of the episode works to establish the changes in the characters' lives since the last instalment, and sets up the event which will bring the group back together, 'a Madchester thing at the town hall', which also works to assert the film's subcultural context and to connect it to the autobiographical element of the serial: 'that was a really important time in my life, with The Stone Roses kicking off', says Meadows

(Anonymous 2015). There are numerous comedic situations: a continuation of the school dinners jokes; Kelly pointing out the homoerotic subtext of Harvey and Gadget's fascination with wrestling; the re-introduction of Flip (Perry Fitzpatrick) and Higgy (Joe Dempsie), two larger than life characters who viewers first met as Sergio Tacchini-wearing bullies in '86, but who are now dressed in shell suits, stonewashed jeans and cowboy boots and listen to Def Leppard, conspicuously marking their difference from the central group; and at Woody's parents, an attempt by Mr Squires (William Travis), his former boss, to recruit him to his new business venture is framed in slapstick fashion when he explodes comically from a cupboard in the living room.

These moments are variously framed by the punctuation shots of the Sheffield landscape, re-orientating and situating the domestic narratives. The disco is largely shot in slow motion, as Meadows returns to one of his tried and tested devices to emphasise the group's togetherness and immersion in the music, specifically 'Fools Gold' by The Stone Roses. The sequence is interrupted by the activities of Flip and Higgy, as Flip has sex with a woman over a snooker table while she sniffs a bag of weed held in Higgy's hands. This apparently comedic scene is intercut with further slow motion montages, as if to convey both a contrast between the two subcultural groups that the two generic registers are attempting to balance. Indeed, in line with the formula, the episode's conclusion moves towards a more sombre tone. The night ends when the group fight with Smell's new boyfriend and his friends; it is another subcultural conflict, this time Goths versus Baggies, and this event triggers another montage. In line with the formula, and the film once more, this one is soundtracked by a Ludovico Einaudi piece and shows slow motion images of the gang smoking and chewing, coming down off their speed in Gadget's and Harvey's flat, and a bereft Shaun crying over Smell.

This pattern thus works to emphasise a persistent affirmation of the communal, the serial's comedic elements, and the suggestion of individual trauma that, as we have already discussed, binds the drama. However, as the series develops, the limitations of these strategies begin to reveal themselves. Just as the first episode is structured around a communal event, so too the second, set in 'Summer', operates. This time, Harvey, Gadget, Shaun, Trevor and Kelly attempt to find a rave, bump into Flip and Higgy along the way, and eventually come across a New Age gathering. These scenes are intercut with a barbecue at Woody and Lol's, attended by Milky, their children and Lol's mum and partner, amongst others. As the group come up on their 'E's, another montage ensues, but this time, rather than using a piece of music that is contemporary to the period, Meadows deploys a track by Evangelist, 'Never Feel This Young', released in 2015. Evangelist was Gavin Clark's final project before his death, with the critically acclaimed album released posthumously. Meadows said that Clark 'elevated my early work from student tat into something resembling art'

(Niven 2015), and the choice of phrasing is significant – Clark's music works in unison with Meadows's montages as an intrinsic element of his poetic transformation of otherwise mundane locations and settings, with *Somers Town* a particularly potent example. Here the music works like Einaudi's (tellingly Einaudi is a collaborator on this track) to de-historicise the setting and to suggest a tonal shift. This is confirmed through pivotal scenes involving Shaun and Kelly. The montage ceases when Shaun wanders into a caravan and encounters an older woman, taking a break from the dancing, Shaun begins to talk to her, and, full of the euphoria of his first Ecstasy experience remarks, 'Yeah, it's . . . It's special here, like, it's so different you know, to anything else.' Meadows then returns briefly to Woody and Lol's home, Woody and Milky are asleep, and Lol is attempting to wake her partner to discuss the prospect of Combo's impending return. We then return to the caravan, where the conversation turns to Shaun's father. Shaun begins speaking about him in a wave of emotional release, with the dialogue, and Shaun's delivery of it, appearing in an authentically stream of consciousness manner: 'Crying's not going to bring him back . . . But if he'd have seen me down here, you know, having the time of me life and sat here having fun . . . He'd be, like I say, he'd be sat there going, "Fucking, Shaun, love you to bits, mate."' It is the first time in this series that we have witnessed Shaun speaking of his father, and where previously the grief manifested itself in hatred and violence, there is now a sense of acceptance. Turgoose's performance feels improvised, the words flowing incoherently but with emphatic candour, as if to convey the intense emotional experience of Ecstasy. As Shaun begins to sob, the woman embraces him, and the camera, handheld, moves in further so that we dwell on Shaun's hands as strokes his new friend's back for comfort. Here, the duration of the take is key, just under three minutes, which accentuates the immersive intimacy of the moment. The scene relies on Turgoose 'playing himself', our broader knowledge of the relationship with the *This Is England* film, and on Meadows's willingness to suspend the stylised register in favour of a conspicuously raw aesthetic, which feels all the rarer for its placement here.

Indeed, after the scene, the montage is reinitiated with a different song by Evangelist, 'God Song', as the focus shifts to Kelly. Meadows adopts a jerky, out of focus aesthetic with jump cuts indicating her worsening state. She goes into a caravan with three men to smoke heroin and, in what is a harrowing scene, the men are at various points shown to be penetrating her while she appears heavily under the influence of drugs. Flash cuts of close ups of the other characters' eyes intercut the scenes, along with images of Mick and Chrissy having sex in '86 – this is not a memory that Kelly could possess and indeed, she will not learn that Mick raped Trev or that Lol killed him until the next episode. The scene therefore presents this moment of sexual abuse as thematically linked to those that haunt the serial. In the morning an emotional

Kelly tells Gadge, 'I'm a fucking slag', not recognising what she has endured as rape and revealing the extent of her internalised misogyny. As the family's revelations are revealed in the next episode, Kelly's drug dependency worsens and she cuts off ties from her friends, sister and mother, but at the end of '90, at Woody and Lol's wedding reception, she returns. She and Lol reconcile and it is revealed that Smell is no longer addicted to heroin:

> Lol: Are you still doing it?
> Kelly: No, I haven't done it for a few weeks now . . . It got to a bad place.
> Lol: Did it?
> Kelly: Yeah.
> Lol: Was you . . . just smoking it or was you injecting?
> Kelly: Might as well be honest . . . I just want to see a future with everybody.
> Lol: There is one, I promise you, Kell.

The two return to the room and Kelly is literally returned to the gang. Typically, another slow motion montage is deployed, re-establishing the group, with Einaudi's familiar piano score as accompaniment. Thus, Kelly's storyline is underdeveloped, despite the brutal representation of her sexual abuse and drug dependency, and once she leaves the gang the breadth of narrative dispersal is not sufficient to contain the complexity of her narrative.

This is not the only self-conscious reference to the series' representation of the past. While Gadge's 'nostalgia' comment might have seemed flippant, Combo's parole board speech at the start of episode three seems to be similarly designed to draw attention to a conscious sense of the series reaching its conclusion with a thematic tying of loose ends: 'You see, the past does matter. It kind of shapes the future, if we face it.' As the montage ends and the credits roll a title reads: 'In Memory of Gavin Clark 25.01.69–16.02.15', and another Gavin Clark song begins, his track with Toydrum titled 'I've got a Future', which hauntingly repeats the line 'I've got a future with you'. This moment is a reminder of Meadows's own embeddedness within the narrative, of the real trauma that exists outside of the text, of the relationships that have formed and strengthened over its eleven-year life, of the fiction's reliance on lived experience, and the intense emotional labour involved in the mining of personal histories for dramatic ends.

These moments bring forward the intrinsic features of Meadows's work: the symbiotic convergence of performance, dialogue, and *mise en scène* that are intuitively familiar, with a heavily conspicuous, but no less affecting willingness to heighten and re-contextualise these elements through music and montage. Through our analysis of the television dramas we have seen how the transition to seriality has curtailed the more nuanced examination of the dynamics between place and character that define Meadows's earlier work for the big screen, but taking a holistic view across his oeuvre, there is a clear formal and ethical commitment to realist practice in common with his new realist contemporaries. Just as Hopkins's repetitions, Hogg's heightened sound design and Arnold's visceral address similarly work to poeticise their subjects, Meadows is concerned fundamentally with a stylised approach to the representation of lived experience, one which affirms the lyrical potentials of everyday life. In this sense the new realist film-makers continue to be united by their shared poetic concern with depicting the often symbiotic and intersecting relationships between environment and identity.

5. CLIO BARNARD

If Shane Meadows, Andrea Arnold, Joanna Hogg and Duane Hopkins can be seen to share a commitment to the lyrical representation of national landscapes and the environments which shape and constitute their human subjects, then Clio Barnard, whose work to date comprises three feature films, pursues an analogous artistic project. Like Hopkins, her approach to *mise en scène* is accented through the repetition of leitmotifs which both build poetic rhythm and enable symbolic meaning, in a further example of image-led narration. Like Hogg, Barnard repeatedly places emphasis on elements of atmospheric sound, generating a conspicuous aural emphasis which adds texture to her highly formalised visual compositions; like Arnold, her films oscillate between sensory, visceral and painterly compositions to foreground an empathic engagement with character (both human and non-human) while interrogating the locations they inhabit; like Meadows, location is presented figuratively and is central to meaning making; and like all of her contemporaries, Barnard has used non-professionals in her work, not merely as authenticating agents of realism, but as resources of lived experience and rich personal narrative. More broadly, like all the film-makers we have discussed so far, Barnard pointedly positions her work as moving beyond an apparently conventional mode of realist practice towards a stylistic approach which is more pointedly ambiguous and which transcends the illusion of surface verisimilitude, as she claims:

I think I'm a bit suspicious of naturalism and realism [. . .] Life is complicated and doesn't really have neat storylines. There are always several different versions of a story you could tell at any one time, so it's more fractured and complicated than that. I think that's why I want to put the two together somehow: the artifice and the real. (Anonymous 2013b)

I have discussed already the ways in which critics and film-makers alike draw upon a conveniently homogenised understanding of the realist tradition as a discursive mechanism to illustrate difference or departure. Barnard is therefore not alone in seeking to trouble popular understandings of British realism, and yet it is possible to suggest that her films, in multiple, distinctive ways, work to realise its limitations and reframe its parameters. As we will see, her three features to date enter into critical dialogue with the illusion of realist truth telling, seek to frame poetically the landscape as a mechanism for understanding the very construction of our lived environment, and expand this project to position physical space as analogous to and in convergence with human trauma. Thus, on one hand, Barnard has carved out a distinctive niche within new realism as the film-maker who most explicitly engages with and self-consciously critiques realist form. On the other, this self-conscious use of style can also be seen as part of the wider project of new realism to subtly transform and re-contextualise that which is familiar and fundamental to the lived experience.

For example, throughout this book I have drawn upon Doreen Massey's work to help conceptualise the ways in which the new realists' accented approach to everyday imagery enables a complex engagement with space as textured, evolving and formed of multiple layers. Perhaps more than any other element, it is the poetic rendering of landscape that defines the broad tendency of new realism. Indeed, just as her contemporaries do, Barnard recognises 'that 'society' is both 'temporal and spatial' (Massey 2005: 27). As we will see, space in Barnard's films is thus never presented as fixed or static but is instead revealed to be formed of multiple, often conflicting narratives – through the juxtaposed generic intertexts of *The Arbor*, the post-industrial vistas of *The Selfish Giant* that reveal the corrosive presence of the past, and the precarious and exploited internal and external landscapes of *Dark River*, the lived environment is both disturbingly authentic and presented as mutable and lyrically charged. This is where the poetics of new realism are most clearly in operation – in simultaneously marrying the familiar with the lyrical and in the process enabling a critical engagement with the everyday.

Barnard's particular interest in form might be partially understood by means of an awareness of her background as a visual artist. Having grown up in Otley, West Yorkshire, close to Bradford (the setting of her first two features), she studied art across multiple institutions and moved gradually towards film as her medium of choice. Barnard produced pieces for galleries such as MoMA and the Tate Modern, and was, until her feature film work, best known for the experimental short *Random Acts of Intimacy* (2002). The film involved Barnard in interviewing people talking about their experiences of sex with strangers before bringing the recordings together as a set of narratives and having various actors lip-synch the aural fragments. Barnard described the process as 'a rather laborious way of experimenting with a technique in which the sound is verbatim, but the images are constructed' (O'Hagan 2013), but the film reveals Barnard's interest in the limitations of linear realist practice and the artistic possibilities of conceptualising narrative construction as a process of layering multiple and often discordant sounds and images.

This technique was re-imagined and expanded more than a decade later to stunning effect in the shape of Barnard's feature film debut *The Arbor* (2010). In a sign of Barnard's position somewhere between the gallery and the cinema, the film was co-produced by, amongst others, the arts body Artangel, notable for their support of artists producing installations and site-specific works, and the now defunct UK Film Council, and the film's poetic energy emerges from the combination of its arresting formal strategies and its compelling narrative arc. The film centres on the Brafferton Arbor in Bradford (part of the wider Buttershaw Estate) where the late writer Andrea Dunbar lived. Barnard recorded multiple interviews with Barnard's friends and family, most notably, her daughters, Lorraine and Lisa, to form an aural narrative thread which works to unite the film's disparate and multiple elements: actors playing Andrea's family members and lip-synching the audio recordings; a restaging of *The Arbor*, Dunbar's debut play (which was performed at the Royal Court Theatre in 1980, directed by Max Stafford-Clark) using actors in contemporary dress and staged on the estate; reconstructions of multiple scenes from Dunbar's life; footage from numerous BBC documentaries, most notably an *Arena* profile of the young writer; and fragments from the play *A State Affair* (2000), written by Robin Soans, which returned to the estate ten years after Andrea's death. The film therefore represents a collage of narratively and aesthetically conflicting fragments which converge to present a fractured but deeply affecting portrait of Dunbar's life and death at the age of twenty-nine, and the tragedy of Lorraine's life. We learn that Andrea's first-born daughter Lorraine (from a relationship with abusive ex-partner Yousuf) slipped into drug abuse and prostitution after the death of her mother and, in 2007, was convicted of manslaughter following the death from a Methadone overdose of her two-year-old son, Harris.

Following the critical success of *The Arbor*, Barnard stayed in Bradford to direct *The Selfish Giant*. The film explores the relationship between teenage best friends Arbor (Conner Chapman) and Swifty (Shaun Thomas). Both face significant problems: Arbor suffers with attention deficit disorder, his brother is a drug addict, and he struggles at school, while Swifty lives in poverty with his large family, with his mother and father staving off loan sharks. Both, however, are blessed with talents: Arbor's entrepreneurial zeal brings the pair into contact with scrap merchant, Kitten (Sean Gilder), and the two earn money scrapping around their local area, while Swifty is shown to have a gift with animals, riding and caring for Kitten's horses. The film reaches a tragic peak when Swifty and Arbor are electrocuted, having been sent on the precarious mission by Kitten to extract high voltage wires. Swifty is killed and Arbor, while unharmed, is left utterly devastated. Ultimately, Kitten is arrested and the film ends with Arbor tending to one of the horses Swifty had so deeply cared for.

The inspiration for *The Selfish Giant* came from local characters Barnard met while making her first feature, and accordingly the film is laden with intertextual allusions to *The Arbor* and its myriad narrative layers. Such allusions include the central character's place-specific name; the fact that Swifty's mother is played by Siobhan Finneran (Rita in *Rita, Sue and Bob Too* [Alan Clarke, 1987]), which was scripted by Dunbar); and the naming of Kitten after Lorraine's abusive ex-partner in *The Arbor*. More broadly, just as *The Arbor* engages in a kind of critical engagement with realist traditions, so too *The Selfish Giant*'s close relationship to *Kes* (Ken Loach, 1969), enables a self-reflexive element within the film which sits alongside its markedly lyrical treatment of external space. These elements will be returned to in greater detail later, but it is important to acknowledge here the way in which Barnard's films, while formally distinct from one another, operate on an associative level and are yoked together intertextually by geographical and narrative referents.

While set some twenty miles north of Bradford and starring established actors rather than lesser known performers and non-professionals, such as those deployed in *The Selfish Giant*, Barnard's most recent film *Dark River* can be viewed similarly as a companion piece. The film, a loose adaptation of Rose Tremain's novel *Trespass* (2010), is centred on Alice (Ruth Wilson), who returns to the farm on which she grew up following the death of her father (Sean Bean). Here she finds her brother Joe (Mark Stanley), who is angry and depressed and has turned to alcohol to numb the pain of his father's death. The farm itself has gone to ruin, and Alice sets about restoring it and plans to take ownership of the lease. During her time on the farm she is haunted by the memories of abuse that she received at the hands of her father, Richard, and the film equates her traumatic memories with the landscape itself, while the economic pressure that Joe comes under opens up broader questions of land ownership and exploitation. In this sense *Dark River*'s examination of gendered abuse and trauma, and its intricate and multi-layered examination of space as it is lived and experienced, sees it work symbiotically with Barnard's other features to further illustrate the new realist preoccupation with the intersecting relationships of environment and identity. Indeed, Barnard's three films reveal differing threads of realist practice: the neo-Brechtian formal experiments of *The Arbor*, the poetic landscape-driven lyricism of *The Selfish Giant*, and the memory poetics of *Dark River*, bound together by recurrent thematic concerns.

Barnard's films can be seen to occupy a distinctive but harmonious position within the conceptual spaces of new realism. However, one area in which we might productively seek to disturb this cohesion is through her approach to place. In the last chapter we discussed the complexities inherent in Meadows's construction of non-specific landscapes, of forming collages of real space which function paradoxically to appear as both universal and authentic. This is in marked contrast to Barnard's approach, which marks specific locations as central to the political and aesthetic dimensions of her films. Barnard's films might occupy a Northern, cultural geographical terrain, but this is not a patch-work of regional iconographies, it is rather a sustained, intimate and carefully articulated representation of named landscapes which contain defined but multilayered narratives – thus, *The Arbor* might be seen to function as a sphere of interlinking, increasingly local narrative spaces: the North, Yorkshire, West Yorkshire, Bradford, Buttershaw, Brafferton Arbor.

In his work on the cultural construction of the English North, Philip Dodd invokes the notion of a 'Lowryscape' (Dodd 1990: 17), inspired by the famous Salford painter who produced stylised landscapes of the industrial working-class in Manchester. Here 'the North is less a number of particular places with specific histories than a Lowryscape, a settled place with an agreed iconography' (Ibid.). It is clear that in Barnard's films, space is not 'settled', rather it is contested and mutable, playing host to multiple and often discordant and evolving narratives and memories, and her rejection of the 'Lowryscape' in favour of geographical specificity clearly enables pointed explorations of the relationships between environment and identity. In rejecting the homogenising discourse of the North, Barnard's films can be seen to move beyond the estab-lished conventions of regional representation and, more broadly, the reduction of Northern narratives to limiting, parochial aesthetics.

To momentarily consider the popular traditions of Northern working-class writing established in the 1950s and 1960s, Dave Russell suggests that such representations were similarly generic and they were 'little concerned with much of the daily texture of northern life and did not engage at any significant level with regionally distinctive topography, labour relationships, workplace practices or any of the other standard concerns of earlier northern fiction' (Russell 2004: 93). These novels and plays, and the films that followed them, therefore tended towards a non-specific engagement with space and loca-tion which can be seen as formative in shaping a narrow Northern regional imaginary that is still prevalent today. This is an example of what Rob Shields calls 'social spatialisation' where particular iconographies are bound together to form a 'spatial mythology' that organises 'the attitudes, institutionalised arrangements, and practices' associated with regional space (Shields 1991: 207). This is particularly significant in relation to the English North, where the 'space myth' operates to identify the region with particular forms of class-bound stereotypes, contrasting the North indelibly and regressively against the economically prosperous South of England. Shields, building from Higson (1984), describes the way in which the films of the British New Wave capitalise on and further construct this space myth through the tendency towards 'typically a panoramic view over a town, sometimes with a contrasting foreground object . . . blurred by industrial smoke, with the camera focused on the far horizon, past the town itself' (Ibid.: 216). That these landscapes are in most cases wilfully non-specific – often functioning as lyrical interludes in films which are located in amalgamated, generic Northern towns and cities – further indicates the importance of the palimpsest in constructing iconographic Northern spaces. As Shields argues, 'far from being "realist", these shots are entirely selective and *conventionalistic* in that they do not challenge commonsensical, "folksy", categorisations of the region, thereby framing and presenting a one-sided vision of the "North"' (Ibid.: 218). For Shields, these generalised 'Northern towns' are spectacular but emptied, distant and alien townscapes, 'like the commanding panoramas of a general's view over a field of battle: the audience is given a view from a position of spatial power and authority' (Ibid.: 185). Here, a correlation is drawn between the non-specific townscape and its dulling of regional distinctiveness, and the exertion of authorial, spectatorial and subsequently political power in the process of spatialisation – power that is organised and maintained through the continual narration of space myths.

In her survey of the cultural and geographical construction of the English North through film and television, Ewa Mazierska describes the 'discursive power' of 'the South over the North', that which grants the 'authority to tell stories about this region' (Mazierska 2017: 3). This is significant for Barnard because it is against this historical and contemporary backdrop that her highly specific cinematic landscapes assert themselves as distinctive, breaking away from the more conservative elements of a particular strain of Northern place-making in cultural texts associated with the realist tradition and with the region more broadly. This spatial power can also be seen to intersect with modes of gendered aesthetics. Just as we explored the ways in which Andrea Arnold's embodied accounts of female agency worked to dislodge monolithic and masculine organisations of space, so too can we situate Barnard's representation of the North as countering the patriarchal poetics of the Northern space myth – with its alienated male protagonists projecting their existentialism onto monolithic Lowryscapes. To this end, Sue Thornham's work on Arnold is also relevant to Barnard, with Thornham seeing Arnold working against the realist traditions of a '"mastery of aesthetics"', one that 'serves to authenticate a masculine narrative, which in turn, in its repetition through successive realist movements, becomes the history of British cinema' (Thornham 2016a: 137). In occupying and countering these established iconographies, Barnard, like Arnold, reformulates this 'gendering of time and space' (Ibid.: 149).

THE ARBOR (2010)

The Arbor's geographical specificity, its formal self-reflexivity, its privileging of women's voices, and its pointed examination of a working-class realist storyteller whose creative output and personal trajectory differed wildly from her largely male forebears and contemporaries, are therefore all factors that work to position Barnard's first feature as operating against the normative structures mentioned above. As Beth Johnson argues, 'the landscape of Buttershaw and its residents are made visible in Barnard's film, taking their place as important textures and layers of meaning' (Johnson 2016: 280). Here then, specificity is not merely an authenticating aesthetic enterprise – rather, the marriage of locational verisimilitude and narrative texture enables the depiction of an 'emotional history' which combines 'the multiple voices . . . and the sociopolitical and geographically specific landscapes of Buttershaw' (Ibid.: 288). A temporally layered appreciation of the multiple histories that emerges from the focus on playwright Andrea Dunbar is here examined and interrogated alongside a nuanced engagement with the deterministic relationship between location and identity, binding the politics of the personal and the public. As Johnson continues:

> This destructive pattern of addiction was clearly linked not only to the heart of the struggles of these troubled women but also, and more specifically perhaps, to the site-specific reasons for it, connected directly to the spaces and places of social exclusion that had such a direct impact on their lives. (Ibid.: 284)

The engagement with a specific landscape, and with its attendant histories, alongside a radically conspicuous approach to form therefore enables both an exploration of the socio-economic life of the estate, and a richly textured focus on Dunbar and her family. The film therefore presents fragments about Dunbar, her family and her wider community which are anchored by a sense of specified and documented place and testimony but which are radically disconnected from an organising narrative authority. This marks a departure from the conventional approaches to such subjects mentioned earlier, as Barnard herself seeks to disrupt realist traditions:

Housing estates and the people who live there are usually represented on a film in the tradition of Social Realism, a working method that aims to deny construct [. . .] I wanted to confront expectations about how a particular group of people are represented by subverting the form. (Wood and Haydyn Smith 2015: 45)

Again then, just as we have seen from many of the other film-makers explored in this book, Barnard seeks to disassociate herself from earlier traditions of realist practice.

For Sophie Mayer, the film combines 'social realism and contemporary verbatim theatre' to produce 'a very particular, strongly feminist mode of British realist cinema' (Mayer 2015: 86). Through these means, the film's formal and generic collage of 'theatre and film, documentary and fiction, literary and vernacular' (Ibid.) means that it counters the kinds of gendered modes of representation which we have already discussed. This exploration of the politics of representation can also be seen to be triggered at the level of the film's subject matter. As Alison Peirse argues, Dunbar spoke 'for herself and her own experiences, distinct from (and uninterested in) the male, middle-class voices dominating the landscape of Northern social realism' (Peirse 2015: 2). The very act of seeking to represent Dunbar's life by critically re-assessing the modes of representation that she herself departed from in her own work, works to draw attention to and reawaken Dunbar's vital legacy as a working-class artist whose take on realist subject matter was utterly original, as Peirse emphasises:

When faced with the North, poverty and estates, framed within a social realist aesthetic, the critics knew what to expect, having witnessed the politically fiery, engaged work of Ken Loach and Tony Garnett, or the bleak desperation of Alan Bleasdale's *Boys From the Blackstuff* (1982). Yet *Rita* rejected much of the moralising, dignity and commentary on inequality (the 'have and have-nots' as Dunbar puts it) usually found in these dramas. (Ibid.: 9)

Peirse here refers to the critical reception of Dunbar's play, *Rita, Sue, and Bob Too*, adapted for the screen in 1987, just two years before Dunbar's premature death. The film was directed by Alan Clarke, whose particular mode of visceral and self-conscious realism has, as we have already seen, played a formative role in the development of new realism. However, in this case it is possible to view the adaptation through the lens of Barnard's critique of social realism in *The Arbor* – her melding of Andrea's already indistinguishable private and public worlds calling attention to the film as a further example of the way in which her narrative was continually processed and occupied by others. Indeed, examining the later film's cyclical account of the tragic lives of both Andrea and later Lorraine, reveals, for Johnson, the 'male dominance of the past' (Johnson 2016: 285). Both women's lives are controlled by fathers, variously defective or absent, lovers and abusers. The exploitation of Dunbar's creative labour thus microcosmically reveals the extent to which particular modes of representation work to exclude those on the margins, and in this case the corrosive wounds of gender and class exploitation visibly intersect across the film's multiple intertexts.

In calling attention to the contested narratives of Dunbar's life, *The Arbor* remaps histories of class, aesthetics and gender in the English North that had previously been embedded in more conservative modes and traditions of representation. This process has evolved in the form of Adelle Stripe's novel *Black Teeth and a Brilliant Smile* (2017), a work of creative non-fiction which invokes intersecting narrative voices and draws on multiple sources to tell the story of Dunbar's tragic life as an imagined autobiography. Stripe combines an italicised first-person narrative with a third-person mode conveying dialogue, albeit without speech marks, and deploying free indirect discourse. In this sense Stripe's approach can be seen as a literary analogue to Barnard's cinematic rendering of multiple modes to frame, construct and represent Dunbar's life, continuing the radically self-aware realist project initiated in the film and stretching it across mediums. Indeed, it is significant that Stripe also draws on *Rita, Sue, and Bob Too* as an intertext, to illustrate the extent of Dunbar's gendered disempowerment. The first-person register imagines the pressure Dunbar might have experienced from those in her own community, including her father, as a result of the film:

> *When I think about all that money I feel sick. Paddy in the pub thinks I'm in the money now. Keep telling him, I don't get that money you know, it's to make the film. But try telling him that. He keeps asking me to buy him a drink. The whole of Buttershaw wants me to buy their drinks. They treat me different now, since the film crew arrived and since it all appeared in the paper. Dad said I'll do a Viv Nicholson and blow it all on fur coats and cruises. He reckons I'll end up back on the Arbor no matter what happens.* (Stripe 2017: 134)

The intimate immediacy of the present-tense address is filtered through our retrospective knowledge of Dunbar's tragic fate, working associatively with screen representations of Dunbar's life, such as *The Arbor* and *Rita, Sue, and Bob Too*, to enable an engagement with a narrative which paradoxically feels both distanced and immersive. For example, as the chapter unfolds, Stripe alternates the register to convey the unhappy process of the film's production on the Brafferton Arbor:

You write the script. Give it to the production company. They change it. Make it better. Add bits. Then you get paid. We add more. Take bits away. Then we shoot. And even after that we change it again. It gets butchered in the edit.

Alan gestured with his hands, holding both of his palms towards the light.

I don't fucking care what you say. This is *my* script. I wrote it. My story. Not yours. Not anybody else's.

The anger began to rise in Andrea's voice.

That's not in dispute, he said. We know it's *your* story. But film is a different form to theatre. You've already done your part of the deal.

Thought I could trust you. I've seen what you're doing. You won't let me onto the fucking set, and you come in here, throwing your weight around. And now you're changing the ending. You've made Rita and Sue look like a right pair of slags.

Her face turned pink as the fury strangled her.

Andrea, have you ever seen my films? Gritty social realism is my middle fucking name, he said. I've spent the last ten years of my life making films about the working-class, *my class*. (Stripe 2017: 137)

Stripe makes explicit the connections – developed through Barnard's self-conscious approach to form in *The Arbor* and as observed by Peirse – between social realism, authorship, gender and power. Here Stripe presents Dunbar's creative labour as pervasive and fundamental to her very existence, and subsequently exploitable – her work, itself an embodiment of her geographical and social identity, is here literally taken over. Moreover, like Barnard, Stripe's use of contesting voices and discrete and distinct narrative registers exposes the limitations of realism as understood as a privileged mode of truth telling or as enabling the authority of a single story, rather than realism as a layered process which combines multiple subjectivities. Indeed, the Clarke character effectively positions his reality, 'social realism is my middle fucking name', hierarchically against Dunbar's, 'This is *my* script. I wrote it. My story. Not yours. Not anybody else's.' Stripe's and Dunbar's projects both therefore draw on and reveal the limitations of historically established realist forms, illustrating their role in the reductive categorisation of Dunbar's creative output and labour and opening up a critical process of re-evaluation – indeed, we have identified Stripe's novel as emerging from Barnard's film as evidence of this evolving relationship. The imagined debate between Dunbar and Clarke here enables critical reflection on the historical construction of the male auteur and discourses of authenticity and authorship in British film, television and theatre history, and invites us to again read Dunbar's life as shaped by men, both professionally and personally. As Katie Beswick argues, Stripe's novel – and,

I would also add, Barnard's film – enable the development of an alternative history of creative labour:

> The novel usefully downplays Stafford-Clark's pivotal role in discovering and nurturing Dunbar, positioning Liane Aukin and Kay Mellor as key figures in the playwright's development and, in doing so, questioning the gendered 'star-maker' narrative that surrounds figures like Stafford-Clark and affords them such power.
> [...]
> Stripe's novel also makes a useful postpositivist argument, actively playing with and drawing attention to the researcher's role as a creator of history. This point is especially pertinent given Dunbar's position as a working class woman, her untimely death and the role of middle-class white men such as Stafford-Clark in acting as gatekeepers of her legacy. (Beswick 2018: 2)

We might read the exchange between Clarke and Dunbar in Stripe's novel as similarly making visible the unavoidable presence of the 'gatekeeper' as a form of embedded power in Dunbar's story and those countless others that it represents. As we have already seen, Barnard's film can also be seen to render this, with the multiple voices and visual and aural sources – the documentaries and news footage of Dunbar, and clips from Alan Clarke's film – illustrating yet also enacting formally the continual writing and re-writing of Dunbar's professional and personal narrative by those other than herself. Indeed, as Beswick suggests, Max Stafford-Clark, as the director who first brought Andrea's work to the Royal Court Theatre, might similarly be positioned as a 'gatekeeper'. Indeed, it is he who provides a lengthy introduction to the published edition of *A State Affair*, packaged by publisher Bloomsbury with the stage version of *Rita, Sue, and Bob Too*. Here, Stafford-Clark contextualises Dunbar's life and work and frames the two plays through the lens of his own creative role as a director. This is highly significant in light of recent events, where historic sexual abuse allegations emerged against Stafford-Clark in late 2017. The allegations coincided with a touring production of *Rita, Sue, and Bob Too* by Stafford-Clark's company, Out of Joint, and the decision was taken not to stage the play as a result of the controversy. However, following impassioned public debates, Vicky Featherstone, artistic director of the Royal Court, chose to reinstate the production:

> I have ... been rocked to the core by accusations of censorship and the banning of a working-class female voice. For that reason, I have invited the current Out of Joint production of *Rita, Sue and Bob Too* back to the Royal Court for its run. As a result of this helpful public debate we are

now confident that the context with which Andrea Dunbar's play will be viewed will be an invitation for new conversations. (Featherstone 2017)

Tellingly, Stripe herself intervened in the public exchanges following the initial decision, and it is not too far-fetched to suggest that works like *The Arbor* and *Black Teeth and a Brilliant Smile*, in rendering the process by which working-class lives are both dramatised and exploited in the service of particular traditions of art and culture, nurture a landscape in which texts such as *Rita, Sue, and Bob Too* can be received and engaged with in the way that Featherstone suggests.

Stafford-Clark of course is also present in *The Arbor* but his is just one of many disembodied voices and testimonies in the film, with none ever projecting a sense of authority or stability over the narrative(s). He is introduced when Lorraine watches the *Arena* documentary in her prison cell. Barnard alternates between the television operating diegetically – as Lorraine views it on her television set – with shots where the documentary consumes the frame and is unmoored from this context. When the documentary introduces Stafford-Clark, rather than continuing the footage to reveal his actual body, Dunbar switches register, cutting to the actor Danny Webb mouthing Stafford-Clark's words. Tellingly, Webb also plays the drunken and abusive father in the version of the *The Arbor* that is re-staged throughout the film, and this instance of double casting of course further calls to attention the insidious presence of patriarchal forces in Dunbar's overlapping personal and professional worlds. Stafford-Clark tells us 'at that point she was staying in a battered wives home in Keighley . . . 'course she'd never been out of Yorkshire before . . . never been in a theatre . . .'. The last line signals a cut to an image of Andrea from the *Arena* documentary walking through her estate with Lorraine in a pram, and we hear her voice: 'nowadays people want to face up to what's actually happening . . . cos it's actually what's said . . . and you write what's said . . . you don't lie, and say, aw, it dint happen when it did all the time.' We then see Dunbar, smoking, watching rehearsals at the Royal Court, before we return to the estate in the present day with a close shot of 'The Girl' (Natalie Gavin), Andrea's avatar in the play *The Arbor*. 'The Girl' looks directly at the camera and lip-synchs Andrea's voice, taken from the *Arena* documentary: '*The Arbor*, by Andrea Dunbar'. This short sequence thus concerns itself with multiple elements of Andrea's story: her realist practice and its apparent authenticity, her lack of control over her own narrative, the mediating presence of Stafford-Clark, the Royal Court and the layers of power that represent the Brafferton Arbor as a physical and symbolic space, and the play as both historically situated and re-imagined in the contemporary moment, as if to gently displace Andrea's own claims to ownership and authenticity.

Following an extract of the play as it is performed on the estate, Andrea's voice-over – describing her relationship with the play's protagonist – for the *Arena* documentary returns: 'She's like me more than not. I wrote more or less about my feelings.' There is then a cut to an image of the estate from the documentary. The shot appears to be taken from a car window and moves across the recreation ground as we hear Andrea's voice: 'I called the play *The Arbor* because the street I lived on is called Brafferton Arbor, it's always known as The Arbor, and a lot of these things actually happened on the street.' Dunbar's words are accompanied by an instrumental soundtrack distinct from the *Arena* footage that serves to subtly re-contextualise the footage so that it is not presented solely as an extract but as another fragment in the film's collage. Indeed, the footage shows dogs running wildly along the grass, and a second shot lingers on piles of rubbish and household detritus strewn across the field. These archive images directly reference the close shots of the grass and of dogs sniffing at rubbish, including drugs paraphernalia, in the film's opening; these images precede the introductory title: 'Bradford, West Yorkshire'. Moreover, the presence of the dogs is also a feature of those other representations of Dunbar's life and career, that intersect with *The Arbor*. Adelle Stripe's novel frequently mentions their ubiquitous presence on the estate: 'one of the things she didn't miss about Buttershaw was the dogs'; '*1981. Back on Buttershaw. More kids than before. Dogs. Dogs. Dogs.*' (Stripe 2017:103); and Stafford-Clark's aforementioned introduction describes how 'A pack of abandoned and feral dogs roamed the centre of the Brafferton Arbor, the crescent on which Andrea lived' (Stafford-Clark 2000: 1). The last moments of the archive footage conjoin with Lisa's voice-over as she describes the same space through the lens of her own childhood memories: 'a pen thing in the middle . . . full of glass and people having bonfires on the field'. Barnard then cuts to a frontal shot of Christine Bottomley (the actress playing Lisa) lip-synching Lisa's words in front of the space as it exists in the film's present day. As she recounts her memory, Barnard cuts to a tracking shot of the field, as children play on it, an echo of the earlier scene from the *Arena* documentary.

Taken collectively, these scenes illustrate the ways in which the film is able to hold together and integrate multiple visual and aural sources in a manner which at once invites critical awareness and engagement with the construction of narrative and the limitations of the linear models of realist representation, while presenting these seemingly disparate elements in a highly integrated fashion, as Cecília Mello argues:

> the editing employed is far removed from a rapid or fragmented style; rather, it gently interweaves the different intermedial strands as if composing a mosaic. Hence the impossibility of solving this film's paradox by either saying that it introduces fictional elements into a documentary or that it brings the 'document' (such as interviews, letters and television/

film footage) into fiction. The vague impression one has when confronted with its heterogeneous structure is that *The Arbor* cannot be defined in or against these terms. Documentary is no longer the opposite of fiction, and fiction no longer the opposite of documentary, just as cinema is neither the same nor the opposite of other media. (Mello 2016: 119)

This collapsing of generic and formal parameters and the construction of a 'mosaic' of modes of memory, testimony, archival footage, re-enactment and theatre does, Mello goes on to argue, see the film responding to an 'anti-naturalist' tradition of realist critiques 'akin to Brecht's Epic theatre' (Ibid.: 124). This is particularly significant in relation to the place of *The Arbor* within discourses of new realism, given the ways – discussed at the outset – in which such approaches have traditionally been used to service arguments against realist traditions. However, Mello also observes that rather than reject the process of character identification and absorption, the 'mosaic' structure of *The Arbor* enables 'a heightened level of intimacy, which seems to draw the spectator in closer to the stories being recalled' (Ibid.: 114). More specifically, Mello argues that while

the interviews ... appear to embrace distanciation, they in fact go one step further by combining it with emotion, for while their constructed nature is exposed, putting the spectator into a critical thus distanced position in relation to what is being told, they never seem to lose their emotional power, enhanced by the use of a less intrusive medium (the sound recorder) and by the inescapable direct gaze at the camera, sustained by the actors. (Ibid.: 123)

This suggests that rather than efface realism's empathic qualities, *The Arbor* heightens them, with the lip-synching strategies in particular working to locate the audience in a specific and knowable relationship with its modes of address, albeit one which presents conflicting accounts of lived experience and reality. Thus, while Barnard challenges the notion of a single, authoritative mode of truth-telling, *The Arbor* is not merely a critique of realism's limitations – rather, it realises its potentials.

If the film can be seen as a 'mosaic' of realisms, the presence of the Brafferton Arbor in the present moment might be understood as occupying its core. It is the space that holds together the multiple testimonies, that stages the play, that facilitates the recreations, and it is the means by which Lorraine and Lisa share the frame and convey their conflicting memories. Crucially, it is also the location that asserts the film's contemporaneity and provides its quotidian universality. As Peirse notes, the 'staging' of the play on the 'street, the pavements, the bricks and mortar' sees 'the residents all become living

5.1   Real spaces and real lives in *The Arbor*.

embodiments of Dunbar's life' (Peirse 2015: 5), yet the estate and its residents, as Peirse also argues, can be viewed as '"social actors": real people, in their usual environments, behaving (more or less) as they would do without the presence of cameras' (Ibid.: 6). So, while these real spaces and real lives work to situate and contextualise Dunbar's work, they also move beyond the film's immediate narrative demands to acknowledge the presence of indeterminate parallel stories that are similarly located within this location and those like it.

For example, early on in the film Lorraine reflects on her mother's parenting style and implies that Andrea failed to acknowledge the sexual abuse Lorraine suffered as a child. Manjinder Virk is shown lip-synching Lorraine's words in a side-on shot, with the door open as she sits on the stairs. The lip-synching then ceases and is replaced by voice-over as the camera moves gently out: 'can I forgive her? If she was alive today, I'd have a lot to say to her. One of the reasons I hated her is because I couldn't tell her exactly how I felt as a child and the way she brought me up, so no I can't forgive her.' As the voice-over ends the camera pans away from the figure in the doorway and atmospheric sounds fill the gap left by Lorraine's voice. We hear a dog bark, children in the distance, and the hum of traffic, while alongside this the camera continues its movement away from Lorraine's narrative to survey the textures of the pebble-dash wall, and then a fence, and then rests on the identical rows of houses in the street. The whole shot lasts one minute and nine seconds, with the images and sound following the end of Lorraine's voice-over taking up fifteen seconds, to conspicuously evoke a perceptual grounding of the Brafferton Arbor as a real, continuously evolving space; as the site of Andrea's, Lorraine's and Lisa's stories, but of many others, too.

THE SELFISH GIANT (2013)

As mentioned at the outset, if *The Arbor* is rich in intertextual citations and layers of realist narratives unfolding and both pulling against and complementing each other, *The Selfish Giant* draws on the earlier film as a direct reference point, as well as more obviously its loose origins in Oscar Wilde's children's story of the same name. Indeed, *The Selfish Giant* can be seen as another narrative to develop from the Brafferton Arbor in a further affirmation of Barnard's multilayered treatment of the location. As she explains:

> When I was making *The Arbor*, I got to know a lot of kids – one boy in particular called Mattie. I felt frustrated that I didn't have an on-the-ground understanding of what people's lives were like in that situation. That's why I wanted to go back and make another film there. (Sarhimaa 2014)

As we have already discussed, the sense of parallel narrative lives and realities alongside the Dunbars' is felt in *The Arbor*'s subtly expressive use of the estate to restage the play and to facilitate and situate the characters' memories as they unfold, and Mattie's story – emerging as it does from the literal margins of the estate used as a film set – can be understood as one more thread in the film's tapestry. However, while the films can be seen to function in a complementary relationship with each other, *The Selfish Giant* is clearly a more conventional film than its forebear, as Barnard argues:

> Those formal techniques in the *The Arbor* were critiquing the notion of realism and authenticity. That was the reason I used them, to say there's always a gap between what's reality and what's a presentation of it. In a way, with *The Selfish Giant* I embraced the language of realism. But I still don't believe in it. That's why I wanted it to be a fable. [. . .] in *The Selfish Giant*, I kind of accepted an existing form and worked within it. (Sarhimaa 2014)

Barnard therefore explicitly acknowledges the limitations of the realist form as she interprets it here, but also recognises that there are mechanisms for formal experimentation 'within' the form itself. Here, Barnard describes the self-conscious evocation of the fable, for example, with its historical emphasis and fairy tale qualities, and we will go on to discuss the ways in which the film's engagement with its filmic intertext, in the form of *Kes*, operates. Moreover, the sense that realism might offer further possibilities for manipulation can be felt in Barnard's discussion of her collaboration with the director of photography Mike Eley:

> I wanted naturalism – realism but with an edge of something that alluded to the fable, a subtle edge of something more transcendent. What Mike achieved was beyond what I had hoped for; particularly the shots in the power station, of the cooling towers and the sheep in the mist. (Wood and Haydyn-Smith 2015: 49)

What is particularly important about this insight is that Barnard explicitly identifies the film's use of landscape as those moments that go beyond 'straight' realism and enable poetic contemplation. This 'something more transcendent' brings us again to the fundamental tenets of new realism, with Barnard herself arguing for a style that brings into focus and/or transforms that which is familiar.

In the case of *The Selfish Giant*, then, while Arbor and Swifty's narrative arc – from their initial prosperity, Arbor's corruption, Swifty's tragic death and Arbor's subsequent redemption – follows a familiar pattern, these elements are deployed within a broader, more contemplative aesthetic in which the actions of the characters are repeatedly contextualised by the landscape shots. Typically, these shots depict semi-rural, edgeland spaces, conspicuously foregrounding pylons and a disused power station. While these spaces are narratively significant, since it is the pylons that cause the electrocution incident that kills Swifty, their presentation, again to borrow from Barnard, sees them 'transcend' these functions. Indeed, there are in total twenty-five of these landscape shots. They are mostly static, and range from eight to eighteen seconds in length, and frequently they are presented in groups of two or three, with their frequency and duration asserting their importance. The images are accompanied by atmospheric sound – combining wind, birdsong and the sounds of other animals, and frequently, in the case of the pylon shots, the hum of electricity – alongside Harry Escott's ambient score. Their stillness also functions rhythmically as a counterpoint to the often-frenetic dialogue-led scenes. For example, the film opens with a fourteen-second-long take at night, with horses in a field and a row of pylons in the distance; Barnard then cuts to a four-shot sequence from under Arbor's bed as he screams and smashes his fists against the frame, during what we later learn is an episode relating to his attention deficit disorder. A few scenes later, when Arbor (Connor Chapman) and Swifty (Shaun Thomas) take some cable to Kitten's (Sean Gilder) scrapyard to sell, Barnard shows the workings of the scrapyard – with the cable being stripped – in a series of short and close one- and two-second shots, before cutting to three seemingly unrelated shots of horses in a field with the sounds of distant wind chimes, birdsong and the sound of the grass against the breeze, lasting seven, eight and eight seconds respectively. The shots therefore work to create a pattern of imagery that runs through the film and works both against and in response to the scenes involving its human subjects.

We might think, too, of the scene where Swifty's father sells the family sofa, offering a vivid insight into the poverty-line experience of his family, where this is followed by two long takes of the cooling towers in the morning mist, while in the second shot the sheep graze in front of the towers and cars can be heard in the distance. Again, the shots' sustained duration (twelve and eighteen seconds) forces attention onto the atmospheric elements and the striking poetic qualities of the image. In a later scene at the scrapyard, Swifty is shown stroking and gently pacifying the horse, Diesel, after frenzied handheld shots show Kitten's failed attempts to calm the startled animal. This moment of tenderness, illustrating Swifty's talents and emotional intelligence, is followed by three shots of the pylons at dusk, taken from various angles, beginning wide and distant before moving closer to the structures. The first shot lasts ten seconds, as does the second, and the third eight, again fostering a rhythmic quality while also inviting the images to be 'read' and contemplated. Indeed, sound is key in presenting the images as textured, with the currents of electricity particularly audible. The shots are therefore referencing the narrative content in a direct sense – here we might think of them as foreshadowing Swifty's death – and they are fostering a rhythmic dialogue with what comes before and after, effectively pacing the film's lyricism, but they also contain within them the possibility of interpretation through the film's broader thematic framework. Thus, while Stella Hockenhull is right to suggest that the landscape shots in the film provide a 'lyrical interlude' (Hockenhull 2017: 125), they should be seen to go beyond the level of punctuation because of their repeated foregrounding and deployment. Indeed, for Barnard, they are absolutely central to the film's meaning making:

> Landscape is really important in the film. I was interested in liminal places and liminal people – places that are in a state of flux. I wanted to explore the threshold between urban and rural, not industrial or agricultural, but forgotten and undervalued places – just as teenagers are in a state of flux between being children and adults. As well as referencing the past with the horse-drawn vehicles, I also see the film as a vision of the future. The disused power station is a redundant place, the remnants of an unsustainable diminishing resource that made a few people very rich but which became increasingly inaccessible to those with little. It's also Arbor and Swifty's territory, a place where they can get away from the pressure of home and school – a place where they can come of age. I find the pylons,

5.2   The yoking together of past, present and future tenses.

the cooling towers and substations very beautiful – they are giants in the landscape. They are also the viaducts of tomorrow – the remnants from today of an industrial past. (Wood and Haydyn-Smith 2015: 48)

There is much to discuss here. Again, in line with the new realist film-makers we have already explored, the sustained nature of poetic landscape shots is seen as evoking the notion of space as lived and experienced rather than as static and pictorial. In this case, Barnard invites contemplation of the landscapes' multiple temporalities – their yoking together of past, present and future tenses – to enable her lyrical examination of the post-industrial North and its exploitation by capital. The poetic placement of the shots asserts their multifaceted function within the film, and the ubiquitous nature of the images – familiar as they are across the landscapes of Britain – forces reflection on the lived experiences of our own environments, and their narrative construction. Moreover, this presentation of landscape as malleable and layered returns, albeit in subtler forms, to the site-specific poetics of *The Arbor*.

Throughout this book I have sought to identify the importance of image-led narration in new realist films, where, through a variety of means, our attention is drawn to specifically visual motifs drawn from quotidian *mise en scène* that enable a lyrical contemplation of the films' themes. Here, Barnard's landscape shots can be seen as absolutely typical of this poetic tendency. The pylons and cooling towers are both examples of the *The Selfish Giant*'s rhyming patterns – repeated and self-contained distillations of the film's political concerns –

rich in layers of symbolic significance. These structures of figurative meaning and sheer spectacle are also grounded and given resonance by a sense of the mundane and the familiar: the everyday poetics that underpin new realist films.

These compositions are not the only visual leitmotifs in the film. If the film's politics is asserted at least in part through the landscape shots, then its emotional core is inculcated through the visual thread of Swifty and Arbor's hand-holding. The depth of their friendship is represented non-verbally throughout the film, and we might think of the moment where they pick up a discarded pram (for scrap purposes) while walking through a dilapidated shopping precinct with a large mural bearing the word 'LOVE' in the background, or of the two-shot sequence when they play on a trampoline, with the second shot a thirty-five-second take showing them laughing and holding a hammer they have found. The length of the take and the absence of narratively significant information forces attention onto the body, particularly the connection of their hands. This motif has already been signalled at the outset in the aforementioned scene under the bed, when it is Swifty who manages to calm and then rouse the seemingly unhinged Arbor, the latter's submission to his friend signalled by a close shot of their hands clasped together. In the shocking moment when the boys are electrocuted, their hands are again shown clasped together. Following the rush of electrical charge, Barnard cuts to a sixteen-second shot of the horse against the backdrop of the cooling towers, and there is then a ten-second shot of the night sky, followed by three shorter takes (eight, six and five seconds respectively), a twelve-second take of the cooling towers and the horse at dusk before a return to the boys, with a fifteen-second long take of Arbor holding Swifty's blackened hand. Here, *The Selfish Giant*'s key motifs converge with one another at its most crucial point to lyrically draw together the film's political and personal dimensions. The hand-holding motif returns at the film's conclusion when, in a repetition of the earlier scene of Arbor under the bed, the grief-stricken child is visited by a vision of his best friend, who returns to once more hold his hand. Again, Barnard emphasises and forces attention onto touch, with the final shot of this sequence a twenty-five-second-long take with the hand-holding its focus. This is therefore another of Barnard's rhyming patterns, with the film's beginning, ending and its climactic moment anchored by a non-verbal motif.

Like many of the films I have discussed, *The Selfish Giant* deploys highly formalised visual and aural motifs to inculcate its particular thematic emphases, with these often drawn from the sphere of the ubiquitous and the quotidian, both acknowledging and poeticising familiar landscapes, gestures and sensory experiences. It is no surprise then that when seeking to engage with the emerging traditions of new realism, critics have read Barnard in line with film-makers such as Andrea Arnold. As mentioned in the chapter on Arnold, Clive Nwonka's critique of new realism is centred around a concern that its poetic approach blunts the potential for a critical engagement with the class system. Nwonka's reading of *Fish Tank* is complemented by an analysis of *The Selfish Giant*, which he sees as representing an 'implicitly fatalistic and uncritical . . . naturalism' that does not arrive at any 'political understanding of Bradford's social world' (Nwonka 2014: 216). Nwonka wants *The Selfish Giant* to 'locate its polemic in a visual confrontation with contemporary forms of capital', but instead sees Arnold's and Barnard's films 'as comfortable in the mode of representation for the working class through sentimentality' (Ibid.: 217), in a restatement of the familiar, Brechtian-inspired criticism of realism's presentation of socio-inequality as always already naturalised. As I argued earlier, the poetic impulse of *Fish Tank* emerges through its highly immersive, subjective engagement with Mia – this is itself a deeply political act, and we should defend Barnard's film on similar grounds. It is her lyrical engagement with the spaces of Bradford and with Swifty and Arbor that generates an image-led exploration of the ways in which social inequality and alienated labour are written into the landscapes of the post-industrial North. It is clear that Barnard is not failing at confronting directly the causes of, for example, Swifty's poverty, because she is not attempting such a critique in the first place. The film's politics are present, as we have discussed, but they are wilfully non-prescriptive and open to interpretation. As Barnard herself argues, it is perhaps unfair to expect a realist text to have a direct political impact:

> It's unlikely that a film like *The Selfish Giant* would lead to direct changes in policy. I think its themes are too broad for that. There would need to be a huge shift in ideology to be able to say it had had a direct effect. [. . .]
> If I were optimistic, I would say we are in a state of flux and that Arbor and Swifty are showing us the way forward. We need a societal coming of age where we understand what we stand to lose if we continue with this ideology of greed. (Wood and Haydyn-Smith 2015: 50)

Nwonka's criticisms of the apparent political failings of *The Selfish Giant* and *Fish Tank* are based partly on a comparison with Ken Loach's more obviously avowed thematic intentions, comparing Barnard's film to *Kes* (1969), and suggesting that the former falls short because

> the very political ambivalence of Barnard's Bradford means very few visual signifiers emerge to demonstrate an ideological correlation to Ken Loach to root the story in political reality – that is, an antagonistic relationship between the social structure and the protagonists that determines their life choice and behaviour. (Nwonka 2014: 215)

Nwonka's wider argument represents a further positioning of new realism against a paradigmatic mode of politically committed Loachian realism.

In seeking to understand *The Selfish Giant*'s position within new realism it is worth interrogating these critiques further. Indeed, as we have argued already, while *The Arbor* can be seen to be explicitly formed as a 'mosaic' of intertexts, Barnard's second film retains a subtler sense of self-consciousness born from its intertextual dialogue with *The Arbor, Rita, Sue, and Bob Too,* and *Kes*. Indeed, although the focus is on two boys rather than one, the comparisons with Loach's film are multiple and wide-ranging. They include Swifty's nurturing craft, expertise and emotional depth that is born from his bond with an animal; a critique of an overly mechanistic model of a capitalist education system which lacks the creativity and compassion to nurture the unconventional literacies possessed by boys like *Kes*'s Billy Casper (David Bradley), Swifty and Arbor; an unsympathetic depiction of a bullying brother and of toxic masculinities more broadly; a tragic ending which equates the suffering of animals with the loss of social and political hope; and a striking treatment of landscape which seeks to make visual the politics of labour and exploitation. Barnard has explicitly acknowledged her indebtedness to the earlier film, talking of how, in preparation for *The Selfish Giant*, she 'watched realist fables' such as '*The Bicycle Thieves, The Apple, Kes*, and *The Kid with a Bike*' (Wood and Haydyn Smith 2015: 51) with her children, while Sean Gilder, who plays Kitten, describes the film as '*Kes* for the twenty-first century' (O'Hagan 2013). Much of the structural analysis apparent in *Kes* comes from its engagement with Billy's education: the film shows him being bullied and ridiculed by his teachers and classmates, and he is shown to be disengaged and barely literate in class. It is only when he learns about and then finds the confidence to speak about falconry that Billy finds a voice, as the film's writer Barry Hines put it: 'That's what *Kes* is about really – about the fact that Billy Casper's not supposed to be clever, he's not done well at school, but when he gets involved in something, then you get a sense of what his potential could be' (Bhula 1999: n.p.). Hines, himself a former teacher, positions the school as the site for the film's class politics – as the bridge between the emotionally tender portrait of Billy and a wider analysis of what his story means in social terms. Hines's comments on what '*Kes* is about' are echoed in Barnard's discussion of how education functions in her own film: 'I wanted people to understand his [Arbor's] value because he's being written off, in a way, by the education system. What I'm saying is: don't write him off, he's got these incredible qualities' (Sarhimaa 2014). In both films, school is shown as an inhumane, judgemental institution which fails its most challenging pupils. Arbor is excluded and his mother is told that 'mainstream education' is not the right place for her son, after Swifty and Arbor fight with bullies who make fun of Swifty's poverty. When a similar incident occurs in *Kes*, the one caring and nurturing teacher, Mr Farthing (Colin Welland), comes to Billy's aid and uses the incident to make arrangements with Billy to observe his falconry up close.

Barnard's vision of school is altogether more hopeless, however, and there is no such redemptive figure in 2013.

We first see Arbor at school when he is administered his medication by a burly teaching assistant. Barnard holds the static shot for forty seconds, which emphasises the oppressive nature of the setting – the corridor in which the scene takes place feels more like a prison than a school. As Jonathan Romney argues, continuing the comparison with *Kes*:

> The school here may not be as mechanically soul-destroying as Billy's, but for all the liberalism it espouses there's an antiseptic, bureaucratic deadness about its shiny corridors, while cheerful placards in the classroom urging 'Be Positive' come across as empty sloganeering. And the school does, after all, entirely give up on the boys. (Romney 2013)

In drawing similarly on the school as a microcosm of an unjust society, *The Selfish Giant* redeploys *Kes*'s themes in the present tense, and arguably draws even bleaker conclusions than Loach and Hines. As Romney suggests, while someone at least believed in Billy, the same cannot be said for Swifty and Arbor. Indeed, in place of Mr Farthing is Kitten, an exploitative boss whose interest in the children is purely instrumental, in another example of the ways in which *The Selfish Giant* might be viewed as a fable of neoliberalism. Indeed, to evoke *Kes* once more, we might say the symbolic presence of the pit in Loach's film portrays a working-class community which still offered work to its citizens, and, as Romney argues, Kitten's scrapyard can similarly be read figuratively to reflect the economic and social conditions of its setting:

> Kitten's yard embodies the malaise of a dismantled industrial society in which nothing new is made but everything is available to be picked, stolen, scavenged: a selfish economy in which everything is potentially worth a bob or two (the theme gets a sourly comic spin when the father of Arbor's best friend Swifty sells his sofa from right under his numerous children). (Ibid. 2013)

Just as in *Kes*, then, the landscape poetically renders the film's politics. We might think, for example, of Billy reading his *Dandy* comic against the vast backdrop of the pit in a similar way to the boys dragging their horse and cart to Kitten's scrapyard, monetising the detritus of consumer culture – these images graphically render location as illustrative of the particular socio-economic context in which the children's narratives unfold.

As we have already discussed, the heavy emphasis on the edgeland compositions of the cooling towers, pylons and animals works similarly to foster an image-led engagement with the politics of the landscape, one which draws together multiple intersecting narratives of past, present and future, of town and country. As Romney argues, the film is 'as much a study of the porous boundary between town and country as *Kes* was', identifying 'an extraordinary shot late in the film of a landscape that bears the marks of post-industrial disuse, the land and vegetation taking on the look of fatigued, rusted metal, evocative of the inert mineralisation afflicting a world once organic' (Romney 2013). Indeed, to turn again to Hines and Loach, we can similarly locate a repeated emphasis on an accented and textured approach to the landscapes of semi-rural Barnsley as one of the central mechanisms of making meaning in *Kes*, as Barry Hines explains: 'In the village where I lived, the miners walked to work across meadows, with skylarks singing overhead, before crowding into the cage at the pit top and plunging into the darkness' (Hines 1999: 200). Hines placed the contradictions of the working-class landscape at the centre of his work, and the evocation of a natural environment of both liberation and containment is, as I have argued elsewhere, a key feature of *Kes*, with its 'poetic evocation of an in-between space – at once romantic, imaginative, rural, and industrial, layered with social, political and economic narrative' (Forrest and Vice 2017: 26). As Romney implies, this is a project that can equally be discerned from Barnard's own poetic strategies, albeit one that is updated to reflect the more uncertain ecological, economic and social climate of the twenty-first century.

These comparisons are particularly significant because they reveal the historical continuities between the poetic strategies adopted by Loach and Hines and those deployed by Barnard. In the process, we see the limitations of those critiques which seek to valorise the political efficacy of one iteration of realist practice over another and reveal instead the porous thresholds of apparently fixed traditions of realism in Britain. If one of the threads that connects the poetic realism of *Kes* to *The Selfish Giant* is the rendering of landscape as both a political and emotional canvas, then we might suggest that this also runs through Barnard's oeuvre in its own right, one that holds together her multiple and diverse forays into realism(s).

Dark River (2017)

As mentioned previously, *Dark River* differs from Barnard's other two films because of its move away from Bradford, and because of the absence of unknown or untrained actors. However, as I have suggested, its multifaceted treatment of setting further develops the aesthetic projects of *The Arbor* and *The Selfish Giant*. Indeed, the focus on a rural location intensifies Barnard's examination of landscape as layered, and often contradictory:

We have a romantic notion of the countryside and now large sections of land are earmarked 'rural idyll' and visitors, or those fleeing big cities, have an idealised view of it. But there's a bit they don't want to see and that's where *Dark River* is set. (Anonymous 2018a)

Barnard's 'rural realism' might therefore be understood as part of a wider critique of popular representations of the countryside which seek both to naturalise and gloss over its inherent power dynamics and perpetuate a myth of the rural landscape as pictorially fixed and temporally static. Making the distinction between 'rural cinema' and 'heritage cinema', both Paul Newland, and Catherine Fowler and Gillian Helfield in separate studies examine the ways in which rural locations are depicted on film. Newland suggests that, rather than presenting the countryside as 'spectacle', rural cinema tends to explore in more dynamic and nuanced ways 'the relationship between the lands and its inhabitants, and how this relationship develops in terms of a merging of physical and social landscapes' (Newland 2016: 12). As we have already seen, the concept of 'merging' in and of the landscape is central to the poetic and political projects of Barnard's earlier work – in *Dark River* we can add the psychological realm as an intersecting sphere. Indeed, Fowler and Helfield similarly remark on the way rural cinema establishes a textured relationship between 'lands and inhabitant', but suggest, too, that 'another key element of the rural landscape is its emotive, nostalgic power as an idealized space and community – the land imagined or remembered as a dream and that finds its most visceral evocation through the imagery of earth and sand and flesh and bone' (Fowler and Helfield 2006: 6).

As Fowler and Helfield also argue, 'the rural tends to be less an expression of venerability than of vulnerability: the rural inhabitants [. . .] occupy the lowest rung on the socio-economic ladder of the surrounding nation' (Ibid.: 5), and in this sense Barnard's expansion of her landscape project from the edgelands to the countryside also provides another means of addressing questions of class politics. Indeed, the film's central dramatic tension comes from Alice's and Joe's claims on the land following their father's death, their failed attempts to make the farm economically viable, and the looming presence of a water company that is seeking to exploit their precarious situation and buy the tenancy. Barnard has observed the way in which

> [t]he countryside has been gentrified now and those tenancies are insecure. All the assets belong to landowners and it's pretty impossible to make a living . . . All the tenant farmers I met were lorry drivers too to have a second income. So as well as being about politics of the body – how Alice was treated as she grew up – *Dark River* is also about politics of the land too. (Anonymous 2018a)

Here, then, an explicit and uncomfortable connection is made between Alice's traumatic return to the farm as site of childhood abuse and the farm itself as a symbol of the economic precariousness and exploitation that afflicts the rural working classes.

For example, in the first part of the film, Alice (Ruth Wilson) is shown in a coastal location, working as a sheep shearer. While there she tells a man, who appears to be a romantic partner, that her father has died and that 'he promised the farm to me'. Then there is a cut to her father coming to the door, silently, then a close shot of Alice's face as she shuts her eyes, and then a wide long shot of the cliffs, the sound of the wind highly conspicuous, before a closer shot of Alice against the sea. There is then a cut to a rural Yorkshire landscape, and the next shot is in what appears to be the farmhouse. The camera moves towards a dilapidated dresser in a deserted room, picking out photographs of the family. These early moments illustrate how editing, sound and *mise en scène* will operate as the mechanisms by which Barnard will bind the external and internal environments of her protagonist, and more specifically will seek to represent her trauma. Her arrival is accompanied by the track 'An Acre of Land', written and performed especially for the film by PJ Harvey and described by Barnard as 'a children's rhyme' that 'hints at a corrupted childhood. I hope it makes people think of land ownership, and land as a commodity' (Anonymous 2018b). Alice's Land Rover Defender is shown in three external long shots moving through pylon-laden landscapes (a visual nod to the landscape poetics of *The Selfish Giant*), and a fourth then shows Alice's vehicle moving towards the farm, before we move into the car with an over the shoulder shot. Alice then gets out of the car and we share a spectacular point-of-view shot of her surroundings, before two shots taken from amongst the grass give a sense of the texture and feeling of the landscape, rather than just its visual qualities. Alice is then shown smiling as she shuts the gate, which is followed by three more environmental shots: two of sheep in the field, and one of a rabbit, as the music fades. Here the frequency and volume of the aerial shots work to further emphasise their meaning making qualities, just as in *The Selfish Giant*.

As Alice approaches the house, the wind appears more prominent on the soundscape, as another point-of-view shot is deployed, this time showing a washing line with overalls hanging on it, and suddenly the loud external sound is muted and replaced by childhood laughter – the presence of Joe's overalls has, it is suggested, triggered this memory of childhood. As Alice then moves around the house the sound becomes distorted, and the wind in particular is manipulated to produce an unpleasant atonal noise – here a feature of the external environment is transformed through allusion to the character's internal realm and the house itself becomes a subjective landscape. We then see another image of Alice's father, which prompts her to leave the house. There

5.3   Layers of landscape and memory in *Dark River*.

follows an abrupt cut to the young Alice (Esme Creed-Miles) submerged under water. She then surfaces with a teenage boy and a match cut moves to Alice in the present-time narrative swimming at Janet's Foss waterfall. Here the match cut works to bridge the past memory with the present experience. Three external long shots then show Alice at night walking across the moorland, before she is then shown arriving at the house. Alice is again greeted by a vision of her father, as he gets into bed with the young Alice. Again, sound is heavily distorted, and breath, as a sensory evocation of the trauma, is made emphatic on the soundtrack. Another match cut takes us from the young Alice to Alice in present time, as she lies in bed, with the sound of the sheep moving in the grass soundtracking the scene.

These devices are used throughout the film to reveal the porousness of the external and internal realms and the emotional and political themes they represent, with distortions of sound, the repetition of landscape shots, the visual and aural flashbacks of the father and of childhood scenes signalled by match cuts which connect memory to place and/or sense. Just as in Barnard's previous films, then, *Dark River* draws on a highly structured, formalised mode of realist poetics. For example, the repeated shots of doorways, and of the crack of light under the door from the corridor and Alice's childhood bedroom, work to generate a lyrical emphasis on the notion of the threshold which might similarly be called upon in the scene where Joe (Mark Stanley) talks about selling the tenancy with the representative of the water company. Here, the open door between them divides the chaotic internal space and the spectacular but vast and imposing landscape beyond it, and the importance of the motif is made explicit when an angry Joe responds to Alice's claims that she can save the farm: 'How's it ever gonna work? You're scared every time you set foot in the fucking door.' These recurring symbolic patterns can be seen to work in much the same way as the hand-holding shots and the images of the pylons and cooling towers in *The Selfish Giant*; as quotidian spaces and gestures that assert a sense of external verisimilitude, and that are utilised symbolically to emphasise broader themes. This is perhaps more acute in *Dark River*, which draws on the notion that one's outer setting both informs and can be seen to represent one's inner, emotional life, with the house physically housing, and therefore releasing when its doors are opened, Alice's memories of abuse. For Barnard, then, the film's examination of external and physical pain, of traumatised landscapes and bodies, is necessarily delivered through stylistic means.

To support her research for the film, Barnard was awarded a £30,000 Wellcome Trust fellowship to work with medical and scientific specialists on memory and trauma, since, as she describes, she was particularly interested in 'PTSD and intrusive memories', arguing that in 'film-making, these are visual intrusive memories, but in reality it's mostly audio and sense memory, often without the context – so a lot of work with people suffering from PTSD is putting those traumatic memories into a context' (Anonymous 2018b). Here, then, Barnard explicitly makes the case for a sensory, experiential realism, what Pamela Hutchinson calls the presentation of 'physical verisimilitude and psychological traces together on screen' (Hutchinson 2018). Thus, if new realist poetics can be defined through the films' accented explorations of the dynamics between environment and identity, Barnard can be seen to follow in this tradition, expanding its parameters to explore psychological realism. Indeed, just as Hogg's manipulated use of natural sound works to both situate her characters in authentic, shared locations and to draw out aspects of their emotional lives, so too Barnard uses sound to produce a highly textured sense of 'being there' in a locational sense and 'being with' in the psychological realm.

As I have argued, Barnard's films announce their artifice and probe the boundaries of form, and yet they are continually grounded by an authentic sense of place. This approach to location exerts heightened, poetic emphasis upon the sensory experience of the environment, on its symbolic significance in relation to questions of structural and identity politics, and as a mechanism to explore the inner states of her characters. Thus, while we can locate the distinctiveness of her films in their self-conscious and disruptive relationship with the formal parameters of apparently established realist conventions, it is the persistent examination of landscape poetics and politics that sees Barnard's work converge with that of her contemporaries.

CONCLUSION:
NEW REALISM IS DEAD,
LONG LIVE NEW REALISM?

As I write this conclusion, Shane Meadows's latest mini-series *The Virtues* (2019) has just premiered on Channel 4. It is now six years since he made a film for the screen, and thirteen years since *This Is England* confirmed him as a major figure in British cinema. Meadows, Danny Leigh observes, has 'upended the hierarchy that said directors must aspire to graduate from TV to film [. . .] reckoning . . . that television allowed him to make better work, for bigger audiences – in a medium with an established place for working-class talent' (Leigh 2018: 25). Meanwhile, the work of film-makers such as Steve McQueen, Andrew Haigh and Lynne Ramsay in Hollywood constitute what *Sight and Sound* last year labelled an 'Atlantic Drift' (Massa 2018: 26), whereby the favourable economic and creative conditions offered in the United States have seen British film-makers move away from domestic settings and subjects.

And yet, Joanna Hogg's latest film *The Souvenir* (2019) has just been released and, although executive-produced by Martin Scorsese, the film finds Hogg on familiar ground. It is perhaps her most directly autobiographical work and, as Guy Lodge tells us, Hogg's realist style is still palpable: '*The Souvenir* is as much a work of social realism as the more rawly styled kitchen-sink dramas of Ken Loach' (Lodge 2019).

Hogg then, like Barnard, maintains distinctive geographical, thematic and formal consistencies, which point to the enduring presence of new realism, and yet Hopkins has not made a film since *Bypass*, and, as we have seen, Meadows's and Arnold's artistic attentions have diversified significantly in the last decade. It is fair to say, too, that while new realism is felt deeply in films such as Hope Dickson Leach's *The Levelling* (2016) and Francis Lee's *God's Own Country* (2017), British contemporary cinema is undergoing a long overdue diversification, in terms of genre, authorship and subject matter. As Will Massa puts it, directors such as 'Shola Amoo (*A Moving Image*, 2016), Babak Anvari (*Under the Shadow*, 2016), Rungano Nyoni (*I Am Not a Witch*, 2017) and Sarmad Masud (*My Pure Land*, 2017)' represent a 'truly heterogenous talent pool' that 'may even help to usurp the long reign of the British poetic realists' (Massa 2018: 27). Massa's pitting of these film-makers against the 'poetic realists' recalls my discussion at the outset of this book about the ways in which cycles of film-making in Britain, specifically 'realisms', emerge in opposition to those which have come before. In the process of their formation, they each enshrine their predecessors as a *tradition* – that is, a coherent set of films that share particular tendencies, which can be connected to specific moments in history. Massa inadvertently confirms what I have been arguing throughout this book: that the films of Hopkins, Hogg, Arnold, Meadows, Barnard and others like them, while superficially disparate, taken together form a new tradition of realism that has defined itself apart from and against previous cycles of realist film-making, one that now might indeed be dispersing through other forms, approaches and emphases.

To enable a granular and sustained analysis of its specific formal qualities, this book has consciously avoided discussion of the institutional and production contexts out of which new realism emerges; however, it is at this point necessary to reflect briefly on the historical, industrial conditions that enabled its development. New realism's two most successful and prominent films, *Fish Tank* and *This Is England*, were in part supported by the UK Film Council's (UKFC) 'New Cinema Fund', described by Alan Parker (former UKFC chair) as 'for cutting edge films which were not expected to make a profit but actually were meant to encourage film-makers who didn't really fit into the normal commercial bag' (Doyle 2014: 134). The UKFC was closed in 2011, with the remit of the New Cinema Fund effectively taken on by the British Film Institute's (BFI) Film Fund, which has supported *The Selfish Giant*, *God's Own Country*, *American Honey* and *Dark River*, amongst others, and which similarly works to support projects which might not immediately show 'upfront commercial value', 'which take risks in form and content', and which reflect 'author and place . . . outside of London' (BFI: n.d.).

The case of Andrea Arnold is particularly illustrative of new realism's relationship with this specifically British funding environment. Her films have typified new realism's haptic aesthetic sensibilities, its attentiveness to the intersections of class with other spheres of identity, its lingering and wilfully oblique relationship with landscape, and its poetic indeterminacy, and they have all found support in part from first the UKFC and then the BFI, via funding streams which specifically invite film-makers to think beyond immediate commercial imperatives. Thus, Arnold's most recent feature film lasts 163 minutes, has a meandering seemingly aimless plot with no discernible conclusion, and contains a cast of largely unknown and non-professional actors, with the notable exceptions of Shia LaBeouf. *American Honey*'s realisation is the result of significant trust in Arnold's artistic vision, and that of her collaborators, and of an accompanying funding climate that supports and aligns with the particular strain of realism in which she operates.

The relative freedom that Arnold has been allowed in her film career in Britain stands in stark contrast with her recent experiences working in television in the United States. In a corrective to the perceived greener pastures of the 'Atlantic Drift' narrative, Arnold's work directing the second series of *Big Little Lies* (HBO 2017–) has been compromised severely. As Chris O'Falt puts it, 'the show was yanked away from Arnold, and creative control was handed over to executive producer and Season One director Jean-Marc Vallée' (O'Falt 2019). As Danny Leigh reports, 'it emerged that Arnold had been encouraged both to shoot as she saw fit and allowed to start her own edit in London before, predictably, her most distinctive sequences took the brunt of Vallée's cuts', suggesting a significant betrayal on the part of Vallée and the studio executives (Leigh 2019). The commercial machinery of 'quality television' is shown here to be altogether more hostile than the relative benevolence of British film culture, with Arnold's uncompromising realist style exploited as cachet for a highly marketed cultural product.

New realism has therefore flowered in part because of favourable institutional conditions, conditions that, on account of their specific remits and parameters, favoured a particular 'newness'; a distinction to what had come before. By definition, such conditions – taken alongside the lure of America and television – can be seen to work against the longevity of this particular tradition of contemporary cinema. Despite its continued, if dimming presence in British film culture, realism in its present form is finite.

New realism has elevated its everyday subjects through lyrical emphasis on ubiquitous landscapes, domestic interiors, familiar buildings, routines and habits. New realist films evoke the physical and perceptual conditions that constitute and frame our quotidian realities and render these visible and pronounced, and thus poetic. They make clear the political, emotional and cultural forces that shape and determine our lives, and stir the experiences and memories that we deploy to negotiate, interpret and consume them. Realism is no longer instrumental, it is no longer fixed to a specific effect or defined by a particular appearance, rather it provides a site for multiple reflections, inhabitations and contestations. Unmoored from its hitherto narrow confines, realism has become emotionally literate, poignantly and attentively representative of physical and sensory experience, empathetic, and intuitively, inclusively and excitingly ambiguous.

I have for the first time in this book spoken of new realism in the past tense, and yet this is not an elegy or a retrospective account of a fixed and now closed moment in time. New realism should be understood as having initiated a fundamental reshaping of the boundaries of British cinema beyond what was previously considered possible. Realism, so often understood in pejorative, reductive and monolithic terms, is now re-defined.

REFERENCES

Adams, Tim (2013), 'Interview: Joanna Hogg: "With each film, I go further into my dreams"', *The Guardian*, https://www.theguardian.com/film/2014/apr/13/joanna-hogg-film-further-dreams-exhibition-english-auteur (last accessed 3 March 2019).

Aitken, Ian (2001), *European Film Theory and Cinema*. Bloomington: Indiana University Press.

Aitken, Ian (2006), *Realist Film Theory and Cinema: The Nineteenth-Century Lukácsian and Intuitionist Realist Traditions*. Manchester: Manchester University Press.

Andrew, Dudley (1995), *Mists of Regret: Culture and Sensibility in Classic French Films*. Princeton: Princeton University Press.

Andrew, Geoff (2002), 'Guardian Interviews at the BFI: Lynne Ramsay', *The Guardian*, 28 October, https://www.theguardian.com/film/2002/oct/28/features (last accessed 1 March 2019).

Anonymous. (2008), 'Interview with Writer/Director Duane Hopkins', http://www.betterthingsthefilm.co.uk/interview.html (last accessed 6 November 2009).

Anonymous (2009), 'Somer of Shane', *Interview Magazine*, https://www.interviewmagazine.com/film/somers-town (last accessed 16 March 2019).

Anonymous (2013a), '*Exhibition*: A Film by Joanna Hogg (press pack)' http://www.visitfilms.com/media/product/EX_PressKit_8-1-13.pdf (last accessed 3 March 2019).

Anonymous (2013b), 'Fairy tale film-maker: Clio Barnard interview', *Evening Standard*, https://www.standard.co.uk/go/london/film/fairy-tale-film-maker-clio-barnard-interview-8804864.html (last accessed 22 March 2019).

Anonymous (2015), 'This Is England '90: Is this really the end for Shane Meadows' searing saga?', *Digital Spy*, https://www.digitalspy.com/tv/a665732/this-is-england-90-is-this-really-the-end-for-shane-meadows-searing-saga/ (last accessed 16 April 2019).

Anonymous (2017), 'Oscar-winning Director Andrew Arnold's First Ever Commercial',

Little Black Book, https://lbbonline.com/news/oscar-winning-director-andrea-arn olds-first-ever-commercial/ (last accesses 8 October 2019).

Anonymous (2018a), 'A Product of Your Landscape: Ruth Wilson And Clio Barnard Make "Dark River"', *Electra*, https://www.electramedia.co/blog/2018/2/22/a-prod uct-of-your-landscape-ruth-wilson-and-clio-barnard-make-dark-river (last accessed 29 March 2019).

Anonymous (2018b), 'Interview: Clio Barnard on *Dark River*', *Film4*, https:// www.film4productions.com/news/interview/2018-02/interview-clio-barnard-dark-river (last accessed 29 March 2019).

Antunes, Luis Rocha (2015) 'Adapting with the Senses – Wuthering Heights as a Perceptual Experience', *The Victorian*, 3:1, pp. 1–12.

Bachelard, Gaston (2014), *The Poetics of Space*. London: Penguin.

Barker, Jennifer (2009), *The Tactile Eye: Touch and the Cinematic Experience*. Berkeley: University of California Press.

Barrett, Ciara. 'The Feminist Cinema of Joanna Hogg: Melodrama, Female Space, and the Subversion of Phallogocentric Metanarrative', *Alphaville: Journal of Film and Screen Media*, 10 (Winter), pp. 1–16.

Bavidge, Jenny (2016), 'Brontë Soundscapes: The Role of Soundtracks in Adaptations of *Wuthering Heights* in Brontë Heritage Discourses', in I. Habermann and D. Keller (eds), *English Topographies in Literature and Culture: Space, Place, and Identity*, pp. 116–33.

Bazin, André (2005), *What is Cinema? Volume 1*. Berkeley: University of California Press.

Bazin, André (2005), *What is Cinema? Volume 2*. Berkeley: University of California Press.

Bazin, André (2010), 'The Evolution of the Language of Cinema', in M. Furstenau (ed.), *The Film Theory Reader: Debates and Arguments*. London: Routledge, pp. 95–103.

Beswick, Katie (2018), '*Black Teeth and a Brilliant Smile*: Review', *Studies in Theatre and Performance*, April, pp. 1–2.

BFI (n.d.), 'Our Funding Priorities', https://www.bfi.org.uk/supporting-uk-film/produc tion-development-funding/our-funding-priorities (last accessed 17 May 2019).

Bhula, Mo (1999), 'Interview with Barry Hines and Natasha Betteridge, *Kes*: Programme, West Yorkshire Play House', Barry Hines Papers, University of Sheffield.

Bitel, Anton (2015), '*Archipelago*: Review', in N. Mitchel (ed.), *Directory of World Cinema: Britain 2*. Bristol: Intellect, p. 242.

Bolton, Lucy (2015), 'A Phenomenology of Girlhood: being Mia in *Fish Tank* (Andrea Arnold, 2009)', in F. Handyside and K. Taylor-Jones (eds), *International Cinema and the Girl: Local Issues, Transnational Contexts*, London: Palgrave Macmillan, pp.75–84.

Bordwell, David (1985), *Narration in the Fiction Film*. Wisconsin: University of Wisconsin Press.

Boym, Svetlana (2001), *The Future of Nostalgia*. New York: Basic Books.

Brown, William (2009), 'Not Flagwaving But Flagdrowning, or Postcards from Post-Britain', in R. Murphy (ed.), *The British Cinema Book (3rd Ed.)*. London: BFI, pp. 408–16.

Bruno, Giuliana (2001), *Atlas of Emotion: Journeys in Art, Architecture, Film*. London: Verso.

Caughie, John (2000), *Television Drama: Realism, Modernism, and British Culture*. Oxford: Oxford University Press.

Chion, Michael (1994), *Audio-vision: Sound on Screen*. New York: Columbia University Press.

Cortvriend, Jack (2017), *Making Sense of Everyday Spaces: A Tendency in Contemporary British Cinema*. PhD Thesis. University of Sheffield.

Cox, David (2011), 'Is Archipelago a class act or an empty gesture?', *The Guardian*, https://www.theguardian.com/film/filmblog/2011/mar/14/archipelago-class-joanna-hogg-irrelevant (last accessed 8 March 2019).

Cuming, Emily (2013), 'Private Lives, Social Housing: Female Coming-of-Age Stories on the British Council Estate', *Contemporary Women's Writing*, 7:3, pp. 328–45.

Dallas, Paul (2014), 'Architecture of Desire: Joanna Hogg's Exhibition', *Cinema Scope*, http://cinema-scope.com/cinema-scope-magazine/architecture-desire-joanna-hoggs-exhibition/ (last accessed 10 March 2019).

Dave, Paul (2011), 'Tragedy, Ethics, and History in Contemporary British Social Realist Film', in D. Tucker (ed.), *British Social Realism in the Arts*. Basingstoke: Palgrave Macmillan, pp. 17–56.

Dave, Paul (2013), 'Choosing Death: Working-class Coming of Age in Contemporary British Cinema', *Journal of British Cinema and Television*, 10:4, pp. 746–68.

Dave, Paul (2017), '*Bypass*, Obscure Forces and Ontological Anxiety', in E. Mazierska and L. Kristensen (eds), *Contemporary Cinema and Neoliberal Ideology*. London: Routledge, pp. 121–36.

de Luca, Tiago (2014), *Realism of the Senses in World Cinema: The Experience of Physical Reality*. London: I. B. Tauris.

Dodd, Philip (1990), 'Lowryscapes: recent writings about "the North"', *Critical Quarterly*, 32:2, pp. 17–28.

Doyle, Gillian (2014), 'Film Support and the Challenge of "Sustainability": On Wing Design, Wax and Feathers, and Bolts from the Blue', *Journal of British Cinema and Television*, 11:2–3, pp. 129–51

Dyer, Hannah (2017), 'Reparation for a violent boyhood: pedagogies of mourning in Shane Meadow's *This Is England*', *Pedagogy, Culture, and Society*, 25:3, pp. 315–25.

Edensor, Tim (2015), 'Sensing National Spaces: Representing the Mundane in English Film and Television', in I. Bondebjerg, E. Novrup Redvall and A. Higson (eds), *European Cinema and Television: Cultural Policy and Everyday Life*. London: Palgrave Macmillan, pp. 58–80.

Elliott, Paul (2013), '"Now I'm the monster": Remembering, Repeating and Working Through in *Dead Man's Shoes* and *TwentyFourSeven*', in M. Fradley, S. Godfrey and M. Williams (eds), *Shane Meadows: Critical Essays*. Edinburgh: Edinburgh University Press, pp. 83–94.

Elsaesser, Thomas (2009), 'World Cinema: Realism, Evidence, Presence', in L. Nagib and C. Mello (eds), *Realism and the Audiovisual Media*. Basingstoke: Palgrave Macmillan, pp. 3–19.

Ezra, Elizabeth and Rowden, Terry (2006), 'General Introduction: What is Transnational Cinema?', in E. Ezra and T. Rowden (eds), *Transnational Cinema: The Film Reader*. London: Routledge, pp. 1–12.

Featherstone, Vicky (2017), 'A Statement from the Royal Court Theatre', Royal Court Theatre, https://royalcourttheatre.com/statement-royal-court-theatre/ (last accessed 23 March 2019).

Fife Donaldson, Lucy (2014), *Texture in Film*. London: Palgrave Macmillan.

Fife Donaldson, Lucy (2017a), '"You have to feel a sound for it to be effective", Sonic Surfaces in Film and Television', in M. Mera, R. Sadoff and B. Winters, Ben (eds), *The Routledge Companion to Screen Music and Sound*. London: Routledge, pp. 85–95.

Fife Donaldson, Lucy (2017b), 'Feeling and Film-making: The Design and Affect of Film Sound', *The New Soundtrack*, 7:1, pp. 31–46.

Fisher, Mark (2009), *Capitalist Realism: Is There No Alternative?* London: Zero Books.
Fisher, Mark (2014), *Ghosts of My Life: Writings on Depression, Hauntology, and Lost Futures.* London: Zero Books.
Fisher, Mark and Gilbert, Jeremy (2013), 'Capitalist Realism and Neoliberal Hegemony: Jeremy Gilbert A Dialogue', *New Formations*, Winter 80/81, pp. 89–101.
FitzGerald, Louise and Godfrey, Sarah (2013), '"Them over there": Motherhood and Marginality in Shane Meadows' Films', in M. Fradley, S. Godfrey and M. Williams (eds), *Shane Meadows: Critical Essays.* Edinburgh: Edinburgh University Press, pp. 155–70.
Forrest, David (2009), 'Shane Meadows and the British New Wave: Britain's hidden art cinema', *Studies in European Cinema*, 6:2–3, pp. 191–201.
Forrest, David (2010), '*Better Things* (Duane Hopkins, 2008) and New British Realism', *New Cinemas: Journal of Contemporary Film*, 8:1, pp. 31–43.
Forrest, David (2013), '21st-Century Social Realism: Shane Meadows and new British realism' in M. Fradley, S. Godfrey and M. Williams (eds), *Shane Meadows: Critical Essays.* Edinburgh: Edinburgh University Press, pp. 35–49.
Forrest, David (2014), 'The Films of Joanna Hogg: New British realism and class', *Studies in European Cinema*, 11:1, pp. 1–12.
Forrest, David and Vice, Sue (2017), *Barry Hines: Kes, Threads and Beyond.* Manchester: Manchester University Press.
Fowler, Catherine and Helfield, Gillian (2006), 'Introduction', in C. Fowler and G. Helfield (eds), *Representing the Rural: Space, Place, Identity in Films about the Land.* Detroit: Wayne State University Press, pp. 1–16.
Fradley, Martin and Kingston, Seán (2013), '"What do you think makes a bad dad?": Shane Meadows and Fatherhood', in M. Fradley, S. Godfrey and M. Williams (eds), *Shane Meadows: Critical Essays.* Edinburgh: Edinburgh University Press, pp. 171–85.
Fradley, Martin and Sutton, Emma (2014), '"Disappointingly Thin and Flaccid": Gender, Authorship and Authenticity in Shane Meadows' *Once Upon a Time in the Midlands* (2002)', *Scope: An Online Journal of Film and Television Studies*, Issue 26, https://www.nottingham.ac.uk/scope/documents/2014/february/fradley.pdf (last accessed 22 March 2014).
Fradley, Martin, Godfrey, Sarah and Williams, Melanie (2013a), 'Introduction', *The Journal of British Cinema and Television*, 10:4, pp. 823–8.
Fradley, Martin, Godfrey, Sarah and Williams, Melanie (2013b), 'Introduction: Shane's World', in M. Fradley, S. Godfrey and M. Williams (eds), *Shane Meadows: Critical Essays.* Edinburgh: Edinburgh University Press, pp. 1–20.
Fuller, Graham (2007), 'Skinhead Memories, Violent and Vivid', *The New York Times*, https://www.nytimes.com/2007/07/22/movies/22full.html (last accessed 15 March 2019).
Fuller, Graham (2014), 'Interview with Graham Fuller', *Film Comment*, https://www.filmcomment.com/blog/interview-joanna-hogg/ (last accessed 8 March 2019).
Gritten, David (2012), '*Shame*: Steve McQueen Interview', *The Guardian*, 14 January, https://www.telegraph.co.uk/culture/film/filmmakersonfilm/8994878/Shame-Steve-McQueen-interview.html (last accessed 1 March 2019).
Haillay, Samm and Hopkins, Duane (2014) '*Bypass* Press Notes', http://www.filmpressplus.com/wp-content/uploads/dl_docs/BYPASS-Notes.pdf (last accessed 1 March 2019).
Haillay, Samm (2015), 'How "Bypass" took the direct distribution route', *Screen Daily*, https://www.screendaily.com/comment/how-bypass-took-the-direct-distribution-route/5086187.article (last accessed 3 March 2019).
Hallam, Julia and Marshment, Margaret (2000), *Realism and Popular Cinema.* Manchester: Manchester University Press.

Hallam, Julia and Roberts, Les (2014), 'Film and Spatiality: Outline of a New Empiricism', in J. Hallam and L. Roberts, Les (eds), *Locating the Moving Image: New Approaches to Film and Place*. Bloomington: Indiana University Press, pp. 1–30.

Hatherley, Owen (2009), *Militant Modernism*. London: Zero Books.

Hatherley, Owen (2011), *A Guide to the New Ruins of Great Britain*. London: Verso.

Higson, Andrew (1984), 'Space, Place, Spectacle', *Screen*, 25:4–5, pp. 2–21.

Higson, Andrew (1989), 'The Concept of National Cinema', *Screen* 30:4, pp. 36–47.

Higson, Andrew (2006), 'The Limiting Imagination of National Cinema', in E. Ezra and T. Rowden (eds), *Transnational Cinema: The Film Reader*. London: Routledge, pp. 15–27.

Higson, Andrew (2011), *Film England: Culturally English Filmmaking since the 1990s*. London: I. B. Tauris.

Hill, John (1986), *Sex, Class and Realism: British Cinema 1956–1963*. London: BFI.

Hines, Barry (1999), *A Kestrel for a Knave*. London: Penguin.

Hockenhull, Stella (2014), *Aesthetics and Neo-Romanticism in Film: Landscapes in Contemporary British Cinema*. London: I. B. Tauris.

Hockenhull, Stella (2017), *British Women Film Directors in the New Millennium*. London: Palgrave Macmillan.

Holmwood, Leigh (2009), 'Channel 4's extra £20m for drama to fund Shane Meadows' TV debut', *The Guardian*, https://www.theguardian.com/media/2009/aug/26/shane-meadows-channel-4 (last accessed 22 March 2019).

Hopkins, Duane (2008), 'Screenplay Extract', http://www.betterthingsthefilm.co.uk/interview.html (last accessed 6 November 2009).

Hopkins, Duane (2015), 'If Britain Is Broken – They Didn't Break It', *Huffington Post*, https://www.huffingtonpost.co.uk/duane-hopkins/if-britain-is-broken-they_b_6793542.html?guccounter=1 (last accessed 3 March 2019).

Horeck, Tanya (2011), 'A "Passion for the Real": Sex, Affect and Performance in the Films of Andrea Arnold', in T. Horeck and T. Kendall (eds), *New Extremism in Cinema: From France to Europe*. Edinburgh: Edinburgh University Press, pp. 169–79.

Horne, Alex (2014), 'The New Film "Bypass" Offers a Raw Look at Life in Post-Industrial England', *Vice*, https://www.vice.com/en_ca/article/mv5kv8/bypass-duane-hopkins-interview-293 (last accessed 3 March 2019).

Hutchinson, Pamela (2018), 'Film of the week: Dark River drags a history of abuse into the present', *Sight and Sound*, https://www.bfi.org.uk/news-opinion/sight-sound-magazine/reviews-recommendations/dark-river-review-clio-barnard-ruth-wilson (last accessed 29 March 2019).

Ince, Kate (2017), *The Body and the Screen: Female Subjectivities in Contemporary Women's Cinema*. London: Bloomsbury.

Jacobs, Amber (2016), 'On the Maternal "Creaturely" Cinema of Andrea Arnold', *Journal of British Cinema and Television*, 13:1, pp. 160–76.

James, Nick (2007), 'At the Edge of England', *Sight and Sound*, 17:5, p. 41.

Jameson, Frederic (2013), *The Antinomies of Realism*. London: Verso.

Jenkins, David (2015), 'Robbie Ryan On New Andrea Arnold and Ken Loach Movies', *Little White Lies*, https://lwlies.com/articles/robbie-ryan-interview-andrea-arnold-ken-loach/ (last accessed 11 March 2019).

Johnson, Beth (2016), 'Art Cinema and *The Arbor*: Tape-recorded Testimony, Film Art and Feminism', *Journal of British Cinema and Television*, 13:2, pp. 278–91.

Johnson, Beth (2017), '*This Is England*: Authorship, Emotion and Class Telly', in D. Forrest and B. Johnson (eds), *Social Class and Television Drama in Contemporary Britain*. London: Palgrave Macmillan, pp. 13–28.

Johnson, Beth (2018), 'Don't Look Back in Anger: Manchester, *Supersonic* and *Made of Stone*', in N. Bentley, B. Johnson and A. Zielenicc (eds), *Youth Cultures*, pp. 127–44. London: Palgrave Macmillan.

Johnson, Beth and Andrew, Joe (2013), '*Dead Man's Shoes*: Revealing the Subtext of the Lost Maternal', *Journal of British Cinema and Television*, 10:4, pp. 863–77.

Kendall, Tina (2010), '"The in-between of things": Intermediality in *Ratcatcher*', *New Review of Film and Television and Studies*, 8:2, pp. 179–97.

Kiang, Jessica (2014), 'Venice Review: Duane Hopkins' "Bypass" Starring George McKay Is Garish Style Over Grim Substance', *IndieWire*, https://www.indiewire.com/2014/09/venice-review-duane-hopkins-bypass-starring-george-mckay-is-garish-style-over-grim-substance-272738/ (last accessed 3 March 2019).

Knight, Deborah (1997), 'Naturalism, narration and critical perspective: Ken Loach and the experimental method', in G. McKnight (ed.), *Agent of Challenge and Defiance: The films of Ken Loach*. Westport, CT: Greenwood Press, pp. 60–81.

Kouguell, Susan (2016), 'Tribeca Film Festival: A Conversation with Acclaimed Writer/Director Andrea Arnold', https://www.indiewire.com/2016/04/tribeca-film-festival-a-conversation-with-acclaimed-writerdirector-andrea-arnold-287919/ (last accessed 2 March 2019).

Kracauer, Siegfried (1960), *Theory of Film: The Redemption of Physical Reality*. Oxford: Oxford University Press.

Kuhn, Annette (2008), *Ratcatcher: BFI Film Classics*. London: BFI.

Kuhn, Annette and Westwell, Guy (2012), *A Dictionary of Film Studies*. Oxford: Oxford University Press.

LaBelle, Brandon (2010), *Acoustic Territories/Sound Culture and Everyday Life*. New York: Continuum.

Lawrence, Michael (2016a), 'Andrea Arnold: Introduction', *Journal of British Cinema and Television*, 13:1, pp. 156–9.

Lawrence, Michael (2016b), 'Nature and the Non-human in Andrea Arnold's *Wuthering Heights*', *Journal of British Cinema and Television*, 13:1, pp. 177–94.

Lawrenson, Edward (2004), 'Interview with British filmmaker Shane Meadows', *Sight and Sound*, 14:10, pp. 35–6.

Lebeau, Vicky (2013), '"Stick that knife in me": Shane Meadows' Children', *Journal of British Cinema and Television*, 10:4, pp. 878–89.

Lee, Benjamin (2016), 'Andrea Arnold: I find my adaptation of Wuthering Heights "hard to look at"', *The Guardian*, https://www.theguardian.com/film/2016/apr/19/andrea-arnold-wuthering-heights-american-honey-tribeca-film-festival (last accessed 11 March 2019.

Leigh, Danny (2018), 'The Class Ceiling', *Sight and Sound*, pp. 22–6.

Leigh, Danny (2019), 'Does Andrea Arnold's experience on Big Little Lies suggest that auteurs are doomed?', *The Guardian*, https://www.theguardian.com/film/2019/jul/18/does-andrea-arnolds-experience-on-big-little-lies-suggest-that-auteurs-are-doomed (last accessed 25 July 2019).

Liese, Spenser, (2009), 'What are you looking at?', *Sight and Sound*, 9:10, pp. 16–20.

Lobb, Adrian (2011), '"This Ain't Acting" – On The Set Of This Is England '88', *The Quietus*, https://thequietus.com/articles/07580-this-is-england-88 (last accessed 22 March 2019).

MacCabe, Colin (1974), 'Realism and the Cinema: Notes on some Brechtian theses', *Screen*, 15:2, pp. 7–27.

Macnab, Geoffrey (1998), 'The Natural', *Sight and Sound*, March, 8:3, pp. 14–16.

Marks, Laura U. (2000), *The Skin of the Film: Intercultural Cinema, Embodiment*. Durham, NC and London: Duke University Press.

Marks, Laura U. (2002), *Touch: Sensuous Theory and Multisensory Media.* Minneapolis: University of Minnesota Press.

Marris, Paul (2001), 'Northern Realism: An Exhausted Tradition?', *Cineaste*, 26:4 Autumn, pp. 47–50.

Mason, Paul (2015), 'This Is England '90: when the working class still had hope', *The Guardian*, https://www.theguardian.com/commentisfree/2015/sep/14/this-is-england-90-when-working-class-still-had-hope (last accessed 22 March 2019).

Massa, Will (2018), 'Atlantic Drift', *Sight and Sound*, May, pp. 24–7.

Massey, Doreen (2005), *For Space.* London: Sage.

Mayer, Sophie (2015), *Political Animals: The New Feminist Cinema.* London: I. B. Tauris.

Mazierska, Ewa (2017), 'Introduction: Imagining the North of England', in E. Mazierska (ed.), *Heading North: The North of England in Film and Television.* London: Palgrave Macmillan.

Meadows, Shane (2007) 'Under my Skin', *The Guardian*, https://www.theguardian.com/film/2007/apr/21/culture.features (last accessed 22 March 2019).

Mello, Cecília (2016), 'Art and Reality in *The Arbor* (2010)', *Acta Univ. Sapientiae, Film and Media Studies*, 12, pp. 115–28.

Morgan, Daniel (2010) 'Rethinking Bazin: Ontology and Realist Aesthetics', in M. Furstenau (ed.), *The Film Theory Reader: Debates and Arguments.* London: Routledge, pp. 104–30.

Murray, Jonathan (2015), *The New Scottish Cinema.* London: I. B. Tauris.

Murray, Jonathan (2016), 'Red Roads from Realism: Theorising Relationships between Technique and Theme in the Cinema of Andrea Arnold', *Journal of British Cinema and Television*, 13:1, pp. 195–213.

Nagib, Lúcia (2016), 'The Politics of Slowness and the Traps of Modernity' in T. de Luca and N. Barradas Jorge (eds), *Slow Cinema.* Edinburgh: Edinburgh University Press. pp. 25–46.

Newland, Paul (2016), 'Introduction: Approaching British Rural Landscapes on Film', in P. Newland (ed.), *British Rural Landscapes on Film.* Manchester: Manchester University Press, pp. 1–23.

Newsinger, Jack (2013), 'Structure and Agency: Shane Meadows and the New Regional Production Sectors', in M. Fradley, S. Godfrey and M. Williams (eds), *Shane Meadows: Critical Essays.* Edinburgh: Edinburgh University Press, pp. 21–34.

Niven, John (2015), 'Gavin Clark obituary', *The Guardian*, https://www.theguardian.com/music/2015/apr/09/gavin-clark (last accessed 22 March 2019).

Nwonka, Clive (2014), '"You're what's wrong with me": *Fish Tank*, *The Selfish Giant* and the Language of Contemporary British Social Realism', *New Cinemas: Journal of Contemporary Film*, 12:3, pp. 205–23.

Nwonka, Clive (2017), 'Estate of the Nation: Social Housing as Cultural Verisimilitude in British Social Realism', in D. Forrest, G. Harper and J. Rayner (eds), *Filmurbia: Screening the Suburbs.* London: Palgrave Macmillan, pp. 65–78.

O'Brien, Mike (2016), 'Interview with Joanna Hogg', *Take One*, http://takeonecinema.net/2016/interview-joanna-hogg/ (last accessed 3 March 2019).

O'Falt, Chris (2019), 'Big Little Lies' Season 2 Turmoil: Inside Andrea Arnold's Loss of Creative Control', *IndieWire*, https://www.indiewire.com/2019/07/big-little-lies-season-2-andrea-arnold-lost-creative-control-jean-marc-vallee-1202156884/ (last accessed 25 July 2019).

O'Hagan, Sean (2013), 'Clio Barnard: I'm drawn to outsiders – interview', *The Guardian*, https://www.theguardian.com/film/2013/oct/12/clio-barnard-selfish-giant-interview (last accessed 22 March 2019).

O'Hagan, Sean (2016), 'Andrea Arnold: "I always aim to get under the belly of a place"', *The Guardian*, https://www.theguardian.com/film/2016/oct/09/andrea-arnold-interview-american-honey-shia-labeouf-sasha-lane (last accessed 11 March 2019).

Peirse, Alison (2015), 'Speaking for herself: Andrea Dunbar and Bradford on film', *Journal for Cultural Research*, 20:1, pp. 60–72.

Penz, François (2018), *Cinematic Aided Design: An Everyday Life Approach to Architecture*. Abingdon: Routledge.

Pethő, Ágnes (2015), 'Between Absorption, Abstraction and Exhibition: Inflections of the Cinematic Tableau in the Films of Corneliu Porumboiu, Roy Andersson and Joanna Hogg', *Acta Univ. Sapientiae, Film and Media Studies*, 11, pp. 39–76.

Petrovic, Sarah (2013), '"Changing Spaces of Englishness": Psychogeography and Spatial Practices in *This Is England* and *Somers Town*', in M. Fradley, S. Godfrey and M. Williams (eds), *Shane Meadows: Critical Essays*. Edinburgh: Edinburgh University Press, pp. 127–41.

Quinlivan, Davinia (2012), *The Place of Breath in Cinema*. Edinburgh: Edinburgh University Press.

Robinson, Tasha (2016), 'Director Andrea Arnold on the cross-country party that produced American Honey', *The Verge*, https://www.theverge.com/2016/9/29/13109072/american-honey-movie-director-interview-andrea-arnold-tiff-2016 (last accessed 15 April 2019).

Roddick, Nick (2009), 'Do we know where we're going?', *Sight and Sound*, October.

Rolinson, David (2005), *Alan Clarke*. Manchester: Manchester University Press.

Rolinson, David and Woods, Faye (2013), 'This Is *England '86* and *'88*? Memory, haunting and return through television seriality', in M. Fradley, S. Godfrey and M. Williams (eds), *Shane Meadows: Critical Essays*. Edinburgh: Edinburgh University Press, pp. 186–202.

Romney, Jonathan (2009), 'Rural Retreats – Film of the Month: Better Things', *Sight and Sound*, February, http://old.bfi.org.uk/sightandsound/review/4704 (last accessed 2 March 2019).

Romney, Jonathan (2013), 'Film of the week: *The Selfish Giant*', *Sight and Sound*, https://www.bfi.org.uk/news-opinion/sight-sound-magazine/reviews-recommendations/film-week-selfish-giant (last accessed 29 March 2019).

Romney, Jonathan (2014), 'Coming Apart: Director Joanna Hogg revisits the indiscreet misery of the English bourgeoisie in *Exhibition*', *Film Comment*, https://www.filmcomment.com/article/joanna-hogg-exhibition/ (last accessed 10 March 2019).

Russell, Dave (2004), *Looking North: Northern England and the national imagination*. Manchester: Manchester University Press.

Salovaara, Sarah (2014), '"A Relationship is Never a Straight Line": Joanna Hogg on *Exhibition*', *Filmmaker Magazine*, https://filmmakermagazine.com/86407-a-relationship-is-never-a-straight-line-joanna-hogg-on-exhibition/#.XHwT28_7TMJ (last accessed 3 March 2019).

Sarhimaa, Jutta (2014), 'Heavy Metal: Clio Barnard on Junkyards, Heroes, and Fairytales in *The Selfish Giant*', *cléo: A Journal of Film and Feminism*, http://cleojournal.com/2014/08/21/heavy-metal-clio-barnard-on-junkyards-heroes-and-fairytales-in-the-selfish-giant-2/ (last accessed 23 March 2019).

Schwarz, Clair (2013), '"An object of indecipherable bastardry – a true monster": Homosociality, Homoeroticism and Generic Hybridity in *Dead Man's Shoes*', in M. Fradley, S. Godfrey and M. Williams (eds), *Shane Meadows: Critical Essays*. Edinburgh: Edinburgh University Press, pp. 95–110.

Scott, Jason (2013), 'From Local Roots to Global Screens: Shane Meadows' Positioning in the Ecology of Contemporary British Film', *Journal of British Cinema and Television*, 10:4, pp. 829–45.

Shapiro, Joe (2015), *Fredric Jameson, The Antinomies of Realism, Socialism and Democracy*, 29:2, pp. 131–5.

Shaw, Caitlin (2015), 'Remediating the Eighties: Nostalgia and Retro in British Screen Fiction from 2005–2011'. PhD Thesis, DeMontfort University.

Shields, Rob (1991), *Places on the Margin: Alternative geographies of Modernity*. London: Routledge.

Sinker, Mark (2007), '*Control / Joe Strummer: The Future is Unwritten / This Is England*', *Film Quarterly*, 61:2, pp. 22–9.

Sley, Michael (2011), *National Belonging and Everyday Life: The Significance of Nationhood in an Uncertain World*. Basingstoke: Palgrave Macmillan.

Smith, Damon (2010), 'Andrea Arnold, *Fish Tank*', *Filmmaker*, https://filmmakerma gazine.com/1403-andrea-arnold-fish-tank/#.XIZGuRP7SCd (last accessed 11 March 2019).

Smith, Murray (1995), *Engaging Characters, Fiction, Emotion, and the Cinema*. Oxford: Clarendon Press.

Sobchack, Vivian (1992), *The Address of the Eye: A Phenomenology of Film Experience*. Princeton: Princeton University Press.

Stafford-Clark, Max (2000), 'Introduction', in A. Dunbar and R. Soans (authors), *Rita, Sue and Bob Too* and *A State Affair*. London: Bloomsbury.

Steans, Jill (2013), '"No More Heroes": The Politics of Marginality and Disenchantment in *TwentyFourSeven* and *This Is England*', in M. Fradley, S. Godfrey and M. Williams (eds), *Shane Meadows: Critical Essays*. Edinburgh: Edinburgh University Press, pp. 68–72.

Street, Sarah (2009), *British National Cinema*. London: Routledge.

Stripe, Adelle (2017), *Black Teeth and a Brilliant Smile*. Kingston upon Hull: Wrecking Ball Press.

Sumpter, Helen (2014), 'Q&A Joanna Hogg: Exhibition', *Art Review*, https://artre view.com/features/feature_qa_joanna_hogg_exhibition_2014/ (last accessed 10 March 2019).

Thornham, Sue (2016a), 'Space, Place and Realism: *Red Road* and the gendering of a cinematic history', *Feminist Media Histories*, 2:2, pp. 133–54.

Thornham, Sue (2016b), '"Not a country at all": Landscape and *Wuthering Heights*', *Journal of British Cinema and Television*, 13:1, pp. 214–31.

Titze, Anne-Katrin (2014), 'Emergence, part 2', *Eye for Film*, https://www.eyeforfilm. co.uk/feature/2014-06-22-conversaton-with-joanna-hogg-about-unrelated-archipel ago-and-exhibition-feature-story-by-anne-katrin-titze (last accessed 8 March 2019).

Tolley, Gail (2009), 'Andrea Arnold: Behind Glass', *The Skinny*, https://www.the skinny.co.uk/film/interviews/andrea-arnold-behind-glass (last accessed 11 March 2019).

Tucker, David (2011), 'Introduction – "an anthropology of ourselves" Vs "the incom-prehensibility of the real": Making the Case for British Social Realism', in D. Tucker (ed.), *British Social Realism in the Arts*, Basingstoke: Palgrave Macmillan, pp. 1–16.

Turner, Matthew (2010), 'Joanna Hogg: Interview', *View London*, http://www. viewlondon.co.uk/cinemas/joanna-hogg-interview-feature-interview-3934.html (last accessed 3 March 2019).

Wilkinson, Amber (2008a), 'Joanna Hogg talks *Unrelated*', *Eye for Film*, https://www. eyeforfilm.co.uk/feature/2008-09-19-interview-with-joanna-hogg-about-unrelated-feature-story-by-amber-wilkinson (last accessed 3 March 2019).

Wilkinson, Amber (2008b), 'In the Somers Town', *Eye for Film*, http://www.eyeforfilm. co.uk/feature.php?id=513 (last accessed 29 September 2008).

Williams, Craig (2014), 'Interview: Joanna Hogg unravels 'Exhibition', *Cinevue*, https://

cine-vue.com/2014/06/interview-joanna-hogg-unravels-exhibition.html (last accessed 10 March 2019).

Wils, Tyson (2016), 'Phenomenology, Theology and "Physical Reality": The Film Theory Realism of Siegfried Kracauer' in I. Aitken (ed.), *The Major Realist Film Theorists: A Critical Anthology*. Edinburgh: Edinburgh University Press, pp. 67–81.

Wilson, Jared (2012), 'Shane Meadows: The Early Years', https://www.leftlion.co.uk/read/2012/december/shane-meadows-the-early-years-5389 (last accessed 11 October 2019).

Wilson, Jared (2013), 'Shane Meadows and Associates: Selected LeftLion interviews', *Journal of British Cinema and Television*, 10:4, pp. 909–24.

Wood, Jason and Haydyn-Smith, Ian (2015), *New British Cinema*. London: Faber and Faber.

Woods, Faye (2015), 'Telefantasy Tower Blocks: Space, Place and Social Realism Shake-ups in *Misfits*', *Journal of British Cinema and Television*, 12:2, pp. 229–44.

Yacavone, Daniel (2015), *Film Worlds: A Philosophical Aesthetics of Cinema*. New York: Columbia University Press.

Zuckerman, Esther (2016), 'Arnold on her mesmerising party on wheels, *American Honey*', *AVFilm*, https://film.avclub.com/andrea-arnold-on-her-mesmerizing-party-on-wheels-ameri-1798252554 (last accessed 11 March 2019).

INDEX

Woods, Faye, 151, 154, 155
Wuthering Heights, 84, 87, 88, 91, 93, 109–16, 118, 119

Yacavone, Daniel, 49, 57, 58, 70, 76
Yorkshire, 111, 131, 167, 170, 191
Youth Can Do It, 91–2, 102